Migration, Minorities and Citizenship

General Editors: **Zig Layton-Henry**, Professor of Politics, University of Warwick; and **Danièle Joly**, Professor, Director, Centre for Research in Ethnic Relations, University of Warwick

Titles include:

Pontus Odmalm
MIGRATION POLICIES AND POLITICAL PARTICIPATION
Inclusion or Intrusion in Western Europe?

Aspasia Papadopoulou-Kourkoula
TRANSIT MIGRATION
The Missing Link Between Emigration and Settlement

Jan Rath (*editor*)
IMMIGRANT BUSINESSES
The Economic, Political and Social Environment

Carl-Ulrik Schierup (*editor*)
SCRAMBLE FOR THE BALKANS
Nationalism, Globalism and the Political Economy of Reconstruction

Vicki Squire
THE EXCLUSIONARY POLITICS OF ASYLUM

Maarten Vink
LIMITS OF EUROPEAN CITIZENSHIP
European Integration and Domestic Immigration Policies

Östen Wahlbeck
KURDISH DIASPORAS
A Comparative Study of Kurdish Refugee Communities

Lucy Williams
GLOBAL MARRIAGE
Cross-Border Marriage Migration in Global Context

Migration, Minorities and Citizenship
Series Standing Order ISBN 978-0-333-71047-0 (hardback) and
978-0-333-80338-7 (paperback)
(*outside North America only*)

You can receive future titles in this series as they are published by placing a
standing order. Please contact your bookseller or, in case of difficulty, write to
us at the address below with your name and address, the title of the series and
the ISBN quoted above.

Customer Services Department, Macmillan Distribution Ltd, Houndmills,
Basingstoke, Hampshire RG21 6XS, England

Global Marriage

Cross-Border Marriage Migration in Global Context

Lucy Williams
University of Kent, UK

palgrave
macmillan

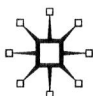

First published 2010 by
PALGRAVE MACMILLAN

Palgrave Macmillan in the UK is an imprint of Macmillan Publishers Limited, registered in England, company number 785998, of Houndmills, Basingstoke, Hampshire RG21 6XS.

Palgrave Macmillan in the US is a division of St Martin's Press LLC, 175 Fifth Avenue, New York, NY 10010.

Palgrave Macmillan is the global academic imprint of the above companies and has companies and representatives throughout the world.

Palgrave® and Macmillan® are registered trademarks in the United States, the United Kingdom, Europe and other countries.

ISBN-13: 978-0-230-21807-9 hardback

This book is printed on paper suitable for recycling and made from fully managed and sustained forest sources. Logging, pulping and manufacturing processes are expected to conform to the environmental regulations of the country of origin.

A catalogue record for this book is available from the British Library.

A catalog record for this book is available from the Library of Congress.

Printed and bound in the United States of America

My children

I can hear them talking, my children
fluent English and broken Kurdish.

And whenever I disagree with them
they will comfort each other by saying:
Don't worry about mum, she's Kurdish.

Will I be the foreigner in my own home?

(Choman Hardi)

Contents

Acknowledgements

My first acknowledgement has to go to my very good friend Dr Mei-Kuei Yu who showed me how important the category of marriage migration is. She introduced me to cross-border marriage migration as a much broader field of study than I ever would have appreciated from my parochial European position. I also acknowledge the debt I owe to my friends who came to the UK as refugees – and whose hopes and dreams continue to be affected by that experience. Thanks are also due to my colleagues in the marriage and migration research group – especially Dr Katharine Charsley and Dr Helena Wray, who have further broadened my view. Without Dr Mecca Chiesa's badgering, this project might never have been launched and without Kalli Glezakou's encouragement it might well have sunk – I hope she will take heart from the conclusion of this task that big projects do finish, eventually. Heartfelt thanks also go to Dr Choman Hardi for her generosity in letting me use her poem, for her support, commiseration and for being a mate. I acknowledge her publisher, Bloodaxe Books, for giving me permission to reproduce her poem, 'My Children' – the sentiments of which seem to me to sum up the dilemma of many migrant parents.

Final thanks go to my steadfast family and especially to B and N who are, and have, living proof of the challenges and delights of cross-border migration for marriage and intimate partnership.

This is book is dedicated to Aileen and Xin Yi.

1
Introducing Cross-Border Marriage Migration

This book takes a broad view of the global phenomenon of cross-border marriage migration and attempts to highlight the migration choices and strategies of individuals, families and communities within political, legal, social and economic structures. It attempts to analyse patterns of migration from the perspectives of the migrants themselves and, using mostly secondary data, will discuss how marriage across borders may mould the migration patterns of individuals and communities. Throughout the book I start from the assumption that citizenship of countries from the Global South is a disadvantage in terms of global migration as, in general, all but the elites of these countries, are disqualified from the migration opportunities that citizens of the developed enjoy. I emphasise, however, that connection to countries of the Global South may confer other attributes that open channels of migration which can be exploited by would-be migrants. By focusing on the migration stories of migrants, this book aims to improve understanding of how migration may be negotiated as well as learn about the affects of migration on migrants and those connected to them. Cross-border marriage migration provides a case study for these far-reaching issues as it is a truly global phenomenon and one which sees migrants moving between the developing countries of the world as well as between developing and developed countries.

The studies drawn on for this book suggest different patterns of marriage migration. Marriage migration, for example, is integral to many transnational communities, that is, those that have established themselves in several countries across the world. In other cases, marriage migration may represent a first migration step which creates a potential for future links between countries. Marriage migration happens because there are structural opportunities for individuals to migrate to

1

join intimate partners but throughout, I assume that migrants have the capacity to act with *agency*, a notion of self-determination that underpins much of this book. In emphasising agency, I recognise that options are shaped and limited by an individual's personal circumstances, attributes and environments as well as by the structures and legislative apparatuses that impact on their lives. *Structure*, here, is represented by the systems and policies of governments but also by social and cultural structures governing communities and families whose members migrate through marriage. Individuals live in environments that constrain certain activities and encourage others and negotiating these different structures is a shared marker of what it is to belong to societies. Structure and agency are always in tension and while the balance differs between people across the world, no one should be seen as entirely bound by structural constraints. Much of the world's population lives in conditions of reduced and constrained agency because of their exclusion from political and economic power structures, but also because of their marginal position in relation to the citizens of developed countries.

Their marginalisation, as individuals and as groups, is a reality but, I argue, should not be seen as a defining characteristic. Studies of migration often emphasise the structural drivers for migration, seeing it as a predominantly 'rational' and calculated activity, but these studies can be criticised for failing to present migrants as people who have larger goals than simple self-preservation and betterment whose migration is motivated by evolving and complex needs and desires.

Discourses emphasising the role of structural factors in personal decision-making are frequently used in debates about trafficking and the sex trade, as this book will demonstrate, but the portrayal of the migrant as innocent victim of circumstance is found throughout the literature on migration. Examples of the objectification and stereotyping of migrants (positively as well as negatively) can be found in literature on economic migration as much as forced migration and it is commonplace in the representation of migrants in government and non-government reports and policies. If agency is the capacity to make free decisions about one's own life, then no-one possesses truly unrestricted agency, unfettered by ethical, cultural or economic restraint, but by the same token, except those who are in living in conditions of bondage, no-one is entirely without agency. Gender roles, imposed or adopted by individuals and communities, provide clear examples (discussed in following chapters) of how community norms can restrict the agency of their members but, as with most structures, what restrains some, in fact, opens avenues of opportunity for others.

Migration in a global world

Although migration has always been a part of the human experience, the twentieth century saw migration expand to become a global phenomenon with migrants moving across the globe in greater numbers and between more countries. This new global reality has been termed an 'age of migration' (Castles and Miller 2009), in recognition that migration and population movement lie at the core of economic and political, national and international relations. Mobility and global interlinking make markets and economic entities ever more tightly interdependent and the expansion of transnational communities and consciousnesses makes the idea of culture and tradition being necessarily linked to 'place' untenable. The work of Arjun Appadurai (Appadurai 1996) and James Clifford (Clifford 1997), among others, has drawn attention to the transnational nature of cultural entities and has demonstrated how, even as nations attempt to strengthen their border control and to manage their populations, so the work of building globe-spanning, transnational communities goes on. The possibility and promise of migration touches not only the elites of the industrialised world but also the poor of the least developed countries. Migration is often an option for the less-privileged who, even if they never migrate themselves, have lives shaped and altered by the migration of others (Conway 2007). Thus, even staying at home, they benefit from migration through the remittances and opportunities presented by their migrant relatives and contacts. The poor may now be the most frequent migrants across the world as well as within national boundaries, as in economically less developed and unstable parts of the world, governments as much as individuals recognise migration as a means of maximising the economic value of people. Migration, in many parts of the world, has become a national as well as an individual strategy.

Globalisation has made the world seem smaller by facilitating communication and by spreading a sense of familiarity through images and other media representations. Previously 'foreign' countries have become 'known', albeit in limited and simplistic ways. But just as those who live in countries of the developed world feel they 'know' about the developing world, so many in the developing world share a sense of 'knowing' the West. The ubiquitous nature of representations of the developed world supports the establishment and maintenance of personal relationships which, formed across international borders, are supported by disembodied communication techniques that maintain social links. Technology allows contact to be made and maintained across the world in the same way as local friends and colleagues are contacted, blurring and, in some cases, masking the real difference between lives and expectations that exist across the world. Research on transnational communities has shown how they produce and reproduce themselves across distance using global communication methods in innovative and complex ways (Williams 2006) and emphasises how transnational communication encompasses the mundane and trivial as well as the momentous.

Cross-border marriage migration exists within the global imaginings of individuals and communities, but is also built on concrete relationships, networks, aspirations and motivations, and is presented in this book as a response by ordinary people to the challenges, opportunities and realities of their lives. Migration, with all its multiplicity of purposes and mechanisms, may be initiated for objectively clear reasons – for experience, to financially support oneself or one's family – but, being an essentially human process, the experience of migration changes migrants and those around them in unanticipated and unplanned ways. Migration lets air into stagnant lives, communities and families and, for better or worse, inevitably changes cultural practice and social environments. Life does not stop for the migrant or those connected to them on migration and, contrary to the apparent assumptions of many policy-makers, migrants and their economic and social contributions cannot be turned on and off at will when political or economic circumstances change. Even if migrants enter a country as foreigners with little or no connection to their place of settlement, they quickly build connections and links. As migrants become part of their country of settlement, they inevitably reassess their relationship to their natal home. This is not to argue that migration is a one-way process, but that migration and mobility promote the reassessment of history, culture and practice and allow individuals to choose ways of presenting themselves and living their lives from a broader palette.

The potential of migration to change and transform is an important theme of this book. I seek to emphasise the complexity of the forces shaping change as well as the myriad outcomes that result from apparently similar migration stories. For many of the women and men whose lives are described throughout this book, migration may be seen as a potential solution to their everyday problems. Migration may be seen as a way out of economic, political and/or social deprivation and may be a short- or long-term response to opportunity or threat. For some, migration is a planned and anticipated event on the life-course but, for others, it may be a drastic step made in conditions of unforeseen adversity. Migration may represent one thing to the community of the migrant and a quite different thing to the migrant themselves and is likely to mean different things to men and to women as well as to the young and the old. Marriage across borders may become a bridge for the migration of other family members and, even in the short term, may increase their contribution to the household that will raise both their family's and their own social standing and economic security.

Towards a conceptualisation of cross-border marriage migration

The migration category of 'cross-border marriage migration' is a broad one that intersects clearly with the category of 'family migration' (Kofman 2004), but is also connected to streams of forced and economic migration. In this book, cross-border marriage migration is understood as migration that results, at least in part, from a contractual relationship between individuals with different national or residency statuses. Cross-border marriage either changes the immigration status of one partner (for example, by increasing their entitlements to reside or to access the social or economic benefits of the country they are resident in), or it enables one partner to enter and to set up home as a non-citizen spouse in a country foreign to them. By this definition, cross-border marriage migrants may not physically move as a direct result of their marriage but their marriage will change their immigration status and grant them greater security, or at least official status, in their country of residence. This difference in citizenship within an intimate partnership, and the unequal relationships it produces, create a crucial tension for the purposes of this book. The migrant cross-border spouses, who are the primary subjects of this study, are non-citizens with an accordingly unequal economic and political status to their citizen (or their permanently resident) partner. Marriage migrants by this definition may have already been living in the country of settlement but formalising a relationship may increase their security in terms of welfare rights and rights of residence.[1] While their rights as partners of citizens may be strengthened, they will not be equal to those of a citizen, and marriage migrants are subject to restrictions on how they live their daily lives – through differential access to welfare services and political representation. Thus, cross-border marriage migrants experience a loss of formal citizenship status and restrictions on their rights in their country of settlement. Their status as a *spouse* and a *dependant* is their defining characteristic in the eyes of the state and their rights as individuals are understood through their social status as wife, husband or partner. This is not to deny that many states claim to protect and promote the human rights of these spouses but to emphasise that their rights are largely dependent on their continuing relationship with their partner. Should a marriage break down before the migrant spouse has established an independent right to residence, the ending of his or her contract with the citizen ends her or his rights in the country of settlement. Her or his future in the country is decided according to local, legal frameworks giving little consideration to the spouse's life and circumstances before and during the partnership.

A migrant spouse receives little official recognition outside of their relationship to their citizen spouse and this makes for a significant paradox in the state's attitudes to marriage and marriage migrants. Many, if not most, nation-states define marriage as of necessity being between equals, yet when one partner is a non-citizen, inequality is institutionalised in the relationship. Marriages, as we will see in later chapters, are judged by the degree to which they match local norms even while these norms are rarely clarified, but merely assumed as common sense and 'natural'. National, normative assumptions about marriage often ignore the couple's private perceptions of their roles as married partners. Privileging the view of the majority ignores the social and cultural meanings of marriage held by the couple and their social group. This reduction and simplification of complex inter-personal relationships make the relationship, and the people in it and connected to it, vulnerable to stereotyping which has led to the stigmatisation of some migrant spouses and to the diminution of their lives to caricature. An example of this is the popular notion of 'mail-order brides' – i.e. marriages that have been arranged by agencies, perhaps via the Internet, that are often judged as 'mismatched' at best and abusive at worst. Such criticisms and stereotypes are based on assumptions that marriages between older men and younger foreign women must inevitably be exploitative of either the man – duped by a gold-digger, or the woman – obliged, because of her poverty and disadvantage, to marry someone she could never love. When marriage is between people unconnected by established links of kinship or ethnicity, marriage may be tested as to the degree of personal commitment within the marriage – do couples love each other? Is their relationship based on emotion rather than convenience or money? Do they intend to stay together on a permanent basis? When marriages are within transnational ethnic groupings the state may have other, or additional, concerns such as the degree to which the couple are committed, and acceptable, to the country they live in. Stereotyping in such cases is often based on a reductionist view of culture and tradition. Communities are reified as unchanging in their social and familial practices with stereotypes informing the immigration and social policies that directly affect the lives and well-being of migrant spouses and their families. Such reductionism leads to the conflation of arranged marriage with forced marriage and to the explanation of extreme behaviours such a 'honour killing' as a practice solely the responsibility of specific ethnic groups and cultures, distinct from broader social contexts.

A focus on status differences between spouses allows the inclusion of partnerships made post-migration within the definition of cross-border marriage. This highlights that the study of marriage migration is one of evolving personal and social relationships seen against a backdrop of immigration control and policy. The downside of this definition of cross-border marriage or intimate partnership as primarily a contract between citizen and non-citizen, tends to reduce intimate relationships to bureaucratic events and downplays their personal and community significance – this is not my intention. I will argue that the contested definitions of acceptable family formation influence marriage migration patterns as the state examines and attempts to shape relationships according to national agenda and criteria. States may judge the validity of a marriage by the partners' ability to contribute and to integrate into the state, while the married partners themselves may see their marriages as grounded in personal and community relationships reflecting their own aspirations and personal and social mores. The state's overt actions in establishing legislative frameworks and policies to restrict and shape who and how people become permanent residents as spouses, are viewed in this book, as one way in which national identity and national ideologies are defined and managed. The processes of maintaining social and national norms are not merely in the hands of the state, however, and I will argue that nations are shaped and defined by actors at many levels including by employers, welfare and education service providers, as well as by families and the community in general. In this, I follow Aihwa Ong and argue for recognition of the role of agencies beyond the state that 'in myriad and mundane ways suggest, define, and direct adherence to democratic, racial and market norms of belonging' (Ong 2003: 15).

Throughout this book I will address the interaction of structure and agency by contrasting the public narratives of marriage migration, (by which I mean the popular stories told about people who marry across borders) with the more private perspectives of marriage migrants and their communities. Marriage migration, I will argue, is highly variable in its form and can be seen as part of an individual strategy as well as a familial one; as a strategy of transnational communities as well as a discreet and complete move between countries. It can be used to inform how some migrants negotiate national borders as well as how families are reunited after migration. A definition based on complexity and variability, in contrast to simplistic state and legislative definitions, does not impose any one view of what a marriage or intimate partnership should be. It argues for an understanding of marriage migration as a form of migration that can be identified objectively within migration streams but which has multiple and complex meanings for migrants themselves. In this way, cross-border marriage migration can be used as an example of how the simplistic categories of migration commonly employed by national and supra-national bodies can be used, negotiated and in some cases manipulated by migrants working to their own personal and community agenda.

Quantifying cross-border marriage migration

Although there is little doubt of the global significance, even dominance, of marriage migration within regulated migration movements across the world, a review of the literature shows significant problems in quantifying the numbers of global cross-border marriage migrants. These problems largely relate to the lack of clarity that exists in defining what marriage migration is, who marriage migrants are and to the under-theorisation of family migration in general (Kofman and Meeto 2008). These are some of the central questions that this volume intends to address but at the present time, understandings of marriage migration depend largely on the history and manifestation of marriage migration in any given context. These issues have been discussed more fully in Chapter 4.

Definitions and terminology

The academic and other literature referred to in this book employs various different terminologies to describe this broad field of study and it is testament to the under-development of the study of marriage migration that a clear terminology has not yet been established. Terms used include broad ones such as 'family-related migration' (Kofman 2004) which reflects the author's interest in a broader field than marriage alone. Other terms that approach the topic from the perspective of migration theory or the quantification and qualification of migration trends use terms such as 'spouse migration' (Khoo 2001) and 'family-forming migration' (Lievens 1999).

In my view, these terms are unsatisfactory as the former implies that the migration of husbands and wives can be studied in isolation from other forms of migration and the latter implies knowledge of the meaning of marriages which may well be more complex than 'family formation' alone.

More specific terms include 'transnational marriage' (Balzani 2006; Charsley 2006; Charsley and Shaw 2006; Beck-Gernsheim 2007), used to emphasise the place of the marriage within established, transnational, ethnic communities. 'Transnational marriage' stresses the role of marriage alongside other the transnational activities by which family and kin-based structures are preserved, traditional institutions and practices maintained and reciprocal relationships, that include marriage, kept up. Some writers have used the phrase 'transnational marriage' to refer to marriages that by my definition would be 'cross-border' (Yang and Wang 2003; Abelman and Kim 2005; Hilsdon 2007) as, while the development of transnational links may occur in the future, the marriages described join individuals with different citizenship statuses but do not link family or community groups. Marriages made across borders may also be referred to in the literature as international (Lin and Ma 2008), intercultural (Chen and Huang 2006), intermarriages (Roer-Strier and Ben Ezra 2006), cross-cultural marriages (Breger and Hill 1998; Wise and Velayutham 2008), or mixed marriages (Gorny and Kepinska 2004; Rodriguez Garcia 2006) – all of which emphasise a cultural, ethnic, religious or social *difference* between the marriage partners regardless of other commonalities that may exist. 'Commercially arranged marriage migration' (Lu 2005) or 'intermediated' or 'commodified marriage' (Wang and Chang 2002; Yang and Schoonheim 2006) are terms that have specific reference to the ways in which marriages are arranged or brokered.

In this book, I have used the phrase 'cross-border marriage' to describe the types of marriages I am interested in, as it is broad enough to encompass the differences between marriages made across borders and also is a neutral term that avoids value judgements or reference to social or ethnic characteristics. The term cross-border marriage has been used widely in academic literature (for example, in the articles in Constable 2005b and Piper and Roces 2003b) and has the advantage of including both marriages made *within and between* communities. It can therefore straddle the separation between studies of transnational marriages and marriages made between people from different communities that are otherwise classified as 'mixed' or intercultural. My view is that terms such as mixed or intermarriages are culturally essentialist and carry with them the implication that people can be effectively separated by a perceived attachment to one group or to another and that groups are static and clearly delineated. Given that individuals can belong simultaneously to multiple groups and communities, privileging differences, such as those relating to culture or religion, over similarities, perhaps in class, social group or interests, can be unhelpful in determining what a couple have in common. The term cross-border marriage also has the very clear benefit of indicating the potential difference in formal citizenship between the married partners – a difference that is very important in this study.

Outline of the book

The chapters that follow are based on a wide-ranging literature review of academic and non-academic resources relating to cross-border marriage migration. It has been acknowledged by other writers that migration is a topic usefully studied from many different theoretical perspectives and academic disciplines (see Brettell and Hollifield's 2000 edited volume, for example) and in collecting data for this project, I have tried to do this. I have included research and analysis from anthropology, sociology, legal studies, geography, political science and to a lesser extent, economics. Underpinning this review is a basic concern to study the field from the perspectives of cross-border marriage migrants themselves and in my analysis of published work I have taken a feminist approach – emphasising the importance of everyday experience and listening to the voices of those women and men directly involved in marriage migration. Inspired by the work of feminists such as Eleonore Kofman, Nira Yuval-Davis, Lois McNay, Aihwa Ong and others, I view gender as an essential factor in understanding social and cultural practice and accordingly, in understanding migration patterns and trends. Assumptions and expectations about gender shape opportunities for migration as well as the consequences of migration. Gender, discussed in Chapter 2, thus plays a major part in shaping the who, how and why of marriage migration. Chapter 2 focuses on how gender can operate in determining and defining migration patterns and critically evaluates what cross-border marriage, as a distinct migration stream, has to add to migration theory and to the understanding of the impact of gender on social processes. I argue that studying marriage migration challenges many of the assumptions of the more simplistic migration theories and concur with Bailey and Boyle (editorial 2004) that migration theories have not taken sufficient account of the dynamics of household and intra-household relations and that economic rationalities alone are not enough to explain migration choices. This study of cross-border marriage migration shows the importance of emotional factors as they relate to family and community aspirations but also as they relate to the dreams and desires of individuals. Marriage migration is shown to be a powerful force in challenging gender roles but can encourage conservatism as well as change. Negotiation of roles between public and private settings is shown to be a key challenge for many marriage migrants and Chapter 2 discusses gendered assumptions as they operate in public and private settings. This tension, between public and private, is essential as a background to any discussion of the place of migrant women in public discourses of integration and assimilation and in the debate of migrants' place between structure and agency.

As already indicated, the concept of agency in migration and in the consequent (re)negotiations of identity and the self, is key to this study. In Chapter 3, I will elaborate on my understanding of the concept of agency as it relates to the cross-border marriage migration. As well as defining agency, the chapter will discuss how potential cross-border spouses are able to purposively choose or refuse cross-border matches and how agency, or the lack of agency, affects the life of migrants in their country of settlement and in their ongoing contacts and relationships with their natal home. 'Agency' will be linked to De Certeau's definition of tactics and strategy (De Certeau 1984) whereby tactics are seen as the domain of the weak and strategy the domain of the powerful. Agency will be shown to operate in two key ways – through acts of transgression and resistance and as innovation. I argue that through transgressing roles and norms, cross-border marriage migrants can advance their own ambitions and can achieve their goals in creative ways. This may allow them to negotiate a path between structures represented by the powerful institutions of family and state entities. The combination of resistance and creativity may allow them to achieve their ambitions from a position of relative disadvantage. This chapter emphasises how the most marginalised and excluded cross-border marriage migrants may find ways to act with agency and argues that ignoring their achievements depersonalises them and contributes to the undermining of their social worth and their essential humanity.

Chapter 4 sets out to introduce the reader to the broad and rapidly expanding research on cross-border marriage. It begins with a discussion of how marriage as an institution has been conceptualised and then attempts to contextualise marriage migration within global migration movements. As already noted, the family has been under-theorised within migration theory and I include a short section here to discuss how family migration and, more specifically cross-border marriage migration fits into global migration trends and patterns. This section is followed by a discussion of transnationalism in which I define how I understand transnationalism and its limits, for the purpose of this book. Finally in this chapter, I will consider what motivates migrants to marry across borders and will challenge the common assumption that marriages are primarily contracted across border for some objective *gain*. Clearly people migrate in the hope of benefit, but I argue that assuming benefit is purely economic ignores the personal, community and social gain migrants marrying across borders may be hoping for. The review shows that the majority of work on cross-border marriage migration is either research carried out on marriages contracted within communities (intra-community marriages) *or* research on marriages between members of different ethnic and cultural groups (inter-community marriages). It is my contention that there are many similarities between the motivations, the mechanisms and the experience of cross-border marriages, no matter who is marrying whom, because of the differences in power and opportunity of the partners – citizen and non-citizen. I argue that focusing on ethnic, cultural and religious similarities and differences excludes other personal and social factors that produce commonality and difference.

Chapter 5 will discuss power, stigma and violence in migration and cross-border marriages. I include such discussion as, I will argue, women migrants are often the subject of violence and abuse but are more often *assumed* to be vulnerable and the victims of violence. The research that already exists on controversial topics such as honour crimes, mail-order brides and the trafficking of women describes a nuanced picture that is very different from media-driven images and one-dimensional stories of exploitation and force. Women and their families described in these reports are often presented as racialised victims or perpetrators whose experience is often defined by and reduced to their ethnicity and their victim status. While not denying that many women suffer appalling and indefensible violence, this situation is not unique to women who are migrants or in cross-border marriages. This chapter will address the manifestation of the abuse of power, force and violence in the area of cross-border marriage migration and will challenge understandings of marriage migration which over-emphasise perceptions of the weakness and vulnerability of women in relation to the power, violence and dangerousness of men. The effect of stereotyping and the stigmatisation of some marriage migrants will be considered and it will be shown that policies controlling and regulating migration and marriage migrants may be complicit in this. Debates on the prevalence and nature of violence in marriage are complicated by stereotypes of women and men in cross-border marriages as uneducated, culturally 'backward' or as conforming to racial stereotypes. Women and men in cross-border marriages are also often viewed as manipulative and exploitative and may be sexualised and exoticised in the public imagination. The actions and motivations of cross-border marriage migrants are often simplified by prejudicial assumptions that often increase their vulnerability and this chapter will address the threat and the reality of violence in cross-border marriages as well as the forms that violence may take. This chapter therefore will draw on the debate about forced marriage and so-called 'honour' crimes, the notion of mail-order brides and the 'victim-discourse' of trafficking and people smuggling. It will also consider government responses to violence against women and migrants and how the enforced dependency through residency status that is contingent on a spouse may itself make women vulnerable to abuse.

Chapters 6, 7 and 8 attempt to demonstrate how notions of transnationalism may be used to enhance our understandings of cross-border marriage in particular and migration in general. Chapter 6 presents case studies of marriages that are properly 'transnational' in that they are shaped by the transnational community structures that the marriage partners belong to. These marriages are contracted, at least in part, because of established community links and play a significant role in the maintenance and development of the transnational projects of migrant communities. Using marriage within South Asian communities, the chapter draws on the extensive literature describing marriages in which one partner moves from their shared, ancestral country of origin to live in a country of settlement. This chapter will use the nuanced published literature to demonstrate the complexity of marriage choices available to many transnational groups and to demonstrate the interplay between personal, cultural and institutional factors that determine migration and marriage choices. Structure, such as traditional gender roles and expectations, will be shown to remain significant but migrating spouses may be able to act with agency in surprising and subtle ways. The chapter will consider why it may be that marriage remains common within South Asian communities despite their social, political and economic integration in many countries of settlement. It goes on to consider the structural mechanisms relevant in the organising of transnational marriages and discusses the implication for individual agency within those structures.

Chapter 7 focuses on cross-border marriages that are not clearly 'transnational' and which are made between individuals marrying outside of their natal communities. I will draw on research from East Asia that focuses on marriages contracted across cultural and national borders, that is, the so-called inter-cultural marriages, sometimes known as 'mixed marriages', that are becoming more common both as global travel for leisure, education and employment increases and as population demographics and social patterns change. In East Asia, research has typically focused on cross-border marriages that are, in part, the result of economic imbalances in the region which juxtapose the strong economies of Taiwan and South Korea with the less developed economies of China and Southeast Asia. Inter-cultural marriage in East Asia, in many cases, has different causes from cross-border, inter-cultural marriage in other parts of the world but the effects on the spouses migrating for the purpose of marriage in terms of isolation, dependence on their new spouse and vulnerability, for example, may be similar to those experienced by cross-border marriage migrants moving to join partners in Australasian, European or North American countries. As in Chapter 6, the role of structural factors such as family relationships and policy will be considered as will the potential for migrants to exert their individual agency in choosing cross-border marriage and in building their future lives. It will be argued that while these marriages can be clearly differentiated from the transnational marriages described in Chapter 6, they may be the first steps in the development of transnational communities which may, in turn, lead to further transnational marriage.

Chapter 8 will consider cross-border marriage migration within refugee communities – a field that has so far been under-researched. I claim a special category for marriage in refugee communities as I argue that they are the result of a different kind of migration logic from the marriages described in Chapters 6 and 7. Unlike these marriages, refugee marriages are not contracted in conditions of social stability and take place as societies are being broken down and re-made after political, social or environmental disaster. As such, marriage in refugee communities may represent the efforts of individuals and groups to promote the immediate security and protection of themselves and those close to them as well as, or instead of, re-building communities that have been displaced and disrupted. Thus, marriages may be contracted within ethnic or cultural communities and may be transnational and follow traditional patterns. Alternatively they may be made between ethnic and cultural groups. I bring them together here in recognition of the particular circumstances that apply in communities with refugee backgrounds that may be motivated by a very real need to use marriage as a way of protecting family members in danger as well as a way of rebuilding and re-establishing communities separated by war and conflict. In this chapter, I first address transnationalism as it relates to forced migration. In some communities, the notion of diaspora may be particularly important as it emphasises the maintenance of the values and ways of communities shattered by conflict and exile. I consider the role of structural factors such as family relationships and policy as well as the potential for refugees to exert their individual agency in choosing cross-border marriage.

Chapter 9 attempts to critically analyse the effect of policy in the home countries and countries of settlement of cross-border marriage migrants. Policy, represented by international migration regimes and by legislation relating to migration within countries, has a major impact on determining who and how people across borders. Policy shapes opportunities for migration often on gendered lines, and opens and closes different forms of migration. Policy in countries of settlement is concerned to control flows of migrants and may be explicitly designed to prevent migration except through a few, highly regulated avenues. One of these avenues is migration for family formation and family reunification but, rather than opening channels for all migrants wishing to form intimate partnerships, I argue that local definitions of what constitutes a recognised 'partnership' for the purpose of cross-border marriage differs from country to country and some of these differences will be discussed. This chapter considers how attitudes to migrants are influenced by national ideologies as well as by history and will put a special emphasis on how attitudes to women as migrants differ across the world. Throughout the chapter I show how policy may make migrants vulnerable, even when the stated aim is to protect the rights of migrants. Legislation has often failed because legislators have been unable or unwilling to appreciate the complexity of the phenomenon they are trying to regulate. As a result, policy has led to vulnerable migrants becoming increasingly disempowered as their personal rights (as opposed to their rights as spouses) have diminished. I argue that policy inevitably imposes 'structure' on migrants that undermines their agency, and it is a structure erected to uphold the interests of the country of settlement above the interests of migrants.

Chapter 10 sets out to look in more detail at what life may be like for migrants who have married across borders. I argue that many cross-border marriage migrants may have little knowledge of the countries they are marrying into or even what will be expected of them as wives and husbands or mothers and fathers in that country. I consider why migrants choose marriage across borders and consider what it is that they are hoping to achieve through their choices. The chapter includes a section on how and whether contacts with the migrant's country of origin are maintained post-migration and I discuss how migrants may manage the different expectations that may exist between married partners. The issue of developing a sense of identity and belonging in a new country is considered, especially in countries where migrants, and migrant women in particular, may face discrimination and prejudice. The integration of migrants and their acquisition of citizenship, formal and informal, are an important part of adapting and becoming part of the country of settlement. The 'space' the state may allow for their integration and for the integration of their children is explored. The final section in Chapter 10 considers problems in marriage and marriage breakdown, highlighting some of the consequences for migrants if their marriages fail before they have established an independent right of settlement.

This book concludes with Chapter 11 bringing together the main themes presented in the book. It will include discussion of the future significance of global cross-border marriage migration and advocate for a more positive approach to a globally significant migration stream. I will argue that by promoting better understandings of why and how cross-border marriages are arranged and lived, the lives and futures of many migrants can be improved, communities strengthened and social cohesion enhanced. My final conclusions in brief are that cross-border marriage migration is a significant and growing form of migration that has lessons for our understanding of all forms of migration. Studying marriages through a lens of ethnicity and tradition alone is insufficient to understand the decision-making processes of marriage migrants, and researchers and policy-makers alike need to pay more attention to the individual needs, circumstances and aspirations of marriage migrants. I have argued that an approach to understanding marriage migration decisions needs to be sensitive to the agency of migrants and that the study of migration and of cross-border marriage needs to hear the voices of those mostly closely engaged in their negotiation and arrangement. As marriages across the world are increasingly made between citizens of different countries and cultures, more and more children grow up with dual, or multiple, heritages. Policy-makers urgently need to take heed of the complex social challenges raised for the well-being of individuals, families and society in general. These issues, highlighted in relation to cross-border marriage migration, are closely linked to discriminatory discourses about migrants in general and closer attention to the individual within the homogenised category of 'migrant' or 'cross-border marriage migrant' is needed to promote both the human rights of migrants and the efficacy and fairness of immigration policies.

Chapter 11 concludes with suggestions for future research based on the gaps in current knowledge identified in earlier chapters. Research recommendations identify general areas of research including the need for improved quantitative research and data collection, longitudinal research projects, as well as more specific areas such as research with refugee communities and with the children of cross-border marriage migrants. I advocate for research that keeps the needs of marriage migrants, their dependants and their families firmly at the forefront of analysis so that policy can be informed by data that is nuanced and grounded in experience. I argue that cross-border marriage migration should be addressed as a type of migration in its own right as it straddles the divisions between forced and voluntary migration, and does not always sit easily within the category of 'family migration'. While it cannot be bracketed easily within any of the other type of migration, such as economic or labour migration, it has elements in common with them and insights from the study of marriage migration have the potential to illuminate other areas of migration study and vice versa.

The study of cross-border marriage migration has much to teach scholars of migration in general. It provides us with a contemporary (but extremely long-standing) and dynamic example of how migrants continue to negotiate borders for their own and others' benefit and provides us with examples of transnationalism operating across the globe both as a personal and a community strategy. This study will illuminate how both well-established and newly established transnational communities adapt and maintain themselves. Further, this study speaks of how citizens are made and of how individuals can build their own forms of public and private citizenship even in situations of enforced dependency and in the face of discrimination. Studying the lives of cross-border marriage migrants brings issues of agency and especially gendered forms of agency into focus and allows an analysis of the minutiae of the negotiation of personal aspirations. Researchers who have focused on this group of migrants have focused on the personal narratives and representations of marriage migrants and these studies are important for what they have to say about marriage migration but also because of what they tell about migration in general. These studies challenge the many stereotypes of migrants that attempt to place them into one or other broad category of migrant and reveal the complexity of motivation for migration and the *human* beneath the stereotype.

2
Gendering Migration

This chapter sets out to highlight the importance of understanding gender in the study of marriage and migration. It will be argued that the critical work of feminist scholars such as Eleonore Kofman (1999; Kofman *et al.* 2000) and Patricia Pessar and Sarah Mahler (2001; Mahler and Pessar 2006) among many others, has demonstrated the importance of gender as a key, but often under-estimated, factor in understanding migration. It has been argued since the 1980s that the value of gendered perspectives on migration has not so much been unknown or under-studied, as overlooked and neglected by policy-makers (Kofman 1999). This neglect continues today as while policy-makers and legislators commonly advocate 'gender guidelines', there remains a tendency for 'gender' to stand for 'women' and for the more subtle lessons of gender-sensitive research to be ignored. Gender identity, conceptualised as a socially and culturally produced construct that is durable but not immutable (McNay 2000), informs the decision-making of individuals and guides the actions of men, women and their communities. This chapter will argue for the importance of gender-sensitive research and policy and will consider how understandings of gender roles inform how marriage is seen in different cultures. Marriage practices and principles are based on deeply entrenched social, cultural, political and economic logics but inevitably, these change and evolve in response to changing circumstances. Actual and potential migration is described here as an important catalyst for change in gender relations and, consequently, on marriage practices and ideologies. This chapter will discuss the impact gender norms and roles have on individual and collective decisions to marry and to migrate and will begin with a discussion of how academics have sought to 'gender' migration studies.

Gendering migration studies

Since the 1990s, feminist academic voices have exhorted policy-makers and mainstream migration theorists to place gender at the centre of the study of migration and specifically to recognise its centrality to the decision-making of individuals and groups migrating across borders (Chant and Radcliffe 1992; Callamard 1999; Pessar and Mahler 2001; Mahler and Pessar 2006; Piper 2006). Academic research which included gendered perspectives and which highlighted female migration has long existed, but was largely discounted or ignored by policy-makers and the public (Morokvasic 1984). More recently, work largely carried out by feminist academics has succeeded in drawing attention to the significance of gender in migration and, from a starting point of studying the migration patterns of women, has highlighted the importance of gendered social, political and cultural factors in determining how and why people migrate. Early work in this vein challenged the notion of the 'trailing spouse' that described women's migration as little more than the direct or indirect result of the migration of male heads of households (Chant and Radcliffe 1992). This assumption of a passive form of migration meant that the independent migration of women, along with children and the elderly, was barely recognised even as global migration movements included increasing, and eventually equal, numbers of women[1] and men (Castles and Miller 2009). While women's migration is seen as dependent on the actions of the men who they travel with, to or from, it remains 'secondary and associative' (Palriwala and Uberoi 2005: vii), and the resulting structural biases in the collection and analysis of data mean that some female-dominated streams of migration go unrecognised in statistics designed with the masculine-based conceptions and categories in mind. As Eleonore Kofman (2004) has noted, the focus on the individual in migration obscures family-related migration and the dominant economic focus of migration studies maintains the dichotomy of male producer/female reproducer. This obscures evidence of women as active migrants in their own right. For example, large numbers of women travel as domestic workers but may travel in small groups that are less observable in official statistics. If they travel as part of family groups, their role as initiators and motivators for migration is rendered invisible. Men and women migrants are present in different concentrations in different migratory flows and men and women migrate through different channels taking advantage of gender-specific labour markets (Piper 2006: 139). Greater sensitivity to these gendered streams of migration has led academics and others to look more closely at how gender and changing notions of gender roles impact on migration patterns.

The study of gender in migration has advanced from being an extra variable – the 'add women and stir' approach (Kofman *et al.* 2000: 22) and subtler studies bring gender perspectives into research on the experience of all migrants rather than just women. Gender-sensitive studies investigating male perspectives are still rare but gender in its broadest sense should clearly be factored into analyses of all migration and migratory movements (Mahler and Pessar 2006: 29). Gendered approaches to the study of migration have benefited from the analytical framework of intersectionality, and transversalism (Yuval-Davis *et al.* 2002; Yuval-Davis 2006) which conceptualise gender as a variable along with other social divisions such as class, race and ethnicity and encourage women's migration decisions to be seen in light of the complexities of women's personal and social attributes as well as their economic and political opportunities.

Laws regulating migration are often highly gendered and reflect the gender biases and normative assumptions of the countries that operate them. Gendered regulations may govern the types of work men and women migrants can do (Tyner 1996) or may be reflected in gendered assumptions about the veracity of asylum claims of women and men (Mahler and Pessar 2006: 40);[2] see also Bhabha (1996, 2007). As we will see throughout the book, social representations of women and men have the power to frame the social, political and economic opportunities of individuals at all stages of the migration process. Gender shapes the degree of choice people have over how and whether to migrate; it shapes the social meaning migration has for the individual as a member of their specific social group and it shapes the perceptions of the migrant by outsiders (such as policy-makers and enforcers) too. Edward Said's classic work *Orientalism* (1978), describes the power of representations to influence how 'outsiders' are perceived by insiders. Migrants are archetypal outsiders who have crossed physical and emotional borders even when such border crossing is socially condoned and sanctioned. Writers describing representations of women migrating to marry foreign men hark back to Said's work on the explorations of the stereotypes and assumptions made about orientalised (or simply migrant) women (Robinson 1996; Ito 2005; So 2006). Women are not the only objects of gender-based stereotypes, however, and women too draw on unrealistic, idealistic or misleading representations of men they hope to marry in the West (Thai 2005; Johnson 2007; Yea 2008).

Migrants are rarely able to control or even influence the way they are represented and their representation is generally more meaningful to the portrayers than to the portrayed. Migrants are seen as simplistic and dichotomous caricatures, as dangerous 'pollutants' (Malkki 1995) undermining national integrity (Crowhurst 2007) or as plucky, hard-working people seeking to better themselves. Refugees, for example, may understand their flight in very personal ways, perhaps as a heroic continuation of political struggle or as evidence of failure or tragedy but on arrival in a country of refuge will be viewed according to the local narratives on refugees and asylum seeking. Much has been written about the representation of migrants and of the 'othering' process that turns them from individuals with personal stories to members of homogenised groups (Grillo 1985; Baker and McEnery 2005; among many others) categorised as 'asylum seeker', 'refugee', 'economic migrant', 'irregular migrant', migrant wife or husband, with little or no regard to their individual story and motivation. How this highly gendered process of 'othering' affects migrants will be returned to in later chapters.

Emotive representations of migrant women, such as those recorded by Carol Freeman in her study in South Korea, affect the life chances of migrants and their dependents. Freeman found women were represented as either 'powerless victims of a government-sanctioned form of trafficking in women or ... as heartless opportunists who actively exploit the South Korean men they marry' (Freeman 2005: 81). These dichotomous views of migrant women in general, and marriage migrants in particular, emphasise how distant migrants may be from their portrayal while still having to live with those depictions. Representations of migrant men are equally stereotypical and unhelpful and numerous writers have commented on how the attributes of migrant men are devalued and stereotyped while white masculinity goes uncriticised (Ong 1996; Yuval-Davis *et al.*, 2002; Manalansan IV 2006; Engebrigsten 2007). Naturally, migrant groups themselves stereotype and Kunz (1973), has described how different 'vintages' of refugees may dismiss the claims to asylum of their fellows who arrive at different times and who have had different experiences of persecution. The stereotyped and homogenised discourses that migrants may adopt, like those of the society in general, are not gender-neutral and are informed by the gendered assumptions the powerful make about the weak. These discourses tell us how gender roles and mores feed into migration debates from the perspectives of the settled and may inform how gender influences the migration choices of people on the move.

Group narratives about gender roles can be significant as a means of delineating the boundaries of the group and help define who belongs and, consequently, who does not. That said, gendered inequalities originate beyond communities as well as within them and the role of the wider community in influencing and shaping gendered practices often goes unacknowledged when minority communities are being scrutinised. Minority status, and the experience of racism and social exclusion that so often goes along with it, can promote a defensiveness that leads to the re-assertion of community boundaries and to the imposition of social controls that are often gendered. Gender norms and behaviours which control women and their fertility have had a central role in the history of group identity formation and an important place in the establishment and maintenance of nationalist ideologies (see Yuval-Davis 1997; Handrahan 2004; Kaufman and Williams 2004) . Women are often treated as ethnic boundary markers because of their assumed natural place in the domestic life of the community through their roles as producers and reproducers through childbirth and through the education and cultural indoctrination of children. Women tend to have an indirect form of citizenship in that they become citizens through others. Joyce Kaufman and Kristen Williams write: 'She is a citizen in so far as her duties and obligations are to produce and educate future citizens and to subordinate her identity and citizenship to the male head of the household' (2004: 421–2) and this statement is particularly appropriate to the citizenship of female cross-border marriage migrants. Betty De Hart writes in a similar vein that women 'give birth to members of the nation-state, but also reproduce its ideology, and the symbolic and legal borders of the collective' and as a result face greater, or a different form of, scrutiny than male migrants (2006b: 52). These long-standing norms may become increasingly significant and subject to revision as members of groups migrate.

Making migration studies gender-sensitive has the potential to add nuance and, where gender is incorporated as a central, determining factor in migration patterns (rather than as just an extra variable) gender has the potential to act as a corrective lens to help understand migration patterns. Mahler and Pessar's important article has shown how 'although not frequently credited with making contributions to theory building, analyses using gender have and can make a difference to understanding how people decide to migrate, why they migrate at all, and why they occupy varying occupational statuses' (2006: 29). Their work demonstrates the power of gendered perspectives to illuminate migratory processes from the initial identification of migration as a possibility, for whom and how, through the decision to migrate, to how life as migrants, settled minorities or even returnees may be lived. Jacqueline Bhabha asks how gendered and other stereotypes play into our understandings of and relationships to migrants and she cites Fiske and Taylor's concept of 'cognitive miserliness' – 'using stereotypes to do just enough mental work to get by but cutting corners in terms of accuracy' (Bhabha 2007: 17). A gender perspective enables and supports our thought processes on migration and encourages us to see beyond the stereotypes of migrants to the gendered and socially positioned individuals behind them.

Migration, marriage and change in gender roles

Migration transforms the opportunities of migrants, positively as well as negatively, so it is reasonable to anticipate that migration may also alter the gender roles assumed by migrants. Academic literature provides examples of how these changes may occur, often focusing on how migrants balance their lives away from their countries of origin with their continuing relationship with their natal countries, but change cannot be assumed to be away from traditional gender roles. Research shows that there is no automatic relationship between migration and increased personal freedom and migrants, and migrant communities do not necessarily reject traditional norms on migration. Many, in fact, draw increasingly heavily on traditions and practices in order to maintain a sense of themselves and a sense of cultural authenticity away from home (see Baumann 1996, for examples). Louisa Schein (2005) has written about the assumptions that country-of-origin parents may make about the progressiveness of Western-based partners only to find them holding more traditional ideas than are common in the country of origin. A similar point has been made by Roger Ballard (2004) with reference to South Asian diaspora-based 'pardeshi' communities who find the privileged 'deshis' from Delhi or Islamabad more westernised than they are. Migration may not deliver the gains migrants hope for and Mirjana Morokvasic has noted how 'The increased participation of women in certain migratory flows does not always reflect more freedom of movement, but rather a proliferation of precarious jobs where, as in the case of trafficked women, their mobility may be very restricted' (2004: 22). This observation demonstrates the importance of separating out the concepts of mobility and migration. Migration may promise new possibilities for women but in reality may just funnel them down certain migratory routes rather than open up a wider range of choices.

The degree to which migrants adapt their social practices, including gender norms, on migration depends on numerous factors including their own personal desires; the nature and opportunity provided by any transnational social spaces they might belong to; their emotional if not spatial connection to home; and on the practical demands of their new lives (Eastmond 1993). What seems clear is that the majority of migrants adopt gender roles that hybridise the roles they bring with them from home and the roles they develop in response to their lives as migrants. This hybridity, which may result in individuals adopting different gender roles in public and in domestic settings, is part of the negotiations of everyday life which might go unnoticed outside the scrutinised world of the migrant. The everyday is a complex and unruly setting for 'the shifting, often messy and contradictory relationships between ideal conditions and everyday practices within transnational families and in gendered relations in migration' (Manalansan IV 2006: 241).

Many authorities argue that migration is generally a positive experience for women as it increases their freedom of opportunity and allows them to break free of gendered forms of oppression and disadvantage. Marita Eastmond found that the social world of the Chilean women she studied expanded and they took on 'a broader repertoire of roles, including greater participation in economic and other public spheres' (1993: 48). She found that migration reduced the social control they experienced but that they missed the emotional support of their former social networks. In contrast to women's more public roles post-migration, Eastmond found that Chilean men's worlds became more private and socially disconnected on migration. Once migrated, especially to the developed world, there is often a trend for families to become smaller in comparison to the extended families of home. Away from the scrutiny of in-laws and other community members, women may also be able to transgress the gender boundaries within the family. Studies have shown, however, that women's newfound public and economic roles are often taken on in addition to their more traditional domestic roles. As a result, gendered roles carried over from the country of origin may not be replaced but simply added to. This experience is shared with women across the world who have found participation in public settings has added to their existing domestic roles. As Bridget Anderson's work has shown (2000), buying-in female migrant domestic labour has been a solution to this impasse but one that is only open to the privileged. Matsuoka and Sorenson quote a professional Eritrean woman describing her experience in Canada thus:

> I worked back home, so it was natural for me to look for a job right away. My child was still young. Back home I could have hired someone to take care of my child and house. But it was not possible here.
>
> (1999: 223)

This woman was working and trying to manage her home along traditional lines while additionally, as one of the few Eritrean women in the community, she was expected to prepare meals for the family's many male guests.

Katherine Charsley and Alison Shaw's study of Pakistani marriage migration found 'potential and actual transformation of gendered status' (2006: 331), and described the Pakistani marriages in their study as representing an important mechanism for change and an example of the dynamism of transnationalism. Patricia Pessar and Sarah Mahler provide case studies of how gender roles may be affected by migration and, on balance, argue that migration tends to break down gender roles except when partners marry as a unit. In these cases 'men expect their wives to preserve established gender roles and women usually oblige' (Pessar and Mahler 2001). The possibility of migration also serves to support gender roles that are changing in countries of emigration as the chance to migrate and maybe marry abroad allows women, and potentially men, to achieve aspirations and to live lifestyles that would not be possible in their home countries. Economic independence may be more achievable for the population of the Global South if they migrate rather than stay at home (as demonstrated by Ester Gallo's work discussed below), but Martin Manalansan's work (2006) has shown that migration may promote far more than economic change. Manalansan argues that migration provides opportunities for establishing new ways of being and cites Carrillo (2004) in arguing for the recognition of 'sexual migration' which 'far from a normalising process when migrants move for the purposes of biological and heterosexual reproduction, suggests that transnational movements enable queer practices, identities and subjectivities' (Manalansan IV 2006: 225). Hung Cam Thai's work (2008, 2005) describes how cross-border marriage migration can facilitate the marriage of people the community may consider 'unmarriageable' because of their non-traditional attributes, for example, an over-educated or independent-minded women or an under-educated man.

Transnationalism, discussed in more detail in Chapter 3, is, of course, a gendered process and the 'convertibility' (Thai 2008) of different assets and resources in different countries and contexts means that different gendered attributes gain or lose value as they cross borders. The notion of convertibility in transnational communities is an important one that has major ramifications for this study. Attributes that in one context work against an individual may work to their advantage in another. Much of the work on marriage and migration assumes the convertibility of assets within transnational groups as an important driver for marriage migration. Gendered roles are clearly assets that are convertible across borders as Thai's study demonstrates. He describes the lives of US-resident, low-income men of Vietnamese origin (known as Viet Kieu) whose perceived low achievement makes finding a marriage partner in the States difficult. 'Both the low income and the absence of a college degree in the United States meant that Teo felt he had little opportunity for social mobility... and in Teo's eyes to acquire social status, particularly in the Vietnamese American marriage market.' Returning to Vietnam, Teo's inadequate social assets were masked by his financial ones and 'The immediate convertibility of money is linked immediately to the convertibility of status and esteem' (Thai 2008: 42). In this example, convertibility is mostly linked to financial assets but the convertibility of negative assets in one setting to positive ones elsewhere can include educational, cultural, linguistic, religious, familial and personal attributes. Marriage migration can upset traditional notions of hypergamy by making women and men who are considered poor matches at home, desirable in transnational contexts, and specific examples of convertibility in marriage across borders will be discussed in the following chapters. Even outside transnational communities, migration similarly upsets traditional notions of who will make a good match and who will make a success of their lives. As the experience of marriage migrants shows, however, migration does not lead automatically to either an improvement in women's opportunities or a diminution and that even when change may seem positive from the outside, the protagonists themselves may hold different views.

The effect of marriage on the lives of women is another debated issue and marriage, whether contracted at home or across borders, may change the lives of women more than it changes the lives of men. Louisa Schein writes: 'In China, it will not be possible for men to take such a transformative step in their lifetimes; instead they will *qu*, or "get", a wife or daughter-in-law but remain firmly tethered to their class and locational positioning' (2005: 57). For many women, marriage means taking charge of their own home and household; gaining new responsibilities, status, and possibly independence from natal family. Marriage may extend a woman's responsibilities as she takes charge of the domestic sphere in addition to her other public roles while her husband may continue to operate much as ever he did before marriage. In the case of the Sudanese refugees described by Katarzyna Grabska (forthcoming), marriage for a migrant man seeking a wife in the refugee camps or villages represents the carrying out of an important social obligation. Marriage, however, results in his return home, alone, to his bachelor life while for his wife marriage means complete separation from the past as she leaves her natal home to become part of her husband's family. In exogamous marriages, a bride has to cope with the challenges of married life, the loss of her family and social networks and, possibly, with a new role of daughter-in-law in her husband's family. Katherine Charsley's work (2005) argues that in societies where exogamy is, or has been, the norm, girls are prepared for this inevitable rupture from a young age. When migration reverses the roles to mean that men have to leave home to live with their new wife's family, the men's lack of preparedness for such an abrupt change can result in great unhappiness and loss.

Many women gain material and social status through the process of migration. Many become wage earners and gain independence and self-determination through their participation in labour markets. Many migrant women become able to choose how they spend their money and many opt to support their natal family as remitters. Esther Gallo's study of Malayali migrants in Italy demonstrates how the material resources women brought into their families leads to marital relationships being 're-interpreted…more than the simple inversion of the conventional dependence of the wife on her husband' (Gallo 2005: 244). Research with migrants from the Philippines has explored in great detail how migrant women may have multiple reasons for seeking work overseas. Mahler and Pessar have referred to migration from the Philippines as 'arguably, the best-documented case of gender-induced and sculpted migration' (Mahler and Pessar 2006: 48), a claim supported by Tyner (1996), and list the ways in which gender has affected migration. Their work follows the gendered processes of migration flows influenced by colonial and post-colonial history, by national politics as well as by the need of individuals to support their families. Studies of migration from the Philippines (Gardiner Barber 2000; Yea 2004; Del Rosario 2005; Ito 2005; Faier 2007, 2008; Hilsdon 2007; Lauser 2008) show women migrating in apparent confirmation of traditional gender roles, as domestic workers, for example, but also tracks their desire to break free from gendered social bonds by finding foreign husbands or leaving their existing ones. Throughout, however, their activities remain informed and motivated by links to home and family. Migration from the Philippines is described in these studies as being both traditional and modern but also as being actively shaped by female migrants using their gender as an asset and a resource. Where women have gone before, there is evidence men are following and Andrea Lauser describes how men from the Philippines are also travelling as marriage migrants and that 'relatively well-established, older unmarried or widowed Philippine women in Western countries have emerged as coveted wives for young Philippine men willing to migrate' (Lauser 2008: 101).

Marriage migration, as already discussed, is generally conceptualised as a female-dominated migration stream but significant numbers of men from some communities travel as cross-border spouses. Research in the UK on marriages made within some South Asian communities shows equal numbers of men re-settling as the husbands of British citizens as women settling as wives (Ballard 2004: 15; Shaw 2006). Marriage is clearly not an exclusively female route to migration. There is increasing recognition of the migration of men from the Global South who migrate as partners of Western women, but research-based evidence of this is scarce (De Hart 2006b; Rodriguez Garcia 2006), exceptions being the work of Sanchez Taylor (20060, Takeshita (2007), and De Hart (2007) but research-based literature is outnumbered by sensational and journalistic accounts.

Male, cross-border spouses may be increasing in number but the evidence remains that cross-border spouses are predominately women. A fact partially explained by assumptions about the adaptability of femininity in contrast to the inflexibility of masculinity. In her critique of Bourdieu's writing on gender, Bev Skeggs argues that women do not resist the domination of men as Bourdieu predicted and that women often accept inequalities that they are well aware of. Skeggs argues that it is this 'ambiguity of femininity' (Skeggs 2004: 26) that recognises subordination but does not seek to change it, that has enabled women to adapt and accommodate the difficulties of their lives whether as migrants or not. Women are typically assumed to follow rather than to lead, to maintain rather than innovate, and women across the world are brought up with the assumption that they, unlike their brothers, will physically leave the home yet remain tied to both their new and old 'homes' by bonds of love and care. The image of woman as carer first and foremost presupposes women will be able to adapt to life in new countries; that domestic settings can be replicated and that the role of 'carer' is universal and natural. Anika Liversage's research with professional marriage migrants (Liversage 2009) is just one example of research arguing that women do not migrate to take on domestic roles but that the stereotype of woman as passive reproducer and carer endures, limiting their professional options. She writes: 'This unwanted domestication occurred because the women could not get *into* the labour market, not because they could not *leave* the home due to pressing domestic duties' (Liversage 2009: 131, italics in the original). Although there is little research available on the social consequences of male marriage migration (i.e. when men travel to set up home abroad), what little research there is emphasises how men struggle to adapt to changes in social settings and to their enforced dependence on their wives (Ballard 2004: 13; Charsley 2005). It may be assumed that women marriage migrants share the same feelings but may be culturally programmed and equipped to accept these struggles and may possess gendered strategies to deal with the problems they face. Gendered assumptions about women's capacities also make it unlikely that women who suffer from the changes brought on by migration (loneliness, isolation, homesickness) will receive recognition as men may do. Their depression or lack of well-being may be mis-attributed, for example, to culture or to factors relating to tradition rather than to migration.

Public and private roles

Women's public roles, as examples and representatives of collective respectability and honour, combine with their private roles, as nurturers and child-raisers, to inform women's roles as markers of community norms. Women's bodies in many cultures represent the honour of the community as a whole and, as a result, women's freedom of self-expression is reduced and limited. This, I would argue, is the norm across the world. These themes will be returned in Chapter 5, in which I will discuss how these attitudes lead to abuse and violence against women. Here these themes will be used to underpin the argument that women are widely assumed to have a special role in the domestic sphere, in nurturing the family, in the raising of children and in ensuring cultural continuity. Irene Gedalof (2007) has written persuasively that the assumed passivity of migrant women, (demonstrated not least by the culturally reified practice of arranged marriages), inhibits their integration and belonging beyond their ethnic communities. Gedalof argues that it is the private worlds of immigrant families, represented and maintained by women, that rouses the majority community's suspicion and places migrant women as both the symbol and the nurturer of 'otherness'. She writes: 'She stands, in her ignorant sameness, for the limits of difference that cannot be absorbed without shaking the stability of identity' (Gedalof 2007: 90). Gedalof's work is based on studies in the UK but has resonance across many countries with significant migrant populations and in countries that fear the establishment of migrant communities. She argues that discourses characterising migrant women as actively maintaining cultural difference place women as both victims of patriarchal, traditional society and as barriers to change because of their nurturing role within (im)migrant families. The assumption is that these women, enmeshed in their communities and unable to speak English, or the dominant language, do not participate in the economy and society beyond their immediate families. Gedalof writes: 'She is a problem defined by her linguistic isolation and limited awareness of cultural difference, and by her entanglement in the "backward practices" of arranged marriage and gender subordination' (2007: 90).

The widely held attitudes Gedalof seeks to highlight are significant in popular understandings of cross-border marriage, in which the differences between arranged and forced marriage are still poorly understood. These attitudes affect both public policy relating to cross-border marriage and the lives of marriage migrants post-migration. This view of women as unassimilable is not unanimous, however, and Gedalof's work has most resonance in relation to migrant women living within settled transnational communities. Carol Freeman's work in South Korea (Freeman 2005) argues that the South Korean state views women as more assimilable than men – demonstrated by the fact that non-Korean husbands have only been allowed formal citizenship since 1998 while non-Korean wives of citizens have long been able to naturalize (Freeman 2005: 108). The impact of Gedalof's work, in my opinion, goes further than local, UK debates about forced/arranged marriage and it has implications for the analysis of marriages involving migrants across in globe. The unequal and unrecognised responsibility women bear for providing care within families across the globe places particular pressure on migrant women who may been seen as possessing desirable domestic attributes yet also be suspected of maintaining and nurturing unwelcome difference.

The contribution women migrants make to their families, communities and to society in general is under-estimated in much the same way that caring and domestic work in general goes unrecognised and undervalued. Louise Ackers has argued that caring, as an important motivation and contribution, is generally invisible in migration theory (2004:

390) and that this lack of acknowledgement impairs our understanding of migration choices and patterns. Policies that privilege the migration of 'skilled' migrants, defined by their academic or vocational qualifications, further discriminate against potential migrants whose skills are unrecognised by systems focused on crude economic measures of participation (Yuval-Davis *et al.* 2002: 519; Kofman 2005: 458). The trend in the developed world towards privileging skilled migration is clearly established[3] and, given gendered disparities in access to education and economic participation, migration patterns will continue to be gendered according to the different forms of social and economic capitals migrants can call on. McCall (1992), cited in Skeggs (2004: 23), describes gender as a secondary form of capital as it is hidden behind the perception of gender as being universal and natural rather than a social construct. Skeggs argues that gender needs to be 'symbolic legitimated' before it can be recognised as a form of cultural capital (2004: 24). In immigration systems, gender clearly does not receive this symbolic legitimation but within communities and families, it may do. Skeggs notes Bourdieu's positioning of women's as 'capital bearing objects' rather as subjects in their own right who can accumulate capital (Skeggs 2004: 28) but, as some of the marriage migrants described in this book will show, women, and particularly wives, may carry a significant symbolic value that reflects back on the men and the families they join. Women are often assumed to be the 'gendered ethnic centre' of their group (Breger and Hill 1998: 15), with the group's ideology revolving around women's symbolic roles in families as mothers, carers and cultural signifiers as well as producers and maintainers of the 'emotional capital' that is shared within families (Reay 2004).

Conclusion

This chapter has attempted to provide a background to the discussion of how gender roles and differences operate within migration systems and within migrant communities. The issues raised here will be returned to throughout the chapters that follow and they inform the evolving debate on the often contradictory ways in which migration and the actions of migrants are gendered. Katy Gardner (2006) notes that historical studies of migration have challenged the assumption of women as exclusively dependant migrants but women clearly face different constraints on migration than male migrants do. Marriage may provide a means for migration but may just 'reinscribe their [women's] subordination within normative gender paradigms' (Mooney 2006: 399).

Traditional assumptions about female migrants as the 'trailing spouses' of pioneering men are being deservedly challenged but the fact remains that women's migration decisions are usually made in response to the actions of men whether as positive actions to join them or negatively to leave them. Women, whether migrants or not, have different aspirations and concerns from men and caring for family and other loved ones remains a *raison d'être* for many women. The place of care, and caring responsibilities, in relation to the migration of women, and, for that matter, of men, has not been studied with as much subtlety as the subject deserves. Research for this book, however, has uncovered a wealth of studies that record the voices of migrants who identify the search for fulfilling family lives as key drivers of their migratory decisions and aspirations. However marriages may be contracted, the majority of marriage partners aspire to love and partnership and this can easily be forgotten when faced with the kinds of negotiation of space and structure that are the norm for would-be cross-border marriage migrants. Marriage migration is just one route across borders but it is argued here that this route, the shape it takes, its opportunities, drawbacks, pitfalls and compromises are subtly gendered and have multigenerational implications for the migrants and their families in both countries of migration and countries of origin.

3
An Agency Approach to Understanding Marriage Migration

The concept of individual agency is increasingly being used as a lens to study migration and the decision-making of migrants and as a challenge to accounts of migrants' lives that assume their vulnerability and which position them as a victim of circumstance such as poverty, global inequality, criminality or immigration regimes. It is a concept that is often used with little clarity of definition. It is a slippery concept, as it is concerned with an individual's interior self and with why, faced with similar external circumstances, people act differently. Agency perspectives inform an understanding of the individuality of human subjects but require subjective judgements about motivations, aspirations and intentions. Studies of agency are often studies of the undercurrents behind the observable actions of people and groups and researchers interested in identifying when their subjects have acted with agency are obliged to interpret the meaning of actions and outcomes from scant evidence. In addition, studies of agency are necessarily studies of individual reaction to highly complex events and circumstances that are subject to on-going assessment and re-assessment by those involved.

The core sociological notion of 'agency' is central to this book and it is my contention that an analysis comparing factors that promote the agency of migrants balanced with the factors that undermine it, the tension between structure and agency, is an important if not essential feature. A focus on the agency of individual migrants as actors within the power structures of family, locality, nation and international institutions promotes a view of migrants as central players in their own lives. This perspective, I argue, is a necessary one to counter the more common representations of migrants who, for pragmatic or political reasons, generalise their experience into broad and impersonal categories such as forced or economic migrants, mail-order or transnational brides.

An individual's agency is situated among conflicting emotions, aspirations and loyalties, personal and community histories, religious beliefs and duties as well as macro-economic and political structures. Researchers interested in the agency of their subjects have to tease out examples and acts of personal agency, as autonomous individuals, from actions made in response to other pressures and influences. Recognising and recording the agency in an individual's story is, in my view, an extremely important goal and one that is certainly worth pursuing despite the inevitable problems it throws up. The effort is justified not only for the purpose of accurately understanding events and histories but also to validate the humanity of the vulnerable and the marginal. This second purpose, to affirm the humanity of even the most disadvantaged by according them respect as autonomous actors, is central to this project.

Human agency is, at least in part, the product of gendered assumptions and I argue that agency, in relation to women, is particularly problematic as women continue to be seen as either possessing power and agency equal to men or being virtually without agency at all. The discussions of research data in this book show how some women migrants are considered undesirable, rather than unfortunate, because of their lack of education and 'liberation' in Western terms. Women's agency and self-determination may be lauded publicly but women considered as lacking agency, or worse still women judged to have rejected agency (for example, by wearing a veil or choosing certain marriages) are condemned. The agency of the weak has generally been judged by the standards of observers looking in from the outside whether by white women commenting on the oppression of black women, by the settled and privileged judging the choices of migrants or by the safe and secure judging the choices made by women in violent personal relations or employment.

An agency approach attempts to hear the stories of the actors themselves. The telling, as well as the hearing, of stories is a complex matter subject to personal and public truths as well as to time and experience as Ken Plummer's work has effectively demonstrated (Plummer 1995). In his conclusion (which, he states, is not a conclusion as such, but an introduction to issues raised by his study), Plummer makes a plea for a deeper appreciation of 'the powerful role of the story telling process in the everyday life of everyday societies' (1995: 179). In my view, the telling of stories publicly and privately, reflects the agency of individuals and groups as they negotiate structures. Stories explain our actions to ourselves as well as to those we tell and are historically and socially situated through what *can* be told, or heard, in any time or setting. Structures, represented by public and private audiences of stories, thus intimately affect what can be told to whom, but cannot entirely control the story and it may be here, in the space between the public and the personal that agency can be found.

In this chapter, I start out by addressing debates over definitions of agency and argue further for the importance of recognising agency in the study of migrants' lives. Following that, I will consider how agency can be achieved through tactics and strategy and will then consider its role in social innovation, transgression and resistance. This discussion is a necessary introduction to the chapters that follow that discuss in greater detail how people claim agency through marrying and migrating across borders.

Defining agency

It has been argued (see Plummer 2001; Clegg 2006) that the pre-eminence of post-modernist thought has focused study on structures as dominant factors in determining action at the expense of the study of human agency. Nevertheless, as Peter Taylor-Gooby (2008) has argued, while notions of agency are increasingly being recognised in the form of the 'rational actor logic', this is only one way of understanding the agency of individuals. Taylor-Gooby writes: 'The way in which it (the rational actor logic) directs attention to the rational aspects of agency and away from the role of social values and emotions generates real problems' (2008: 277). The notion of agency may be attributed to individual rational action as well as to social and non-rational actions as well as all points between; the accounts of agency referred to in this book thus fall along the spectrum between the individual and the social, the rational and the non-rational. Laura Ahearn, in her review of conceptualisations of agency, proposes a 'provisional' definition stating that: 'Agency refers to the socio-culturally mediated capacity to act' (2001: 112) – a definition which articulates the key concepts of action and the mediation of action. Ahearn argues that agency is more than 'free will' and draws on influential thinkers such as Bourdieu, Giddens and De Certeau in discussing the relationship between the simplistic idea of free will and more nuanced culturally and situationally mediated 'agency'. Agency is also, in my opinion, a broader concept that 'autonomy' – which assumes a person's power to act in self-directed ways and is linked to specifically Western ideas of individualism that may have less resonance in non-Western contexts where the community (however defined) may be the appropriate unit of analysis. It is as well to heed Sharon Wray's warning that 'dominant western conceptualisations of agency are often used uncritically; individualistic notions of choice, autonomy and in/dependence often pervade accounts of agency' (2004: 24).

Debates about the nature of agency coalesce around the balance between an individual's autonomous, political or socio-economic position and their ability to act within power structures such as family, community, national and international institutions – the so-called agency–structure debate. Advocates for the human rights of migrants and other vulnerable people may emphasise the pre-eminent role of various structures in dictating the life choices and chances of migrants focusing on the 'structural violence' inherent in immigration controls worldwide that systematically discriminate against citizens of the developing world. While the power and inequity of such structures are undeniable, agency remains a possibility and focusing on structure at the expense of individual agency has led to an underestimation of the capacity of migrants and the less privileged in general to act purposefully and/or even rationally. As Graham Scambler has noted: 'Agency may be structured, but it is not structurally determined' (2007: 1083), arguing that it is the interaction and negotiation *between* structure and agency that is of most interest. This debate will be returned to later in Chapter 5 in discussions of force and violence, but it is important to note here that a focus on the structural without engaging fully with the personal can lead to misunderstandings and to the practical disempowerment of migrants. As Nicole Constable (2006) writes, recognising structural inequality as a major reason for migration and/or marriage has its limitations arguing: 'This logic is not necessarily wrong, but it is not the *only* way to tell and understand the story. Moreover, if it is read as the story, it obscures significant variations among and between women and through time' (Constable 2006, italics in the original).

Steven Lukes discusses how the 'insufficient recognition' of identities (Lukes 2005: 119) can fix people in dependent (or equally, in dominant) positions if care is not taken to hear the personal stories behind their more commonly understood explanatory story. Lois McNay refers similarly to 'misrecognition' by which an individual is 'denied the status of a full partner in social interaction as a consequence of institutionalised patterns of value that deem some certain individuals less worthy of respect and esteem than others' (2000: 189, n.1). Misrecognition or insufficient recognition has a profound impact on migrants given the 'patterns of value' that discriminate against them and which are institutionalised through their contingent status in their country of settlement as well as through policy, practice and representation. Kathryn Robinson's work with cross-border marriage migrants in Australia provides a good example of misrecognition, describing how women were judged to be simultaneously submissive and scheming. Robinson's close examination of some high profile cases involving cross-border marriage migrants shows how their perceived 'transgression of the ideology of romantic love allowed the women to be branded as grasping opportunists, nothing better then prostitutes. The more sympathetic version has them as sex slaves' (Robinson 1996: 56). Recognising and validating the purposeful activities of the weak and disadvantaged celebrates their humanity and creativity and adds nuance to often simplistic depictions of policy 'subjects', whether the subjects of welfare, migration or any other kind of policy (Hoggett 2001).

To balance the emphasis on structure, and in doing so to encourage the telling of other stories, the following section will consider the role of the self in establishing and generating agency.

Agency and the 'self'

In the introduction to her study of human agency, Margaret Archer argues that personal identities are combinations of the 'I' of the self-conscious person we become and the 'me' that is ascribed to us by our families, communities and the societies we operate in. This notion of an interior sense of self combined with relationships with the outside world, positions the agency of an individual 'between the "I", who an individual seeks to become and the "Me", whom they have been previously constrained to be' (Archer 2000: 11). For Archer, evaluating our circumstances and acting in practical ways makes us who we are and 'our continuous sense of self, or self-consciousness, emerges from our practical activity in the world' (ibid.: 3). Archer summarises: 'In short we are who we are because of what we care about: in delineating our ultimate concerns and accommodating our subordinate ones, we also define ourselves' (ibid.: 10). Assumptions of a dichotomy between self and structure is also challenged by critics opposed to the Cartesian dualism it presupposes, see Diana Coole's work, for example (2005: 136), and Archer sees our social selves being defined at the intersection of structure and agency, where personal identity develops from self and structure.

Agency, then, can be seen as the interaction between our self-conscious self and the social context we find ourselves in. It is 'embodied' in that individuals may be more, or less aware of how their environment, social context and upbringing affect their lives and their decision-making. Embodied concepts guide us consciously and unconsciously through adherence to traditions and other social norms that we may see, to varying degrees, as immutable and natural. The enduring nature of these embodied views and ideas tacitly informs our thought processes and 'the body manifests conservative agency by perpetuating embodied rituals that act as a reservoir of sedimented memories to lend a practical continuity to (hierarchical) social life' (Coole 2005: 130). Cultures, be they the cultures of families, religions or nations, drain into these reservoirs of memories shaping our activities and so shaping our agency. A definition of agency as embodiment becomes problematic, however, if embodiment is seen as an essentially conservative force that leads to unchanging cultures governed by unalterable cultural codes. The stereotyping of some cultures as unchanging and conservative (invariably other people's), in contrast to other cultures as adaptable and progressive (usually our own), leads to cultural reification and to a view of some cultures as 'embodied' and therefore static and immutable. Such cultural relativism, in my view, allows cultures to be labelled as backward, unchanging and self-perpetuating and promotes a view of their members as similarly rigid and bound by cultural norms that restrict their agency and implicitly, their humanity – such ideas will be demonstrated in later chapters to have real and demonstrable effects on the lives of migrants.

Even if we can agree on the lasting power of embodied ideas to inform our decisions, people in general and migrants in particular are 'not just cultural artefacts' (Archer 2000: 3), nor are they the 'cultural dupes' (Sandy 2007: 203), that sometimes they are presented as. In Paul Hoggett's view: 'A radical model of agency must illuminate how people break out from the social systems which make up their lives and endure risks that any radical change in one's life course brings' (2001: 51). In suggesting a model of agency that allows for non-rational behaviour and which can cope with the 'paradox and contradiction' (ibid.: 53) of human behaviour, Hoggett anticipates the capacity of individuals to act as both agents and objects and to show different degrees of reflexivity and adaptability. Rationalist models of agency are, in my view, best suited to empowered, resourceful and reflexive agents and may have little to say about the lives of non-reflexive agents who act without thought – the non-reflexive object – dominated by experience which makes them unable to act purposefully; or to the reflexive object who, aware of their domination, may be unable to improve their position (Hoggett 2001).

The 'capabilities approach' advocated by Martha Nussbaum and influenced by the work of Amartya Sen (Nussbaum 2000), argues for basic human capabilities that are 'informed by an intuitive idea of a life that is worthy of the dignity of the human being' (ibid.: 5). The capabilities approach is universalist and related to the achievement of individual goals, something Nussbaum considers particularly relevant to the study of women's lives whose personal goals are so often subsumed in the goals of others. The capabilities she suggests as central to human functioning include the most basic of capabilities to enjoy a normal, healthy life span and to experience the giving and receiving of love and care. Nussbaum's list of capabilities also include more abstract capabilities such as the capability to have an emotional life, to play and to demonstrate practical reason in relation to one's life through critical reflection on life plans and possibilities. Nussbaum argues that severely disadvantaged and deprived groups may not even aspire to the autonomy others take for granted or strive for, but it is important that we imagine how such groups might claim these goals. I will argue that the studies discussed in this volume show how migration can catalyse capabilities and promote claims for autonomy and personal agency.

The impact of cultural and personal upbringing on an individual's capacity for self-determination has been much discussed – most significantly perhaps, by Pierre Bourdieu through his notion of *habitus*. Bourdieu's *habitus* allows for change, adaptation and resistance, but he sees change as something that itself emanates from the 'field'. Bourdieu was at pains to clarify that an individual's *habitus* is not a static worldview but a 'system of *dispositions*, that is of permanent manners of being, seeing, acting and thinking, or a system of *long-lasting* (rather than permanent) schemes of schemata or structures of perception, conception and action' (Bourdieu 2005: 43, italics in the original). Bourdieu describes *habitus* as a style, that informs a person's practical actions, discrepancies and exceptions – it describes how the 'me' that Archer sees as imposed by context and culture exists within the 'I' that individuals know themselves to be. Agency, thus, can be seen as emerging from the balance between the traditional logic of the *habitus*, an individual's experience and opportunity and their own personal attributes. 'It is important,' Laura Ahearn writes, 'to ask how people themselves conceive of their own actions and whether they attribute responsibility for events to individuals, to fate, to deities, or to other animate or inanimate forces' (2001: 113). Sensitivity to agency promotes a re-centring of study on the individual and *their* understanding of their lives.

An agency focus, I argue, allows us to study the lives of migrants in what Sayer, cited in Smith (2001: 118), refers to as an appropriate 'time-space setting', that contextualises events yet holds the actors at the centre of their own story. As objectified people, who tend to be discussed in absentia more often than consulted, migrant women and men are too often subject to the power of commentators who ascribe them a role and decide '*who* is sufficient of an individual to produce a unique performance in a role' (Archer 2000: 12, italics in original). Margaret Archer considers 'unscripted performances' (ibid.: 7) the mark of an active agent, but I argue that in relation to migration and migrants, many of these performances (for example, agreeing to take up an employment contract overseas or agreeing to an arranged marriage) are not credited as positive decisions on the part of the subordinated individual but are interpreted as resulting from duress and/or the circumstances of migrants' lives. Women 'even as subordinate players, always play an active part that goes beyond the dichotomy of victimization/acceptance, a dichotomy that flattens out a complex and ambiguous agency in which women accept, accommodate, ignore, resist, or protest – sometimes all at the same time' (MacLeod 1992: 534, cited in Ahearn 2001: 116). Such actions and decisions are often judged post-hoc, after hindsight allows reflection on how things went wrong, but credit for an individual's place in those actions is still deserved and should be valued.

The notion of an unscripted performance is useful in determining a balance between coercion and self-determination and an example provided by Laura Agustin shows how even while outsiders may identify a person as a victim (with its connotation of innocence) the actor may see herself as 'guilty' and of being complicit. Agustin describes a Colombian woman in detention in Bangkok as wracked with guilt for having broken the law in an attempt to enter Japan. According to Agustin, 'While this woman had been a victim, she had also made choices and felt responsible' (2003: 33). The implication is that she felt it was her 'unscripted performance', knowingly breaking the law to enter Japan, that had led to her present position rather than her disadvantage or the unfairness of global immigration control. Emily Chao (2005) presents another 'cautionary tale' of women's agency. Chao's research shows how Chinese women have eloped, or allowed themselves to be kidnapped, and married away from their home locality. Chao describes how women were blamed for the mistakes they had made and for exhibiting the agency that got them into trouble.

Women who independently seek employment or marriage in more prosperous areas make themselves more vulnerable to kidnappers... Women who leave the familiar to cross distant borders may be perceived as seeking out danger thus calling into question their morality. Women who leave their home region are associated with dishonesty, misguided behaviour and the fostering of social disorder.

(Chao 2005: 40–1)

The central question that this book must address, therefore, is how to recognise and validate the dignity of individuals making and suffering for their mistakes while still addressing the inherent inequalities that make simple aspirations so risky and so heavily punished when they go wrong.

The next sections will attempt to apply theoretical concepts of agency to the literature relating to cross-border marriage migration to demonstrate the dimensions of agency and to show how women and men can act as agents during migration. Migrants may be able to express agency in a range of different ways and the following sections will consider agency as strategic and tactical; as a form of transgression and resistance and as a creative and innovative process. These categories are not mutually exclusive nor clearly bounded but I use them here in an attempt to explore how migrants are able to draw on their personal agency.

Agency, strategy and tactics

I have argued that the agency of individuals and groups is defined, at least in part, through relationships to the structures, in the form of the institutions, formal and informal, that control lives and shape opportunities. This view of agency sees personal opportunity engaging and negotiating with environments which mould our futures but do not dictate them. As Scambler argues:

There is agency even among the coerced and destined... choice is structured, and post-modern culture favours a 'rhetoric of choice' that is often (a) an ideological device covering for a profiteering consumerism, and (b) a legitimatory device allowing for the political attribution of deviance to those who choose 'irresponsibly'.

(2007: 1092)

The rhetoric of choice, therefore, can mask powerlessness, blame a victim for their victimhood and can contribute to misunderstandings about the real possibilities open to individuals or groups. The rhetoric of choice can also ignore the constraints an individual faces from their circumstance, history, status or upbringing yet still blame and label people for failing to achieve or for transgressing. Reya Chow argues for the importance of tactics in the light of the 'new solidarities', represented by nation-states and interest groups that continue to essentialise culture and maintain 'conservative notions of territorial and linguistic propriety' (1993: 17). Being on the fringes of society and possibly belonging to a group considered deviant (and many migrants certainly are) may bring with it some room for manoeuvre, however. The marginalised may be freed from family and community control, but more particularly for this discussion, may be living outside the reach of the social and economic control of the state. The agency of the weak has been discussed by De Certeau (1984) and Scott (1985) who have both demonstrated how agency and self-determination can be achieved by even the most disadvantaged in society and that their very weakness may be a form of strength. Migration clearly provides an opportunity for individuals and groups to claim a sense of agency, to strategise and to employ various tactics.

Our focus here on agency makes it useful to distinguish 'strategy' from 'tactics' following De Certeau's lead. Strategy is defined by De Certeau as

> the calculus of force relationships which become possible when a subject of will and power can be isolated from an 'environment'. A strategy assumes a place that can be circumscribed as *proper (propre)* and thus serve as the basis for generating relations with an exterior distinct from it.
>
> (1984: xix, italics in original)

Strategy, then, presupposes the agency of the individual through their command of their environment. The agent who can strategise is the one who can make decisions about their future from a position of strength and who looks to the future with a reasonable degree of confidence that their plans will come to fruition. In contrast, a tactic is

> a calculus which cannot count on a 'proper' (a spatial or institutional localisation), nor thus on a borderline distinguishing the other as a visible totality. The place of a tactic belongs to the other. A tactic insinuates itself into the other's place, fragmentarily, without taking it over in its entirety, without being able to keep it at a distance. It has at its disposal no base where it can capitalise on its

advantages, prepare its expansions and secure independence with respect to circumstances.

(1984: xix)

By De Certeau's definition, tactics are more likely to be available to migrants than strategies as, except for those migrants possessing financial or other resources, it is unlikely they will be able to separate their ambitions from their environment (see Williams 2004, for examples). Tactics clearly can be very effective in achieving goals and aspirations if indirectly and, typically, there are many steps to take before a target can be achieved. Tactics may also require the agent to take risks and to commit themselves to certain binding agreements (such as claiming asylum or signing an employment or marriage contract) with insufficient information to base their decision upon. I argue that differentiating strategy and tactics shows how only the best connected and resourced migrants can employ strategy to marry across borders – the majority must rely on tactics. The tactics open to migrants vary significantly depending on the individual characteristics of the migrants, the countries they wish to migrate from and the countries they wish to migrate to. Agency, as represented by strategy and tactics, is further produced and defined by the individual and by relevant social groups such as the existing or prospective family members in the country of destination or of origin.

Migration has been seen by many authorities as a field of opportunity and has been used to demonstrate how the apparently powerless can manipulate circumstances and use tactics to achieve their goals. Arjun Appadurai, (1996) for example, has described the opportunities globalisation has created for potential migrants who can advance their ambitions through the various 'scapes' he proposes. One effect of globalisation has been to make migration a realistic, or least an imaginable, prospect for increasing numbers of people across the world. This supports Pessar and Mahler's argument 'for incorporating cognitive as well as corporal actions in studies that examine transnational agency'(2001: 8). Jennifer Johnson-Hanks has described how lives are 'navigated in reference to their horizons' (2007: 878) and observes that there are certain points in life when horizons broaden and the conjunction of marriage with a possible migration route makes different futures become imaginable. Johnson-Hanks has developed this notion into the concept of 'vital conjunctures' and it can be argued that both marriage and migration represent a vital conjuncture defined as 'a socially structured zone of possibility that emerges around specific periods of potential transformation in a life or lives' (Johnson-Hanks 2006: 22). The migration of community members, friends or family may have an important role in determining what futures are possible for all community members and may provide alternative visions of the future for individuals and for those around them. Further, it may be argued that the articulation of the two separate vital conjunctures represented by marriage and by migration provides both the aspiration and the tactics necessary to achieve change in one's life and that marriage *or* migration may be either the means or the end.

My own research (Williams 2004, 2006) has demonstrated how refugees may be able to use their marginal position to transgress both social and institutional restrictions and that migration, by shaking up communities and conventions, allows migrants to build new relationships, alliances and skills. Other writers have also described how the liminality of migrants may set them free from established community norms (Turner 1999) and how their marginal position in institutional structures may allow them space for tactical behaviour (Wang 2007; Hunt 2008). Hongzen Wang's work on Vietnamese marriage migrants in Taiwan has described how the marginality of the women in his study gives them certain options for acting with agency but warns of how their resistance can be romanticised (2007). His work demonstrates that while these women do possess agency, it is extremely limited.[1] Another example of this partial agency can be found in Roger Ballard's work where he describes how gender segregation allows women to gain 'an enhanced capacity to pursue their own ends on their own terms' (Ballard 2004: 3) but warns that in claiming a female-centred space, those spaces too can develop discriminatory power imbalances of their own. Tactics and the weapons of the weak may produce (often short-term) advantages for some but do not necessarily promote the material or social well-being of migrants nor necessarily encourage wider social justice.

Agency as 'transgression' and resistance

Agency, and particularly the agency of women, can result in the transgression of gendered social roles and responsibilities, resistance to patriarchy and other kinds of gendered domination. In the discussion above of tactics and strategy, I have argued that individuals may find opportunities to act with agency even in situations of weakness. As a disadvantaged group and one that is powerless relative to other groups, migrants in general and migrant women in particular must negotiate their aspirations in relation to various power bases. Migrants must first negotiate with the power of nation-states to gain entry to their proposed country of settlement (some may have had to negotiate exit from their country of birth as well). Most will have had to negotiate with their own families and communities to migrate whether they migrate as workers, students, refugees or brides and grooms and some will have travelled without the blessing and support of their kin and community. A migrant, then, may have had to transgress traditional norms and gendered assumptions in order to leave home in the first place. Many migrants are unaware of what their lives as migrants will be like until they have embarked upon them and many may find themselves engaged in occupations or living in ways that would be viewed as transgressive or as shameful in their home context. Transgression therefore does not in itself imply agency while actively resisting roles imposed on individuals by society does. An example of this is Joyce Kaufman and Kristen Williams' research in the Balkans which argues that the choice of a mixed or cross-border marriage may be construed as a political statement and that the women making these non-traditional marriages are claiming for themselves a role and an identity beyond the 'narrow nationalist definition' that their community has assumed for them (Kaufman and Williams 2004: 427). Anne Marie Hilsdon's work with entertainers from the Philippines working in East Malaysia (2007) identifies their agency as a form of resistance to the social norms imposed on women and men in the Philippines and in East Malaysia. She writes:

> The impetus of Filipinas to agency and autonomy in East Malaysia is underpinned and fuelled by a migrant imaginary closely aligned with the diasporic themes of freedom, mobility and economic opportunity. This drives attempts to establish an independent lifestyle and redefinition of negative discourses, while attempting to subsume the latter under legitimised notions of 'making it abroad'.

> (2007: 189)

Hilsdon's work, in common with other writers, identifies ways in which migrants (most often women) demonstrate their agency by resisting discriminatory interpretations of their lives and choices by redefining how they are presented. Lieba Faier's work (discussed in more detail later, 2007, 2008), for example, argues that migrant women married to Japanese men adopt a very public rhetoric of love to explain and make their less-than satisfactory and stigmatised marriages socially acceptable.

Defining an act as transgressive or as against the social norm necessarily relies on an agreed definition of what the social norms are and, again, places researchers in the position of determining the norm of those they study. Researchers and commentators thus classify some behaviours as normative and others as transgressive when, in reality, a broad range of behaviours may be acceptable in any given society. The research cited throughout this book provides evidence that undermines simplistic understandings of social attitudes and traditions as migration is shown time and again to confound assumptions of immutable 'traditional' behaviour by demonstrating how traditions can be adapted and reinvented if needs dictate. The same research shows, however, that societies' norms adapt to suit the powerful, rather than the weak, and that the logic behind many of the innovations in cultural practice discussed later, is to benefit men and masculine concerns rather than to foster greater opportunity in society more broadly. To use the example of changes in Pakistani marriage practices that have been prompted by transnational marriage (discussed in Chapter 6), women have undeniably been able to take advantage of those changes, but male priorities and perspectives have driven the changes themselves.

Agency as innovation

Migration and the personal and social changes that accompany it affect the communities that migrants move to and from, and the ways in which groups of people are affected by the presence of migrant members of the group, may depend on many different factors. Margaret Archer has argued that:

> Each new 'generation' of agents either reproduces or transforms its structural inheritance, but this heritage itself conditions their vested interest in doing so, their aspirations for stasis or for change, the resources they can bring to bear, and the strategies which are conducive to structural morphostasis or further morphogenesis.
>
> (2000: 308)

These vested interests and aspirations can be seen operating through the agency of marriage migrants. The consequences of different generations of migrant agents ripple around communities of origin, broadening the realm of the possible and influencing the choices of the next generations to travel or to remain, to innovate or reaffirm convention. Agency is generally understood to refer to the capacity of an individual to act purposefully and transformatively. The power to act, and to act creatively, is key to agency and as Margaret Archer has written: 'It is possible for human beings to become agentially effective in these ways, that is in evaluating their social context, creatively envisaging alternatives, and collaborating with others to bring about its transformation' (2000: 308). In migration, we see human beings acting creatively and taking the decision to migrate in the hope of transforming (or indeed maintaining) their own or their community's well-being.

Agency, as a creative process, is marked by innovation and risk-taking and it is generally recognised that successful migrants are those who are prepared to accept risks and seize opportunities as and when they present themselves (Fischer and Martin 1997). Successful migrants, that is, those who can establish themselves in a country of settlement, are those who are able to identify opportunities to challenge the status quo and use the spaces within the institutional structures that control their lives to achieve their goals (Farmanfarmaian 1992). For Lois McNay, agency has a 'generative logic' which explains how 'when faced with complexity and difference, individuals may respond in unanticipated and innovative ways which may hinder, reinforce or catalyse social change' (2000: 5). These 'unanticipated and innovative ways' of responding to circumstance are the stuff of migration decision-making and, as the discussion of cross-border marriage migration following will show, migrants respond in highly creative ways to achieve their personal goals. A dynamic view of agency embraces the adaptability shown by many migrants and allows for the extra-personal as well as individual characteristics that 'include the role of cognitive process such as the imagination as well as substantive agency' (Pessar and Mahler 2001: 8). Acting with agency from a marginalised and disadvantaged starting point requires lateral thinking and imagination – characteristics that may differentiate migrants from those who stay at home. Mulki Al-Sharmani's work with Somali women in Cairo provides fascinating insights into how women may use their migration options in sometimes surprising ways to challenge the status quo and improve their family's lot. Al-Sharmani recounts the story of Shamsa who responded to her husband threat to marry a second wife by moving from Canada to Cairo, a move that she realised would force him to support the family. 'Shamsa decided that having her husband become solely responsible for supporting the family would discourage him from pursuing a relationship with another woman' (Al-Sharmani 2006: 65). A further advantage being that the relocation made it cheaper for him to support the family and also allowed her to run her own business to supplement the family's income without her husband knowing. Shamsa's story is an example of creativity in finding solutions to problems but also represents a challenge to family dynamics as well as some calculated risk taking. This story is described here as being a migration story but could also be interpreted as a marriage story showing how a married couple negotiate their relationship. Negotiation is part of marriage, with or without migration and, as Janet Finch (1989) argues (cited in Eekelaar and Maclean 2004: 512), negotiation takes place within established structures and it is 'understanding' which emerges over time.

Much of the literature reviewed in this book demonstrates how women migrants are active agents – shaping their migratory experience in ways that diverge from their traditional roles and renegotiating or reassessing their embodied attitudes to their aspirations. Anika Liversage, in her study of professional non-Danish women married to Danish citizen men, describes how they have re-orientated themselves to the changes in their lives brought about on migration to Denmark in three distinct ways:

> through making use of the immigrant identity that they acquired during the immigration process; through acquiring a new professional identity by re-educating themselves either in their old field or in new ones; or through returning to their home country and thus returning to their old, pre-migratory identities.
>
> (Liversage 2009: 21)

All of these three options imply a certain degree of agency but do not mean that these women necessarily achieve lives they themselves consider to be personally acceptable.

Conclusion

To conclude this discussion of agency as it relates to marriage and migration, I will discuss the agency of women and particularly of non-Western women. I do not argue that the agency of women is intrinsically different from the agency of men but that our recognition and representation of it are affected by inevitably gendered perceptions. Our view of gender may also be influenced by over-generalised and unsophisticated interpretations of non-Western, third-world women as being *different* from other women in terms of their aspirations and their potential. Young Rae Oum (2003) has proposed that rather than attempt to define a universal set of ethical standards to judge the behaviours of women in the developing world, we should recognise the limitations of women to control their environments and accept them as 'negotiating, calculating, situated and fluctuating everyday agents' (Oum 2003: 438). The reality of gendered roles informing what is possible and acceptable means that women across the globe achieve their goals in different ways to men and that their decisions and actions are viewed through different interpretative lenses. So, the actions of a man may be interpreted as being brave and the actions of a woman as reckless even when they make the same choice.

Understandings of risk are culturally based (Charsley 2007; Shaw 2009) and a person's right to accept different types of risks is also culturally defined along gendered lines. Women may not have to negotiate the shame of 'losing face' that is typical of the experience of men in many cultures, but women face the shame of having made bad decisions. Women whose marriages have failed overseas and who have returned to their country of origin may never return to their natal villages, preferring to live anonymously elsewhere. Women and men whose choices have gone wrong need respect for their courage and opportunities to regain some dignity but while it may be possible for men to blame their luck or the actions of others, the failure of women is often judged more harshly and in terms of a failure of morality. Women returning home (especially when they return as part of anti-trafficking programmes) may not be able to control how they are represented and their return may be greeted with an assumption of their immorality as well as their foolhardiness. Social assumptions about the capacities of women may mean that they are not able to be the independent actors agency assumes, as their choices and actions are circumscribed. Doing fieldwork with refugees, I met an young Iranian woman seeking asylum without other family members – she told me she had chosen to travel with a young man she had met en route as it was just not possible for her to travel alone. This was not just for physical protection but also because association with a man connected her to an ethnic community that was heavily dominated by single men who did not have a mechanism for supporting or even communicating with a single young woman. Such a woman could in many communities be seen as a social aberration that would cause discord within the group as she could not be properly 'placed'. This example demonstrates how women's agency can be severely constrained by cultural, historical and political structures which may lead women to adopt personally risky tactics in order to gain some agency.

This book hopes to use a nuanced view of the agency of migrants to develop approaches that 'contest the traditional modes of agency ascribed to female migrants and the role they play in maintaining and sustaining transnational networks' (Kofman 1999: 288). In studying the agency of individuals, I have argued that it is necessary for power relationships to be analysed with due attention to their complexity. Just as agency is not purely a function of structure or of self but a negotiation between the two, power is multilayered and as it is possible to be both abuser and to be abused, it is also possible to be 'powerless' but still able to act with purpose. Hongzen Wang observes that 'Hegemony is never fully achieved – it is always negotiated and contested' (2007: 706). The truth of this statement will be tested throughout this book as the nature of hegemony, represented by migration systems and social control, and the contestation and negotiation observed in the process of marriage and migration, will be discussed.

4
An Overview of Global Cross-Border Marriage Migration

This chapter sets out to introduce the various domains of academic literature that touch on the subject matter of this book. These domains stretch from the macro- to the micro- and include studies using demographic and economic methods focusing on the impact of cross-border marriage on political economies; sociological works analysing social change and the social effect of marriage across borders as well as anthropological studies focusing on the meanings of marriages to individuals and their cultural groups. The chapter will demonstrate that while there is considerable academic interest in certain types of cross-border marriage and marriage migration, there is little cross-fertilisation between the different areas of study. It is the aim of this chapter, however, to bring the different strands in the literature together to look for common themes and positions and to identify areas in which inter-disciplinary work could inform understanding. Given the size and steady expansion of work in this field, the aim here is not to comprehensively describe all the academic studies that are relevant to cross-border marriage migration but to introduce some key academic debates that provide a context for the more detailed exploration of marriage migration in later chapters.

The literature on cross-border marriage migration, as it stands, can be roughly divided into two domains: (1) describing and analysing marriages contracted within community groups (marriages which in some ways relate to or reflect existing cultural traditions and norms); and (2) literature which describes marriages that are inter-cultural and which bring together partners sharing few cultural or historical reference points. Research in the first domain features many qualitative and anthropological accounts of marriages and marriage practices which personalise the discourses around intra-cultural marriages and present emic and nuanced narratives of why and how these marriages are contracted and how they fit into the life histories and life courses of individuals and communities. Emphasis is often placed on the role of marriage in transnational family and community strategies and this function of marriage may be particularly important for members of refugee and diasporic communities (discussed in Chapter 8). Accounts of inter-cultural marriage, in contrast, emphasise the links between marriage migration and forms of labour migration and predominantly, though by no means exclusively, describe cross-border marriage in East Asia where the phenomenon of brides travelling from the poorer countries of the region to the richer ones – for example, from the Philippines to Japan and from China to South Korea – has been studied extensively. In addition to this body of literature on cross-border marriage in East Asia, there is an increasing literature from across the world focusing on marriages between immigrants and citizens.

Rather than follow this conventional division between inter- and intra-cultural cross-border marriages, this chapter will review the current literature on cross-border marriage thematically. The aim in doing this is to show that despite the clear differences in the logic of some types of marriages across borders, there are commonalities too and emphasising these commonalities is a key objective of this book. I will begin by discussing some of the key constructs that will be used throughout this book. Sections will consider marriage as an institution and how migration may sustain or undermine and the interaction of public and private worlds that I argue is key to understanding policy relating to marriage and migration. I will discuss migration theory and the place of cross-border marriage migration within it and will consider why marriage across borders may be the attractive option it seems to be across the world.

The institution of marriage

In this book, marriage and formalised intimate partnerships are seen as products of social norms that define what is a proper relationship in any given society or social entity. Marriage is a way in which men and women take full, adult roles in communities and is an institution that sets out to protect and support family groups defined as (usually) two adults and any dependants they take responsibility for. The normative role of marriage in families and communities means that marriage reflects gendered forms of social discrimination and is an important mechanism for maintaining social hierarchies, particularly in relation to women. Marriage is understood differently by different cultures, communities and therefore nations and these various norms affect the shape cross-border marriage may take. The literature this book draws on is only just beginning to address the issue of same-sex marriage across borders (exceptions being Cooke 2005; Manalansan IV 2006; Holt 2008). For the purposes of this book, it is the effects of legislation, immigration control, social status and rights that are at issue rather than any discussion of how marriage is or should be defined. Marrying across borders, as we will see, is just as likely to be a way of conforming to existing norms as challenging them.

Marriage in classic anthropological terms is a key stage on the life-course and an important marker of transition from youth to adulthood (for example, see the work of Lévi-Strauss 1969). For many people across the world, marriage confers independence and status and signifies a change of social membership, for example, from a child to an adult, from a member of one family to another, from a lower status person to one with more independence and autonomy. The status attained on marriage may, in reality, result in less positive change and a reduction of personal agency. Establishing a legally or socially recognised bond with an individual nevertheless inevitably marks a major life change. Marriages are ultimately made in relation to families, with marriage marking the joining of families or the separation of an individual from their natal family to join their marital family. It is families, or individuals in opposition to families, that define marriage, producing a relationship affected by combinations of tradition, culture and experience and 'the interplay between the institution of marriage and ideas of obligation within personal relationships' (Eekelaar and Maclean 2004: 510). The notion of 'obligation' is an important one and links to the moral economies of families and communities and, when strictly applied, can be a form of symbolic violence used by social groups to control their members. Eekelaar and Maclean argue (ibid.: 534) that obligation can be reinforced externally as well as internally and that the different ways marriage is understood and operates within groups encompass roles 'such as the purely symbolic to the openly instrumental' (ibid.: 537).

Families are sites that establish and reaffirm the values of social groups; they are also sites in which the next generation are socialised into group norms, and marriage helps define who belongs and, by implication, who does not. Restrictions on who one can and cannot marry thus define the limits of a collectivity. Given the significance of marriage in defining and institutionalising social relationships, it is hardly surprising that marriage choice has long been influenced by concern for the division of property and influence, not to mention the maintenance of the privilege of elites. Marriage and marriage choice have always been commodified, whether for the purpose of ensuring land and family assets are kept within a kin group or for the purpose of ensuring vulnerable members of families and communities are adequately cared for. The reality of commodification notwithstanding, the role of 'love' in marriage remains an important part in their arrangement, even if love is something assumed to come to a marriage after the wedding and is demonstrated by the couple staying together and conforming to expectations. The Western emphasis on romantic love and the 'pure relationship' as described by Giddens (1992) has tended to mask the commodification of relationships in many societies but, I would argue, love is just one part of a successful marriage transaction. The capacity of the partners to love each other is often understood as being guaranteed by the process of negotiating the match – a couple properly matched will be able to love each other – and the importance of matching families as well as individuals is assumed in many marriage decisions. When property and/or money are involved in the setting up of marriages, the question of the commodification of human relationships is raised, but here too perceptions of culture and tradition influence our judgement. A fee for traditional or commercial match-making or for a marriage brokering service, a gift of property to parents as dowry or bride price will be seen by some as evidence of unacceptable commodification and potentially as creating a market in brides or grooms. No matter the opinion of observers, however, the meaning of these transactions should surely be defined by the marriage partners and those close to them rather than by outside commentators.

Anthropologists have established classifications of marriage types and patterns and some of these classifications will be used here. Relevant to this study are terms such as exogamy – marriage taking place between social units and typically resulting in the bride moving away from the natal home; and endogamy – marriage taking place within social units. These terms remain useful but as the marriages discussed will show, cultures once classified as either typically exogamous or endogamous may have become more flexible, often while still maintaining a veneer of tradition. The concept of exogamy – that is of women marrying out of their natal communities – is considered to be the most common global marriage pattern so cross-border marriage of brides can be seen as an example of the long tradition of women leaving their natal home to join their husband's family. The assumption of the 'normality' of exogamy, (Lévi-Strauss 1969; Bourdieu 1977), particularly in Asia has, according to Palriwala and Uberoi, contributed to marriage migration being

> largely discounted by demographers and social scientists who have tended to dismiss marriage and migration as a social phenomenon determined merely by kinship and custom, that is, outside the realm of political economy and the operation of modern market forces.
>
> (2005: vii)

The concept of hypergamy[1] similarly encourages the perception of marriage migration as a modern manifestation of a traditional practice and it is often simply categorised as women 'marrying up' from poor to rich areas to improve the life chances of themselves and their families. How hypergamy is measured, and by whom, can be a very subjective matter and in some of the case studies described in later chapters, women appear to accept marriage with partners that would be hypogamous were the marriage not being contracted across borders. Nobue Suzuki, for example, describes how the original 'fantasy' of women from the Philippines marrying in Japan was to enjoy a good life in a 'hypergamous' country. In reality this did not play out for them as their blue-collar husbands turned out to be less advantaged than had been anticipated (Suzuki 2005). The determination of an advantageous match goes beyond simple calculations of economic benefit and decisions are made from positions of relative ignorance. Studies show women marrying to take advantage of the assumed economic strength of affluent economies such as Taiwan, South Korea, Japan or the US only to be disappointed when the reality of their new lives does not match popular imaginings and the evidence of raw GDP (Suzuki 2005; Abelman and Kim 2005; Freeman 2005; Thai 2008). Similarly, brides may indeed be marrying up economically when they move to a more prosperous home but may find themselves disadvantaged without the trappings that comparable wealth would bring in their own countries and facing the isolation and lack of family and social support.

Kalpagam (2005), citing Bourdieu (1977), reminds us that the matrimonial strategies that underlie notions such as hypergamy are aimed at increasing symbolic, as well as material, capital. Non-economic factors are thus important in the calculation of the desirability of a marriage match. The importance of symbolic capital is evidenced by the widely held perception of the US and other developed economies as desirable marriage destinations (Del Rosario 2005). Teresita Del Rosario's work shows how migrants often leave situations of relative affluence in the

Philippines to migrate through marriage to the US where they live in relative poverty. She argues that it is the symbolic meaning attached to the match that makes it hypergamous within the community. Freeman (2005: 192) has demonstrated how ethnicity can also act as a form of capital, raising the 'value' of ethnic Korean women in China who can use their perceived ethnic similarity to make hypergamous matches with South Korean men. Margaret Abraham (2005) reminds us that in many transnational communities, such as the Indian communities she studies, marriage is a collective enterprise not an individual one. The degree of hypergamy represented by any given match therefore, may be a family measurement rather than a calculation for the wife alone. This notion of marriage decision-making as a family activity has been referred to as reflecting 'dispersed agency' by Nancy Abelman and Hyunhee Kim (2005: 102).

Heterogamy (also referred to as intermarriage or mixed marriage) describes marriage between women and men from different communities or ethnic groups in contrast to homogamy (or intramarriage) which relates to marriage between women and men from the same community groups. In my view, these terms have not always been useful and by emphasising ethnic similarities, individuals have been identified as having ethnic heritage as their primary social signifier, but this is clearly not necessarily the case. There has been little critical consideration of the differences (as opposed to the similarities) that may lead a marriage to be considered heterogamous, rather than homogamous, or to be classed as a 'mixed' or intermarriage. Over-emphasising distinctions based on ethnicity or culture means that other factors that may connect people, such as class, profession, interest, experience, belief, are relegated to being of lesser importance. In addition, successful matches may be based on far less tangible connections such as mutual attraction, duty and political activism, to suggest a few. The privileging of ethnicity as a marker of commonality reflects assumptions and simplistic indicators of similarity and difference that this book aims to challenge. It will be argued that the study of cross-border marriage demonstrates the complexity of people's aspirations for relationships, which goes beyond a simple set of characteristics to match.

Anthony Giddens' work on intimacy and the 'pure relationship' argues that relationships in the modern world are based on the desire for mutual love and understanding that is independent of social and other structures around them (Giddens 1992). This notion has been criticised as representing an unrealistic ideal that is rarely lived out in real life (for example, by Jameson 1999). The power of this idealised form of relationship, however, may be seen in the stigmatising discourses, described further in this book (see Chapter 5). These discourses judge some relationship as genuine, i.e. 'pure', and condemn others as false or exploitative if they are considered to fail to match the standard of the 'pure relationship'. Lynn Jameson criticises Giddens' work for its lack of appreciation of the on-going 'gendered struggles with the gap between cultural ideals and structural inequalities' (Jameson 1999: 477) that men and women live with. These struggles, which come from without the relationship as much as within it, are exacerbated and complicated by the experience of migration and the crossing of borders. The very antithesis of the 'pure relationship' is a commodified relationship in which the marriage is seen as being closer to a market transaction than to the individualistic, life-style option envisaged by Giddens. Just as marriages are commodified and based on often careful calculations of compatibility in terms of social and material capital, so intimacy may also be commodified and even if 'true love' (or the pure relationship) cannot be bought, then some of the manifestations of true love – sex, care and companionship – can be.

Families – public and private worlds

Pierre Bourdieu understood 'the family' as a social artefact with a strongly normalising character and Bev Skeggs (2004: 22) summarises Bourdieu's argument thus:

> The family functions as a field in which normalcy or the ability to constitute oneself as the universal is the capital. This enables normalcy to be both a kind of capital within the field of the family and a form of symbolic capital that represents accumulated privilege in other fields.

Cross-border marriage within a family or community may mean that the perceived normalcy of the union, within its social group, gives it a strength and value that inter-cultural cross-border marriages may lack. In relationships that cross cultural borders, as well as national ones, the definitions and assumptions about normal behaviours in marriage and other social contexts may be sites of difference and conflict. Ada Engebrigsten (2007), in her study of marriages in Norway's Tamil and Somali communities, uses Elizabeth Bott's hypothesis that the degree of commonality between partners' close social networks are supportive to the continuing relationship. Applying this idea, Engebrigsten finds that marriages within the Tamil community are more stable than those in the Somali one because of the close ties and shared networks of the Tamils in Norway. Interestingly, Engebrigsten's study compares communities marrying across borders but within ethnic communities and finds the outcomes of these marriages to be very different. This approach is unusual as we will see, as much of the literature tends to homogenise intra-community marriages and treat them as similarly traditional. Engebrigsten's work is illuminating for its sensitivity to both cultural and social difference between migrant communities.

Families are predominantly seen as private sites, but it is important to remember that they are also public and political spaces where broad, social changes are enacted. Plummer writes 'Families, for all their privacies, are structured through laws and politics: they are the site for the reproduction of gender relations and indeed the patterning of power relations between adults and children' (2003: 70). With this in mind, cross-border unions can be seen as bringing together different familial, cultural and national norms in the most intimate of ways. Nicole Constable's introduction to her edited volume on cross-border marriages in Asia echoes this point, stating that 'Each story of cross-border marriage illustrates the importance of social positioning, imagination and initiative, as well as political, historical, social and cultural logics' (2005a: 16). These logics underpin the different dimensions of marriage decisions, which in turn are influenced by economic and political conditions in the context of different imaginations and opportunities.

Cross-border marriage migration, like all marriage, places individuals on the cusp between public and private. Couples in intimate relationships, just as families in general, live by their own often unarticulated and unspoken rules, drawing on the experience of family members and the communities those individuals place themselves within. Depending on the ethos and tradition of the dominant public imagination, public rules and norms effect and potentially intrude on private settings through a variety of direct and indirect means. All families struggle to balance their private notions of themselves with what is publicly held as right and acceptable but families perceived as 'foreign' may find themselves scrutinised more than other families (see for example the work of Irene Gedalof 2007, discussed in more detail in the following chapters). Migrant families are scrutinised in ways citizen families are not and the intimate lives of visa applicants and migrants with temporary rights of residence are considered fit sites for investigation and scrutiny by state authorities. Across the world, potential migrant spouses and their partners undergo tests and examinations on their mental and physical health, their financial status and even on their intentions and future national allegiances. As migrants, the lives of cross-border spouses are governed and regulated by public bodies, with immigration rules conferring the right to reside, to work and to travel. The intrusion of the state, however, is targeted at specific aspects of family life and it remains the case that in private and domestic settings, it is families and communities that control the lives of migrants. Thus despite the state's apparent focus on cross-border marriages, if migrant spouses experience isolation, abuse or violence within their private worlds, they may find they have little recourse to support or redress from the state (see Chapter 10 for further discussion). States seem to be more willing to regulate migrants than protect them.

The significance of cross-border marriage in a global world

Although there is little doubt of the global significance, even dominance, of marriage migration within regulated migration movements across the world, a review of the literature on cross-border marriage migration shows that there are significant problems in quantifying the numbers of global cross-border marriage migrants. These problems largely relate to the lack of clarity that exists in defining what marriage migration is, who marriage migrants are and to the under-theorisation of family migration. These are two of the central questions that this volume intends to address but, at the present time, understandings of marriage migration depend largely on the history and manifestation of marriage migration in any given context. For example, some of the literature studied in researching this book relates to countries with long traditions of in-migration – leading to both large, established minority communities and newer migrant communities. In such countries, for example, the UK or the Netherlands, marriage migration may be understood very differently from countries where migration has historically been outbound and/or where migration is a relatively new phenomenon, for example, South Korea or Japan. The way in which migration patterns are understood and recorded, therefore, may have more to do with the priorities and preoccupations of the citizen population than of the migrants entering the country. Data collected by national or other agencies may tell us little that is comparable across borders as data is framed (for example, as a percentage of total marriages or as the number of marriage or settlement visas granted) by local concerns and preoccupations. The sometimes controversial and always debated nature of cross-border marriage affects both the data collected and the analysis of that data. Local context, in terms of culture, politics and history as well as family and marriage practice, informs how marriages seen as 'aberrant' or problematic are reported and measured. Emily Chao, writing about China where migration within the country is controlled, makes an observation that could be applied to statistics in many countries: 'marriage migration statistics... are less concerned with categorising marriage than with the over-arching objective of tracking and containing populations in their native localities' (2005: 43). Chinmay Liao's (2007) study of UK statistics similarly shows how official statistics are produced with a view to controlling and containing the trend of marriage across borders rather than to aid understanding of the numbers and lives of migrants living as the married partners of citizens. Elisabeth Beck-Gernsheim (2007) considers the challenges of extrapolating data about cross-border marriages from available sources in Germany. The problems she describes are not unique to Germany and official data is rarely designed to separate this specific type of migration from other forms. As a result, estimates of the numbers of cross-border marriages are extrapolated from more general statistics. The lack of data collected specifically for the purpose of estimating the numbers of cross-border marriage, furthermore, has led to the 'recycling' of some statistical analyses in rather uncritical ways, for example, John Lievens' work is still frequently cited as being an indication of current levels of cross-border marriage migration even though it is based on Belgian census data from 1991 (Lievens 1999; Walton-Roberts 2004; Haas 2007). Media interest in migration trends, including trends in marriage migration, have also influenced how and why statistics are collected. So-called 'sham' or bogus marriages, also known as 'marriage blanc', are those by which migrants are alleged to marry a citizen for the sole purpose of obtaining the right to remain in the country. Such marriages are assumed in public discourse to be common and, as a result, legislation across Europe, and elsewhere, has been heavily influenced by a desire to prevent them. These measures will be discussed further in later chapters, but are based on little, if any, reliable evidence for significant numbers of people entering and remaining in their country of settlement on this basis.

Cross-border marriage migration is generally assumed to be a female-dominated migration flow and there is evidence that brides frequently outnumber grooms as marriage migrants. This is particularly so in East Asia where the vast majority of marriages into South Korea, Japan and Taiwan are between non-citizen brides and citizen grooms (Piper and Roces 2003a; Ito 2005; Lu 2005; Davin 2007). Lauser reports that of the 190,000 Filipinos married to foreigners, 90 per cent are women but unfortunately this data is unsourced and no time period is specified, yet the point is made that marriage migration from the Philippines is highly gendered and female dominated (Lauser 2008). Zimmerman and Fix relate that in the US in 1997 half of all new immigrants (the total for that year was 800,000) came to join US citizens as family members and that 'the largest single category of family or any other type of immigrant admitted is spouses of a US citizen' (2002: 64). This trend continues according to Thai (2008: 1) who opens his book by stating that 'international marriage' is the primary reasons for migration to the US. Unfortunately neither Zimmerman and Fix nor Thai record the gender of those spouses. Siew-Ean Khoo (2001) has used a longitudinal survey of immigrants in Australia to study the numbers of immigrants arriving for the purpose of marriage. The survey draws on government data recording the number of visas applied for under categories associated with application as a sponsored or prospective spouse. Khoo argues that the data shows 'a steady rise in the number of spouse migrants' and notes that this stream is 'predominantly female' (9,274 male spouses and fiancée arrivals and 17,458 female arrivals in 1995–96), the sex ratio has varied among different communities (Khoo 2001: 117). Rodriguez Garcia's work (2006) in Spain, however, found that the majority of marriages between citizens and non-citizens were between female citizens and male non-citizens.

Ruri Ito (2005) outlines the history of cross-border marriage (intermarriage in her terminology) in Japan and notes that marriages post-war were generally between foreign men and Japanese women but that by 1975, the trend had reversed. Ito provides statistics from 2000 when 31 per cent of foreign wives came from the Philippines. The assumption of Philippine brides as 'typical' in Japan is reflected in published research on the subject (Piper 1997; Suzuki 2000, 2005; Faier 2007). This is despite the evidence Ito records that migrant spouses from Korea were of similarly significant numbers at 24.5 per cent and from China at 23 per cent. Ito argues that opportunities for migration on a long-term basis have been limited in Japan to professionals and skilled workers but that women on temporary visas could always use the 'loophole' of work as entertainers and/or the 'highly sexualised activities' of bar hostesses as well as having the option of intermarriage (Ito 2005: 53). The reported focus on wives from the Philippines in public discourse, however, demonstrates how the evidence of statistics may be less influential than public perception. Statistics for the number of cross-border marriages in Taiwan (another country in which cross-border marriage has become a matter of public and political debate) show that marriages are typically contracted between foreign women and local men and that the percentage of cross-border marriages is highly significant as a percentage of total marriages. Melody Lu (2005) cites government data for 2002 in which 27.4 per cent of all marriages in Taiwan were cross-border, with the majority of wives coming from Vietnam. Hongzen Wang (2007) cites data that puts the numbers of cross-border marriages higher – 31.2 per cent in 2002 but then reducing to 20.1 per cent in 2005.

In a European context, with its very different history of migration, John Lievens (1999), researching cross-border marriage migration from Turkey and Morocco to Belgium, argues that the higher numbers of brides crossing borders relates, in part, to gendered patterns of labour migration. He argues that this has led to a greater number of male 'potential importers' looking for brides from their home countries (ibid.: 722). This explanation has some merits but, given the numbers of women who have also migrated, and are presumably also 'potential importers', it is of limited value. Lievens' work is strongly influenced by notions of cultural conservatism and, in my view, makes assumptions about behaviours of populations based on reified views of culture and tradition. Shaw and Charsley's analysis of marriage migration among the Pakistani communities in the UK shows that until 1997 most Pakistani spouses were female but that more recently, the sexes have migrated in more equal numbers (Charsley and Shaw 2006: 409). An up-to-date and comprehensive study of family migration to the UK, including marriage migration (Kofman *et al.* 2008), demonstrates the complexities of identifying and following trends in migration as they are shaped and moulded by policy changes.

A review of statistics on the quantification of cross-border marriage migration tells us as much about how marriages are conceptualised and studied as it does about the objective number of migrants crossing borders to form or reunite family units. Comparing the numbers of migrants of any sort is difficult so, beyond recognising that marriage migration is of global significance, I do not intend to try to quantify it further.

Migration theories and the family

Prior to the 1980s, migration theory was dominated by theories based on neo-classical ideas (dating back to Ravenstein 1885, 1889) which saw migration as, at root, a response to a 'push' from negative factors in the home country or area and a 'pull' from the opportunities presented elsewhere. This push–pull theory still has remarkable influence on public policy and in the public imagination which tends to see migration as merely a response to the lure of economic or social betterment in one country in relation to lack of opportunity at home. Other theories of migration (Castles and Miller 2009, or see Zolberg 1989) have linked migration to structural factors such as colonial and post-colonial links and global economic logics but, increasingly, theories of transnationalism, which owe much to systems theory, have been used to understand and model migration patterns. The advances in theorising migration since the 1980s have been most effective in revealing the complexity of decisions to migrate and, rather than assuming potential migrants have equal access to the mechanisms of migration – information, finance, aptitude and social networks to list a few – assume that an individual's ability to migrate depends to a large extent on complex local and transnational resources and webs of support. These resources are understood as highly complex and interlinked and the global positioning of certain families and communities can support their members' movement even when their political, social and economic resources might seem to be insufficient. The pushes and the pulls of a potential migrant's life experience still operate to instigate migration but the simple relationship between disincentive to remain in one country and the draw of another is not enough to explain how, why and where people move. For that, better understandings of social, cultural and migratory capital (see Humphrey 1998; Van Hear 1998) are needed to place individual, family or community decisions within the context of their possible avenues for migration, their aspirations for migration and their capacity and resources to negotiate the obstacles in their way.

Migration streams are increasingly seen as multi-layered, and separations such as those of economic and family, skilled and unskilled, forced and voluntary are breaking down as it becomes clear that migration is driven by a myriad of intersecting processes (Castles 2003, 2007b). Migration has been studied from a wide variety of academic disciplines (as the contributions in the volume by Brettell and Hollifield 2000 attest), and theory has been generated to reflect these different perspectives. Some writers have focused on the prosperity gap between the developed countries of the world and the less developed countries and have described the impact of media representations of life in the Global North as a major motivation for migration. Others have argued that it is the lack of opportunity to immigrate legally that drives cross-border marriage. For example, Agata Gorny and Ewa Kepinska studied marriages between people in Poland and the Ukraine and conclude that the marriages are a consequence of the temporary nature of work visas:

> the fact that a marriage with a Polish citizen enables a foreigner to obtain legal residence in Poland should be perceived as a particular and important non-market trait of a prospective Polish partner. This approach seems justified in the light of the limited possibilities of legal stay in Poland.
>
> (Gorny and Kepinska 2004: 354)

Such arguments may be based on the assumption that many marriages are 'bogus' and contracted for the purpose of obtaining permission to work but undoubtedly opportunities for legal, long-term migration influence marriage strategies.

Studies of cross-border marriage migration often fit within broader discussions of family migration patterns as marrying to form or to re-establish families may be a key objective in migrating. Cross-border marriages may be contracted to allow individuals to break away from existing family structures so it is important to separate marriage migration from more general studies of migration within and through family groups also acknowledge that women and men may use marriage as a means of separating themselves from their natal family as much as to found their own family. Family migration implies migration is for the purpose of bringing separated families together and may result in reuniting refugee families separated by conflict or flight as well as reuniting voluntarily migrant families separated through the migration process. Siew-Ean Khoo's work in Australia suggests five categories of family migration can be observed. She considers two of these categories represent types of family reunion: (1) when migration completes the family relocation process, for example, after refugee movement; and (2) when partners have met abroad for work or study and now choose to live together. Khoo describes her other types of family migration as forms of 'marriage migration': when (3) Australian residents seek partners from another country; (4) chain migration – when previous immigrants look back to country of origin for a marriage partner; and (5) second generation immigrants look for spouses in parental home (Khoo 2001). Khoo's classification, however, describes the types of family migration that conform to the migrant marriages that are administratively possible in Australia and says little about marriage choices and preferences from the migrants' perspectives.

In most of the developed world, family reunification policies define families very tightly, granting reunification rights in terms of vulnerability and dependence. Families and individuals applying for their members to join them must show that the non-resident party relies on them for support. Families fit for reunification are those made up of dependent spouses, children (defined strictly by an age set by the country of settlement) and closely related elderly relatives for whom the already migrant individual must assume full financial and social responsibility. These limits impact upon family relationships and obligations as social responsibilities to cousins, nephews, nieces and other close relatives may not be recognised by countries of migration. Responsibilities to relatives that many communities see as normal and essential may be difficult to honour across national boundaries unless they can be re-framed in ways the country of settlement recognises. Katy Gardner has discussed how caring responsibilities recognised in Bangladesh as simply a normal part of social duties become reinterpreted in the UK to fit formalised, British norms. Accordingly, the concept of care transforms, on migration, to official label of 'carer' (Gardner 2006: 384). Similarly, the 'spouse migration' option may become more attractive to cousins, for example, who cannot migrate on the basis of family ties but could potentially migrate through marriage to community members. Spouse migration therefore, may in some cases be a proxy for broader patterns of family reunification.

Elisabeth Beck-Gernsheim (2007) uses Arjun Appadurai's analysis (1996) of the consequences of mass-media images of the prosperous North to argue that media representations promote cross-border marriages. She concludes from her analysis of studies of transnational marriage motivations and ambitions that 'geographical distance, rather than posing a barrier, is a *prerequisite* for such a union. The marriage comes about *because* the partners do not live in the same country' (Beck-Gernsheim 2007: 277, italics in the original). While undoubtedly media representations of the prosperous West do encourage the migration dreams of many, transnational fields are fields of exchange and the traffic is far from uncritical or one-way between the developed world and the less developed world. Louisa Schein demonstrates how a fantasy of 'the homeland woman' is potent for men in the West (in this case, men of Hmong descent living in the United States) which acts as 'a product of collective fantasy, reiterated in multiple and mutually reinforcing media formats that serve to stabilize this feminine object as a focal point for myriad desires' (2005: 71) This may be an example of Appadurai's observation of the complex effects of media representations and their role in provoking 'resistance, irony, selectivity and, in general, *agency*' (Appadurai 1996: 7; italics in the original). While the mass media-mediated knowledge of the prosperous Global North is significant in forming aspirations, these representations interact in significant and complex ways with local realities. Studies of migration are increasingly demonstrating the complexity of global migration that goes beyond simply South to North, less developed to more developed movement. Just as gender was ignored as a factor in the analysis of migration trends, migration within regions and between countries of the South is still underestimated and poorly understood.

Cross-border marriage and transnationalism

Many cross-border marriage migrants moving into communities that are to some extent culturally familiar may be said to be moving within transnational social spaces and their migration may be part of wider, on-going, transnational projects. Cross-border marriage migration can therefore be interpreted as a manifestation of the transnationalism described by Steve Vertovec as 'a condition in which certain kinds of relationships have been globally intensified and now take place paradoxically in a planet-spanning yet common arena of activity' (1999: 477). I concur with Michael Peter Smith (2001) in that transnationalism can be differentiated from globalisation by which social processes operate in Castells' 'space of flows' (Castells 2000) set free from the specific national entities. Transnational processes and relationships, as Smith has argued, remain 'anchored in' (2001: 3) nation-states whose borders, state policies and imaginations have profound effects on the formation and evolution of communities. Vertovec (1999) uses the term transnationalism to describe communities demonstrating a particular transnational social morphology; a diasporic consciousness; a syncretic mode of cultural reproduction which provide an avenue for transnational capital. Thomas Faist, in a similar way, has described three transnational social spaces: (1) kinship groups – bound by ties of reciprocity; (2) transnational circuits that support instrumental exchange; and (3) transnational communities whose solidarity is based on their shared identity (2000: 194–8). These styles and types of transnationalism could all be seen as promoting cross-border marriage but would have different outcomes for individuals entering states as spouses of nationals. In marriages in transnational communities based on homeland, cultural ties and ethnic or religious identity (such as those described by Balzani 2006 and Kalpagam 2005, for example), there may be continuity in many abstract ways, such as in world-view or cultural logic, but daily life for the incoming spouse may involve a break from the known world both inside and outside the home. This may be in contrast to the experience of spouses marrying within kinship groups, who may be travelling within an extended family and so may experience a greater sense of continuity than spouses marrying within transnational communities that share common identity and history rather than day-to-day experience. In the cases that Shaw and Charsley describe (2006), in which marriage is within a transnational kinship group, wives may have known the family they live with for many years and on marriage, a cousin may turn into a husband and an aunt into a mother-in-law. While the surrounding economic and social landscape alters radically, there is continuity in relationships and expectations. Peter Kivisto has argued that 'participating in the life world of transnational communities can facilitate acculturation into the receiving countries' (2001: 572), thus transnational communities can not only introduce newcomers to the systems and mechanism of daily life, but can also offer them a way of participating in a transnational space that values them and understands their experience.

Cross-border marriages, then, are often made within transnational communities – that is those communities that have a transnational reach and which maintain at least some elements of a common cultural, traditional or religious heritage and which actively promote this heritage through the generations. Equally, but less studied, cross-border marriages may represent the first links between very different families and social entities. The forging of these links may not be grounded in tradition and may be relatively one-sided, with most of the emotional and material investment in the transnational project coming from one partner rather than both, but nevertheless ethnically heterogamous, cross-border marriage, between ethnic or cultural groups, can result from the transnational projects of the marriage partners. Migrant women from the Philippines are most commonly discussed group in relation to transnationalism in this context and several authors (Gardiner Barber 2000; Constable 2003; Mahler and Pessar 2006; Lauser 2008) have described the transnational projects of women from the Philippines who marry across borders. In contrast to discussions of transnationalism within other communities, I argue that for these couples, the marriage itself is not the focus of the transnational project. Whereas most studies relating to transnational marriage identify *marriage* as having an intrinsic value as a symbol of transnationalism, marriage in these studies of women from the Philippines, (although undoubtedly personally significant), has a primarily functional role in that it permits entry into fields that can subsequently be used for transnational projects. These projects focus on the caring responsibilities of women as well as on the management and advancement (perhaps rehabilitation) of their social standing back home.

Transnationalism in some cases, may be concerned with establishing footholds outside the country of birth – footholds which can support families back home, increase the agency of migrants and raise their status. I argue that this is a form of 'asymmetric' transnationalism and contrasts to transnational communities based on shared ethnicity, culture or religion whose transnationalism replicates, or approximates, to the home community across the globe. Communities make use of the advantages afforded by residency status in different ways and cross-border marriage, as a means of gaining residential status, is instrumental in these different transnational strategies. Studies indicate that the transnational projects of many cross-border migrants do not extend to aspirations of linking communities of birth to communities of marriage. Husbands, for example, may have no interest in their wives' natal countries beyond the 'fantasy' of a Filipino family who will repay the remittances sent from Japan by looking after them in a comfortable old age (as Suzuki describes, 2005: 141). This lack of interest in the natal country of wives is commonly described in literature on East Asian countries where, by and large, husbands hold negative views of the developing countries their wives are from. Links between countries of the West may result in greater contact as Ratana Tosakul Boonmathya's work on families of Western men married to Thai women, demonstrates. In her study, Western men show interest in their wives' home countries and often move to live there, learning local languages and becoming integrated (Tosakul Boonmathya 2006). Transnational logics apply to these decisions and these transnational links, along with the asymmetric transnationalism referred to above, may represent the 'transnational circuits', rather than the kinship groups or transnational communities, Thomas Faist (2000) has identified.

These different strategies and the marriages they lead to, or are shaped by, are the subject of closer attention in Chapter 6 where it will be argued that cross-border marriages do not necessarily lead to transnationalism. In cases of inter-cultural marriage, when the new bride knows little of the society she will join, the family's role in the introduction of the spouse to her new life can only introduce her to her new environment in ways that are logical to them and which are often motivated by ensuring she becomes the sort of wife they want her to be (Wang 2007).

I argue that these marriages are not 'transnational' – cross-national but not transnational according to the established definitions cited above.

Why do people marry across borders?

I have argued earlier in this chapter that the institution of marriage is used for both private and public purposes and while marriage is popularly seen as a private affair, the state often uses the institution of marriage to promote national ideologies (Maclean and Eekelaar 2005). These issues will be returned to in Chapter 10, but, given the scrutiny often placed on cross-border marriages, it is important to emphasise here that marriages that involve migration are influenced by all the factors that influence any marriage contract and are not just a product of a desire to migrate. With the possible exception of same-sex partnerships, I contend that no other form of permanent relationship faces the same degree of investigation and examination or is the subject of so much regulation and popular discussion. The identification of marriages made to facilitate migration remains the main thrust of immigration policy relating to cross-border marriage despite the numerous studies showing that motivations for marriage rarely conform to simplistic categories of migrating to marry (acceptable and socially desirable) or marrying to migrate (unacceptable, socially divisive and possibly criminal). Research studies reviewed for this book show motivations for marrying across borders are very variable with economic, social, cultural and political reasons all very important. Marriage migration is one of the few ways in which relatively poor women from developing countries can negotiate national borders to escape poverty and inequality and work towards their personal and family aspirations. It is also one of the few ways in which family members can help their relatives migrate from many countries. Such studies may show women marrying apparently cynically to improve their economic or social standing; but they also show women and men marrying to meet their basic human needs to form families, to find life partners and to participate fully in society.

Cross-border marriages are sometimes conceptualised as 'strategic marriages' with the implication that the cold calculation of potential gain is the overriding factor in settling marriage contracts. The phrase implies that potential gain can be measured in terms of improving migration options and residency rights, by gaining access to labour markets and economic advantage (including welfare benefits), and by consolidating and developing family or community-based resources. Such conceptualisations of marriage frame women, and less often men, as commodities that are traded for the benefit of transnational communities, and while it is undeniable that this is sometimes the case, most of the research cited in this book shows that while cost and benefit are weighed up before marriages are solemnised, they are almost always more than simply 'strategic'. In unpicking the notion of the 'strategic marriage' it is important first to consider what marriage is in the first place. Marriage is always strategic in the sense that balancing the possibilities of 'better and worse' (to paraphrase Christian marriage vows) is always a strategic (or tactical) decision – does one want to throw one's lot in with another individual given what one already knows about them and, by implication, their family? The labelling of cross-border marriage as 'strategic' is based upon stereotyped assumptions about migrants more generally – that they desire above all to enter and remain in certain countries and that once there, they do not fit in. From this starting point, marriage between migrants and citizens (or permanent residents) can be interpreted as part of a plan to advance migration ambitions rather than personal ones.

This discourse was blatantly reflected in the UK's 'primary purpose' rule that required couples to demonstrate that immigration was not the 'primary purpose' of their marriage (see Bhabha 2007: 21). The rule was abolished in 1997 but, along with restrictions on entitlements and residency, it starkly demonstrates the logic behind many of the immigration controls placed on potential marriage migrants across the world. The heir to the primary purpose rule is the current requirement in the UK for migrants without a permanent right of residence to gain official permission to marry[2] – the rationale being that marriages may be strategically (or tactically) contracted to establish a right to remain in the country. Academic research on false, 'sham', 'bogus' marriages or 'marriage blanc' is limited, quite likely because of the problems inherent in defining what is, after all, a subjective judgement.

Globally, migration controls on marriage migration are based on the assumption of migrants as 'rational actors' seeking to gain personal advantage by migrating. This assumption prejudices attempts to marry across borders even in countries in which the accepted norm is for marriage to be a practical as much as an emotional arrangement. There is clearly a double standard working against migrants where marriages involving migration are labelled as 'strategic' while marriages contracted in much the same way but between locals is uncontroversial. Most immigration regimes attempt to control marriage migration by identifying and refusing entry to potential migrants judged to be migrating for economic gain and attempting to circumvent controls through marriage. An additional fear, particularly prevalent in Western countries, is that such migrants will become 'burdens' on the welfare state. The assumption is that marriage migrants are mostly poor, despite evidence showing many if not most marriage migrants are from the better educated and more financially secure classes in their home countries. A second assumption is that a desire to marry and enjoy a happy and emotionally fulfilling family life can be separated from aspirations to an adequate level of prosperity, safety and security. Eleonore Kofman has described the 'multiple personal and familial strategies' that we all employ and writes:

> Women have ambitions and strategies that cannot be reduced to the simple division between economic and personal autonomy, on the one hand, and family migration on the other. One strategy does not preclude other meanings, intentions and strategies... marriage can be the means of gaining independence and participating in a different society, even when the change may occur within a seemingly traditional framework.
>
> (1999: 287)

This statement, which applies to men as well as women, has implications for migration policies in general which typically consider migrants as representatives of their countries or of their cultural groups migrating for economic or social advancement rather than as agents and individuals with myriad and complex motivations.

Conclusion

This review of research relating to cross-border marriage migration has attempted to place this distinct migration stream into its broad context. I have attempted to situate cross-border migration in relation to social traditions of marriage and to emphasise its place within normal, human relationships. In discussing marriage migration as one stream among other streams of international migration, I have given some indication of its significance globally but have stressed the problems and pitfalls with data collected on marriage migration which undermine attempts to quantify how many women and men migrate in intimate partnerships around the world. Migration theory, especially theories which emphasise the multivariate nature of migration decision-making, has much to offer our study of marriage migration, and theories reflecting on transnational migration are particularly relevant to understanding how and why marriages may be contracted across borders. Themes introduced in this chapter, such as the tension between public and private discourse and the objectification of cross-border marriage migration as 'problematic' will be returned to throughout the rest of this volume but it is hoped that this chapter can contextualise the research presented and discussed later.

5
Power, Stigma and Violence in Migration and Cross-Border Marriage

Cross-border marriage migration is, in the vast majority of cases, a voluntary form of migration. There are, however, plentiful examples of how migration for marriage can be forced and these examples generally relate to the trafficking of women and forced marriage. These two crimes are the subject of public concern and debate on how to protect and uphold women's rights. This chapter will discuss how abuse of the power that many actors, individuals and collectives hold relates to cross-border marriage. I will argue for a broader appreciation of the complex ways that migrants, and particularly migrants marrying across borders, become vulnerable and will attempt to challenge commonly held simplistic discourses which locate violence and abuse in the acts of individuals and exonerate wider structural factors that allow abuse to take place. Much of the research on controversial topics such as honour crimes, mail-order brides and the trafficking of women describes a nuanced picture that is very different from media-driven and one-dimensional stories of exploitation and force. In contrast to research, women and their families depicted in the media are often presented as racialised victims and abusers whose experience is defined by and reduced to their ethnicity, culture and 'victim' status. While not denying that many women do suffer appalling and indefensible violence, this situation is not unique to women in cross-border marriages, or indeed to women who are migrants or of migrant heritage. This chapter, then, will challenge discourses that, in my view, over-emphasise the weakness and vulnerability of women. Debates on the prevalence and nature of violence in cross-border marriage are complicated by stereotypes of migrant women and men as well as by state ideologies that are based on the need to control and contain migrants and migration. Women and men in cross-border marriages are stereotyped as manipulative and exploitative and women migrants in particular may be sexualised and exoticised in the public imagination. The actions and motivations of cross-border marriage migrants, as this book hopes to make clear, are simplified by prejudicial assumptions, and this chapter will examine the threat and reality of violence in cross-border marriages as well as consider the forms that violence may take.

Violence and the subjugation of individuals by others never take place in a vacuum and social and state ideologies and policy regimes contribute to the creation of environments in which human rights abuses can take place and, indeed, allow or condone abuses when they occur. This chapter will take a broad view of violence and the abuse of power and will emphasise the multi-causal nature of violence and, with Catherine Lloyd, try to 'avoid the reductive dichotomies such as public/ private, physical/ structural or thinking in hierarchies of violence' (Lloyd 2006: 453). I will begin by discussing how the mis-use of power can lead to the domination of the weak by the strong (or the stronger) and will go on to consider the role of stigma and stereotyping in undermining individual rights. There is insufficient space here to fully address the large and growing literature on vio-lence and, more specifically, gendered violence and I do not attempt to define violence in any definitive way. Violence is defined very dif-ferently by those who live with it and those who commentate on it and actions may only be understood as violence after the event. Shani D'Cruze and Anupama Rao have considered this problem and have noted not only that perceptions of violence are historically specific, but also that 'domination silences and hides the coercive and violent outcomes of power' (2005: 5). That violence silences its victims is par-ticularly true of violence in domestic settings where the private nature of abuse makes escape difficult and where violence may be part of the assumed natural order of things (see, for example, Wehbi 2002). Violence operates by denying the humanity of its victims so is neces-sarily marked by a loss and negation of personal agency and autonomy. Violence is understood here as including both overt acts of physical force and aggression and acts that deny the essential humanity of indi-viduals by limiting their capacity to act purposefully and according to their own best interests. Thus, this chapter will include discussion of overt acts of violence such as forced marriage, so-called 'honour' crimes, domestic violence and human trafficking but will also con-sider the violence inherent in immigration regimes that restrict the human rights of migrants and which encourage their stereotyping and disempowerment.

Sarah Van Walsum and Thomas Spijkerboer ask two important questions about the nature of gendered violence:

> Should it be seen as the expression of men's inherent aggression and women's vulnerability? Or should it be seen as the expression of an ongoing struggle for control: over women's labour, their sexuality and reproductive capacities, their access to resources, their children?
>
> (2007: 5–6)

I would add that violence, gendered and more generally, should also be understood as part of the ongoing struggle by nation-states for control over their population and especially for control over those residing within the state without full citizenship. Rights to reside, in most countries, are granted on a calculation of the 'worth' of any particular applicant and that worth has to be demonstrated and earned. When rights are granted through labour, through attachment to an existing member (citizen or resident) of the state, or through prior experience (as in the case of refugees and highly skilled migrants), migrants place themselves in a position of weakness relative to the state, as any rights they achieve are contingent on the state's interpretation of their lives and circumstances.

Power, violence and domination

Definitions and conceptualisations of power, force, violence and domination are many and various and this chapter does not claim to offer a full summary. I concur with Steven Lukes, however, that power can be understood as when '*A* exercises power over *B* when *A* affects *B* in a manner contrary to *B's* interests' (2005: 37, italics in the original). Domination occurs 'where the power of some affects the interests of others by restricting their capabilities for truly human functioning' (ibid.: 118). Power is concerned with the imposition of one view or interest over another and with the silencing of some to privilege the voice of others. Domination may result from the powers of elites, for example, the power of political classes to dominate and restrict opportunity, or occur through social processes such as patriarchy whereby men exert power over women.

Force and the domination of one person or group over another may be the result of symbolic violence which, as defined by Bourdieu, is a 'gentle violence' that acts through symbolic channels. It is a covert form of violence that may affect people's lives in subtle ways that become normalised and go unrecognised (Bourdieu 2001: 1–2). I argue that policy and legislation, which act to deny, shape and intervene in the marriages and families of migrants, demonstrate the symbolic violence the state employs against migrants and would-be migrants. Social policy towards migrant or partially migrant families in many countries is directed at the institution of the family and at defining what are proper and improper families. I link symbolic violence to the emergence of the powerful stereotypes of migrants, and especially of migrant women, that stigmatise and 'other' them, limiting their agency and self-determination. Bourdieu's concept of misrecognition (Bourdieu 2001) is useful here as the victims of symbolic violence – in this case, migrant women – misrecognise the violence of their situation, interpreting it as the normal and natural result of their social positions as women and as migrants. Symbolic violence renders migrants effectively invisible or only visible in certain roles and positions migrant women (and men) outside the 'normal' in society, placing them outside the protection of state while simultaneously surveilling and imposing restrictions on their agency.

The notion of 'coercion' in conceptualising domestic violence provides further important insights and is useful in the context of this discussion as it can not only help us understand how violence and abuse can occur but also how it operates. Mary Ann Dutton and Lisa Goodman's work describes how the lens of coercive control can reveal the broader context of intimate abuse and control (Dutton and Goodman 2005: 744). Dutton and Goodman argue that for coercive control to operate, an 'expectancy of violence' must be created. The knowledge of the real possibility of violence makes threats of abuse powerful and an individual's vulnerability and disempowerment clear to both the perpetrator and their victim. The social location and context of the violence provide an environment that need not necessarily lead to abuse but which may make abuse more likely. I argue, with Dutton and Goodman (ibid.: 748) that the social isolation, lack of language or cultural knowledge and the precarious immigration status of many migrants set up conditions in which coercion may flourish. Just as migration controls can serve to make migrant women vulnerable, so may the cultural assumptions held about them which may or may not be reinforced post-migration. Women who have migrated for marriage in part to escape poverty, conflict or destitution in their home countries may tend to rationalize violence and abuse as simply part of the deal they have made on migration. Other women may have grown up with a view of abuse as part of their lot in life. My point here is not to

excuse domestic violence and abuse in any way, but to place it in contexts in which institutional and legislative restrictions act alongside all
the other factors that may make women more vulnerable to coercion
and to intimate partner violence.

Veena Meeto and Heidi Mirza (2007) have written of the 'collision of
discourses' that catches 'ethnicised' women and which, they argue, contributes to the way in which honour killings are conceptualised. Meeto
and Mirza argue that women identified as coming from certain communities, generally speaking from Muslim South Asian communities,
are identified as being vulnerable to honour killings. Honour killings
are defined as an identifiable manifestation of a culturally determined
form of violence – and one that is distinct from domestic violence as
it is understood in the majority population. Women from South Asian
communities, and others identified as being vulnerable to violence that
could lead to honour killings, then find themselves in a double bind.

> On the one hand these women are at personal risk from patriarchal,
> cultural and religious belief systems of 'honour and shame' that can
> lead to what has been popularly termed as 'honour killings'. On the
> other hand their personal risk is amplified as they are invisible from
> the protective agencies and social services.
>
> (Meeto and Mirza 2007: 188)

I argue that a similar 'collision of discourses', along with the symbolic
violence apparent in social policies and migration control has a major
bearing on the violence and domination experienced by migrants, and
especially migrant women, worldwide.

This section has introduced the concept of violence as it is understood
in this chapter. The next section will focus on stigma and stereotyping
and how representations of migrants can disempower them and make
them vulnerable to personal and institutional abuse.

Stigma and stereotyping

Jacqueline Bhabha (2007: 17, citing Fiske and Taylor) reminds us that
'cognitive miserliness' can affect how immigration, and other, decisions
are made. Sloppy thinking and an over-reliance on stereotypes, Bhabha
argues, lead not only to discrimination and abuse against women in
the migration system but also to the imposition of assumptions about
women as 'perennial "victims" of the system – defenceless, vulnerable,
naïve agents who were taken advantage of by others' (Bhabha 2007: 19).

Pei-Chia Lan's work (2008) shows this in operation recording how immigration officers in Taiwan test brides against the dichotomous norms presumed to separate a 'good' marriage from a bogus one. Lan's work describes Taiwanese officials testing the authenticity of marriage applicants against 'polarised dichotomies' with the result that 'the complex intentions of migrant women are reduced to flat either–or answers: if they are not romantic fools, they must be either trafficked victims without free choice or cunning criminals with ill intentions' (Lan 2008: 846–7). Such logic is informed by stereotype and has a powerful impact on the lives of migrants from their first contacts with officialdom on application to migrate or to marry to their ongoing treatment as members of families and parents of citizens. With this in mind, we will look at stereotyping and stigma in some depth.

I argue that stigma and stereotyping are intimately linked to the experience of domination and violence that migrants and other minorities face. Stigma and the resulting stereotypes make the stigmatised vulnerable to abuse, reducing the agency of stigmatised individuals and making discrimination acceptable even to the point that the removal of human rights seems acceptable and justified on the basis of promoting the 'common good'. Erving Goffman's definition of stigma makes this clear:

> By definition, of course, we believe the person with a stigma is not quite human. On this assumption we exercise varieties of discrimination, through which we effectively, if often unthinkingly, reduce his life chances. We construct a stigma-theory, an ideology to explain his inferiority and account for the danger he represents, sometimes rationalizing an animosity based on other differences such as those of social class.
>
> (1963: 4)

Migrants, as homogenised and marginalised groups, have little opportunity to challenge the ways in which they are represented, so when these representations are stigmatising, they may find they have little redress. The discussion of agency (in Chapter 3) argued that marginality may have some utility as it places migrants outside the normal controls of the state and, as we will see further in this chapter, some migrants may indeed be able to make positive use of their stigmatised identity as 'victim' to claim some rights. These points made, however, the net effect of stigmatisation and the stereotyping of migrants makes them vulnerable to abuse and reduces their capacity to act purposefully on their own account. Bruce Link and Jo Phelan have suggested a conceptualisation of stigma based on four components: (1) the distinguishing and labelling of human differences; (2) the linking of labelled people to undesirable characteristics; (3) the separation of the labelled 'them' from 'us'; and (4) the discrimination and unequal outcomes that result from labels (2001: 367). Link and Phelan firmly connect the process of stigmatisation to access to social, economic, and political power and state that 'we apply the term stigma when elements of labelling, stereotyping, separation, status loss, and discrimination co-occur in a power situation that allows the components of stigma to unfold' (ibid.: 367). By this definition many migrants, and certainly many of the migrants who are the subject of this book, clearly fall into the category of stigmatised groups and their subordination leads to negative outcomes which, I argue, include many types of abuse and an increased vulnerability to forms of violence.

Stigma, Goffman argues, results from three types of difference – physical deformity, 'blemishes of individual character' and 'the tribal stigmas of race, nation and religion' (1963: 4). During the process of simplification that allows groups and individuals to become stigmatised, I argue migrants become stigmatised for both their perceived 'blemishes' of individual and collective character and for attributes connected by the majority to their race, nation, religion and, as no doubt Goffman would have included had he been writing now, culture and ethnicity. The contingent and temporary forms of residency and citizenship extended to migrants, compounded by negative representations, contribute to their stigmatisation through stereotypes which tie migrants to images of criminality, poverty, desperation, victimhood, untrustworthiness, etc. In many countries of the West, female Muslim migrants have come to stand as surrogates for all immigrant women (Kofman 1999: 285) and negative images of migrant women are often expressions of Islamophobia (Fernandez 2009). The stereotype of a 'migrant' may be based on different ethnic groups in different countries, for example, the ubiquitous image of the Philippine woman as domestic worker in Taiwan or as an entertainer/sex worker in Japan, the Pakistani wife in the UK or the Turkish wife in Germany and the Netherlands. In this way, the shape of the stereotype may differ but the stigma and the effect of the stigma are much the same. Isabel Crowhurst (2007) presents research on the racialisation of migrant sex workers in Italy and shows how trends in migration have affected the stereotyping of migrants. She writes: 'The contrast between the "new" migrant woman, so visible as street prostitute, and the old one, invisible and domesticated, caused a major epistemological rupture in the typical representation of migrants as "deviant males and submissive females"' (ibid.: 244–5). Crowhurst's study shows how in Italy perceptions of migrant women have become separated into two, with 'good' domestic migrants – from the Philippines, Cape Verde and Peru, being separated from the 'bad' migrants from Nigeria, Albania and Romania, who work in the sex trade.

Female and male migrants, we see, are stigmatised differently, with men often seen as dangerous and women as submissive. The stereotyping of men is demonstrated by Rosemary Breger and Rosanna Hill who argue that in the 1940s the assumption was that 'White American men marry only for beauty, while all others marry only to maximise their social position' (1998: 16). This view still has currency and Aihwa Ong (1996) argues that men of colour continue to be devalued while white masculinity remains privileged. Katherine Charsley's work (Charsley 2005) argues that understandings of male marriage migrants need to move beyond their characterisation as merely 'two-dimensional villains' and as perpetrators of domestic violence, racialised and deported (Yuval-Davis *et al.* 2002: 520). Martin Manalansan similarly criticises studies that shut men out of the domestic sphere and depict them as 'pathologically prevented by cultural "tradition" from participating in domestic affairs' (2006: 240). Ada Engebrigsten's work in Norway again observes that Muslim men are viewed as violent and irresponsible while immigrant women remain innocent victims (2007: 744). The communities that migrant men come from are also not immune from stereotyping and denigrating men who migrate to marry, and Katherine Charsley (2005) describes how the so-called 'house son-in-law' (a Pakistani man who has joined his wife's family against tradition) may face a form of social emasculation. Similarly, Ester Gallo (Gallo 2005, 2006) found the husbands of migrant women were disempowered, ridiculed and discriminated against when they joined their wives in Italy.

Annette Hamilton's work on the attitudes of Western men to their relationships with sex workers in Thailand (1997) is largely based on the assumption that Western men who seek brides abroad have had failed relationships at home and are attracted to relationships with Thai women, in part, so that they can 'rescue' them from a demeaning trade. Hamilton argues that there is therefore a good fit between 'the masochistic male who identifies with the abused woman and the "good" woman who sadistically revenges herself through a clever masquerade of passivity and obedience' (ibid.: 165). Doubtless a relationship based on inequality and power imbalance is attractive to some but extrapolating this vision of inadequate men seeking to 'save' fallen women through marriage can only refer to some relationships. Hamilton's explanation of the attractions of marriage with sex workers bears comparison with Denise Brennan's work in the Dominican Republic in which the users of sex workers, who occasionally marry their clients, are presented in a far more predatory manner (Brennan 2002). Writers have often referred to the taint sex work can place on marriages whether or not relationships have actually begun from prostitution (see Cohen 2003: 65) and Nobue Suzuki (2005) describes how Japanese men married to migrant women of certain nationalities are assumed to have found their wives through prostitution.

Pre-existing racism in societies leads to minority ethnic groups being seen as having 'embodied' attributes. That is, attributes considered natural and innate which impose certain characteristics on certain groups. This means that the very presence of their bodies influences interpersonal relationships. For example, women from Southeast Asian countries are often stereotyped as being childlike in physical appearance but at the same time, as being innately sexual (see articles in Manderson, Jolly 1997, and especially, Manderson 1997). Women from Muslim countries may be sexualised by their perceived unattainability, especially those who wear veils. Bridget Anderson has described how attitudes to domestic workers are embodied and she gives examples of employers reluctant to employ overweight workers and who distinguish between workers of different racial and ethnic groups attributing characteristics such as caring, docile or gossipy to specific ethnicities (Anderson 2006: 21, 2003: 108–9). It is the construction of the lives of migrants as 'other' that allows them to be placed so easily into these and other categories. The research drawn on in this book provides plentiful examples of media and public presentations from many countries (often including the home countries of migrants) that present migrants as one-dimensional, and therefore as less than human. Thus a fertile environment for stereotyping develops, allowing caricatures to gain common currency with stigmatisation the result.

So far, I have discussed stereotypical images of migrants in general but in the next section I will focus more closely on stereotypes of marriage migrants and how these stereotypes shape their experience.

Stereotypes of marriage migrants

Cross-border marriages face scrutiny to a degree few other marriages do. They are tested and probed in both formal and informal settings and, when found wanting, their failings are generalised. Marriages between migrants and members of majority communities are stereotyped and problematised in part, because they challenge local norms of what proper marriages should be (Breger and Hill 1998: 17). I have argued previously that in many societies (particularly Western ones) marriages are typified as those aspiring to the 'pure relationship' described by Giddens (1992) – predicated on the equality of the partners who come together and stay together for only as long as both partners wish to maintain the relationship. Lynn Jameson argues that few relationships bear out the ideal of the pure relationship and emphasises that 'The type of intimacy involved in "the pure relationship" necessarily requires equality' (1999: 478). As we will see throughout this book, cross-border marriages are even less likely than marriages between citizens to be truly equal, so setting up the pure relationship as a template for marriage means that cross-border marriages are always likely to fall short. Western traditions of romantic love also tend to place cross-border marriages outside the bounds of the acceptable. While love and romance have a role in marriage in all cultures and traditions, modern Western traditions link them to individualistic discourses, in contrast to other traditions that link them to the upholding of traditional values and the maintenance of collective norms. Arranged marriage and its presumed analogue, forced marriage, seem to be particularly challenging to Western norms as the concept of arranging a socially acceptable marriage, so much a part of Western history, is held up as aberrant and as evidence of the superiority of one set of marriage traditions over another.

Arranged marriage has been key in the identification of 'problematic groups' with marriage between cousins particularly singled out as being simultaneously genetically risky and incompatible with gender equality and human rights (Shaw 2006, 2009; Kuper 2008). The majority view of arranged marriage is a negative one with 'common sense' being invoked to argue that arranged marriages, particularly those involving close kin, are a poor, and probably abusive, substitute for the 'real thing' of a love match. This view of other people's marriage choices being risky and inferior further stigmatises those who opt for arranged marriages as their behaviour is seen so manifestly risky that they become stigmatised for their choice. As Alison Shaw argues, their choices are going against 'advice', in much the same way as the choices of smokers or the obese are, so making them beyond help (Shaw 2009). Much of Irene Gedalof's thesis about the 'construction of migrant women as symbols of unchanging tradition' (2007: 9) is based on the linking of migrant women with the arranging of marriages and it seems that, paradoxically, only by designating arranged marriages as 'forced' can women be seen as actors in these marriages. Women become visible as victims of force but remain invisible as agents capable of choosing an arranged marriage. In making this point I am acutely aware of how duress and choice may be extremely close to each other and how choice may be *so* limited as to be practically indistinguishable from duress. I am also aware that 'choices' made in the past may be reinterpreted as force in the future (I acknowledge Katharine Charsley for her insight on this point), but the point still stands that the agency of women in negotiating the boundaries of force and choice is not acknowledged and that women's agency in taking difficult decisions is rarely recognised by policy-makers. I argue that this particularly applies to women living with men from minority or migrant communities but it is also the case for citizen women facing domestic violence who remain living with abusive men. This argument in no way denies that marriages and other intimate relationships *are* forced upon men and women. Forced marriage is a reality but not one that is exclusively found among minority ethnic communities and not one that can easily be identified or simply measured.

Away from the developed economies of the Western world, cross-border relationships and marriages are also stereotyped and Ruri Ito, in reference to Japan has observed that 'The question of migrant women has tended to disappear into the question of organized crime involving trafficking in women and forced prostitution, or in the question of intermarriage, with the overtone of "mail-order bride" or "Asian Brides"' (Ito 2005: 52). Marriages between citizens and non-citizens in many East Asian countries are generally seen as the product of unequal political and economic relations between the powerful nations of the region and their less powerful neighbours. Ito's argument is that migrant women in Japan, as elsewhere, are not seen as individuals or as fully rounded people but rather as two-dimensional caricatures as victims of trafficking or as brides who have been purchased. Nicola Piper and Mina Roces' collection of papers (2003b) interrogate the relationships between migration, marriage and work in Asia and in doing so provide examples of women challenging the power structures of the state and markets and, even from their positions of weakness and vulnerability acting purposefully and in accordance with their own goals and aspirations. An example cited by Piper and Roces (2003a: 10) demonstrates movingly both the very limited choices available to many cross-border marriage migrants, but also their willingness to confront their situations. In this case 'Ruthie', from the Philippines married to an Australian who had beaten her severely, was prepared to return to her husband saying 'I will just hold on to the blade'. As Piper and Roces argue:

The woman's choice to grasp the blade is an act of courage and agency. The fact that the blade cuts her proves that her agency does not necessarily mean an escape from victimization. Her motives are to gain a husband and to fulfil Filipino womanhood.

(2003a: 10)

This story is not exclusive to an Asian context and the value of symbolic forms of capital, such as the role of dutiful daughter or wife and mother, has weight across the globe. It may be true, however, that the connection of marriage to economic systems and structures is more significant in Asia than in other regions where marriage to a citizen may be the only way to gain citizenship and permanent rights of settlement. The market drivers of female migration in East and Southeast Asia have been extensively studied and cross-border marriage migration in Asia is a phenomenon closely linked to economic structures and mechanisms. The concept of the commodification of marriage and migration in Asia, therefore, has had a particular significance and provides insights that are applicable to the understanding of cross-border marriage migration worldwide.

I have argued in this section that the stereotyping of migrants in general and cross-border marriage migrants in particular has an strong impact on their personal agency and on their capacity to participate and engage in their local communities. The following section will focus on those marriage migrants described by some as 'mail-order' marriages and will discuss how 'commodification' of marriage and migration can represent a form of violence in itself and make migrants vulnerable to abuse.

Mail-order brides and the commodification of marriage

The institution of marriage has long been linked to the commodification of individuals and money; class and status have always been factors in determining the compatibility of marriage partners. When migration is part of the marriage contract, however, and when marriage is between people judged to be culturally, socially or even racially incompatible, the commercial element of marriage and of 'marrying up' (hypergamy), may encourage a view of marriages as commercial transactions involving the purchase of wives or possibly husbands. Understandably such commodified marriages are considered as abusive. Some marriages involving so-called 'mail-order brides' have been placed in this category by commentators on the assumption that poor women, probably already working in the sex trade, have been effectively purchased as the brides of privileged men. An example of this simplistic view is in Sylvia Chant and Sarah Radcliffe's work which regrettably conflates marriage migration with the mail-order bride discourse claiming that

> Another route to overseas migration is through 'marriage', which is often only a thin veil for cheap domestic and sexual services, a typical example here being the 'mail-order bride' business whereby Asian women (mainly Filipinas) are exported to become the wives or concubines of North American, European and Japanese men.
>
> (Chant and Radcliffe 1992: 8–9)

No doubt Chant and Radcliffe have now moderated their view but such easy elision between certain marriages and sex work still occurs. Mail-order brides are generally assumed to have found their husbands (or have been found by their husbands) through brokering agencies or through advertising brochures or, more often than not, through internet advertising services and social networks. This discourse firmly links 'mail-order brides' to sex tourism (Kofman 1999: 282, citing Pettman 1996) and to the trafficking of women (Morokvasic 2004: 18, citing Vartti 2003). It tends to ignore the variety of relationships that may come out of contacts made across borders and as Nicole Constable points out (2006: 11–17), the mail-order bride label is not one that would be recognised by many women who marry in this way. Constable employs the term 'correspondence marriages' as an alternative term as she argues:

> Like the term 'trafficking,' the term 'mail-order bride' tends to define the bride and groom solely on the basis of larger structural inequalities. It denies the possibility of Third World women (many of whom are educated adults) making logical, wise and active choices. While such terms may mobilize sympathy for foreign women as 'victims' they also reinforce certain pre-existing stereotypes of Asian women.
>
> (2006: 14)

The notion of commodification in the literature seems to be used in two related but different ways. Some authorities, notably Hongzen Wang and Shu-Ming Chang (2002) have used the term in its purely economic sense and state that they 'use the term 'commodification' to refer to all profit-orientated activities in the migration flow' (ibid.: 110 n.3). In their study, marriage represents one way among others that agents and brokers can profit from the desire of some to migrate and for others to benefit from their migration. Commodification is also used to mean commercial objectification of people and their attributes. Inevitably these two meanings come together as the presentation of individuals/migrants in terms of their marketable features is part and parcel of the facilitation of migration for economic gain. Wang and Chang's work, although focused on the strategies used by ' "profit-pursuing" marriage agents' (ibid.: 93), nevertheless retains an interest in the effect of commodification on women who must conform to the business interests of the agents and who must 'accept reduced prices, to be "good enough" to marry, and to be married out when there is demand' (ibid.: 109) For Christine So, describing cross-border marriage migration in the US, 'the industry … profits from U.S. imperial fantasises about Third World women as well as from global capital's relentless incorporation of Third World women's bodies as labor' (So 2006: 397) – effectively linking the symbolic value of certain women with broader market-driven processes.

The presentation of women in catalogues, in print or virtually, encourages a view that advertising of this sort is pure commodification. Ericka Johnson (2007: 9) writes of her shock and repulsion on viewing a website that allowed her to place women in her virtual 'shopping cart' and to search the database by variables such as location, hair colour, number of children, etc. Johnson recognised that these online catalogues promote and objectify women as consumer products but her research shows how the women who have placed themselves on these web sites, search for husbands in a similarly consumerist way. Johnson describes the 'catalogue of men' a Russian agent had developed for her female customers to peruse (ibid.: 61) and demonstrates how the women found the impersonal nature of the catalogue empowering as they could pick and choose from a list of available men. Teresita Rosario's study of the marriage migration patterns of women from the Philippines shows how 'Electronic marriages' grants agency to the women and that the Internet can act as a kind of 'refuge' for women seeking relationships overseas (2005: 268). Tolentino, cited in Constable (2006), similarly argues that a simple condemnation of such sites and catalogues ignores women's (and often men's) understandings of them and is increasingly indefensible as more and more privileged women and men advertise themselves alongside Russians and Thais on internet dating sites.

Condemning web pages and other advertising tools when applied to migrant, or potentially migrant women adds to the stereotypical view of women seeking husbands abroad as vulnerable, desperate, powerless or solely 'reproductive workers', whose capacity to reproduce and nurture is their *raison d'être*. Tomoko Nakamatsu strongly challenges the conflation of migrant women with reproductive work, arguing that this narrow view of the place of women in a globalised trade 'tends to dehumanise these women's experience' and downplays the potential of women to use international migration opportunities as well as to be used by them (2003: 183). Kathryn Robinson's work in Australia similarly challenges simplistic views of so-called mail-order brides. She argues that while the acquisition of a wife from overseas may transgress ideologies of romantic love, migrant women are themselves seen as embodying traditional values, including romance, that are perceived as lacking in local women. Robinson writes: 'The particular construction of the 'mail-order bride', the sensual sex slave, and the counterview of the oriental bride as the salvation of traditional family values, can be understood as constructions of the other in the Australian quest for identity' (1996: 60). So while cross-border marriage migrants are objectified and commodified as objects to trade, they are also characterised as possessing valuable personal attributes that grant them a special authenticity and symbolic social value.

This discussion has attempted to demonstrate how stereotyping comes about and how it can affect the lives and prospects of those stereotyped. As with most stereotypes, caricatures of cross-border marriages may contain a kernel of truth. My purpose, however, has been to interrogate stereotypes in some detail and to demonstrate the danger they may hold for cross-border marriage migrants. This discussion has been included here at least in part to provide context and background to the following section which will examine studies of overt forms of violence and control that affect many cross-border marriage migrants and women migrants. The trafficking of women, for sex work or for other purposes, relates to cross-border marriage migration as traffickers may use the promise of marriage to lure would-be migrants away from home but also because human trafficking and marriage migration are linked in the minds of many policy-makers and commentators across the globe. The basis for this link will be evaluated in the next section.

Marriage migration, trafficking and sex work

There are clear connections between marriage migration and sex work in some parts of the world. Women and men find long-term partners through the sex trade and those partners may facilitate migration. Some people may enter the sex trade explicitly in the hope of finding a foreign partner while others' hopes for marriage and migration may keep them in the sex trade (O'Connell Davidson 2001). Sex work is understood by some commentators as inherently violent and as necessarily an act of domination (see Jeffreys 2009, for example) but other commentators argue that it is possible for women to choose to work in the sex trade while recognising that it may only be a option because of the lack of any other (see, for example, the chapters in Kempadoo and Doezema 1998, and Mix and Piper 2003). The divide between the radical feminist position and the so-called 'pro' sex work position is a long-standing and fraught one but taking as it does an 'agency' perspective, this book argues that sex work is a dangerous and demeaning occupation but one that can offer a way for some women to escape economic marginalisation and to move towards their personal goals and aspirations.

There are many academic and professional voices who argue that the agency of sex workers needs greater recognition (Agustin 2007; Dewey 2008) and sex work provides examples of how structure and agency interact. Some writers focus on the agency of women once in the sex trade while others focus on the structures that represent 'deterministic constraints that make prostitution a job opportunity for women' (Law 1997: 232). Humanitarian agencies providing services for women are informed by various ideologies so may encourage their clients to understand their experiences through those same frameworks. These interpretations in turn mesh into the policy structures of national governments and supranational bodies and contribute to what Laura Agustin has referred to as the 'rescue industry' (Agustin 2007). In relation to this study, my concern is to position discourses on the sex trade into the broader global context of migration. Focusing on the sex trade or on trafficking without contextualising it within broader migration streams is, in my view, not helpful in understanding how and why people become involved in these criminal activities as victims or perpetrators. This view is echoed by other commentators, including Lisa Law who writes:

> Privileging the structural aspects of prostitution minimizes the complexity of life choices and agency available to women in the Philippines. Simplifying prostitution to an uncomplicated relation of domination casts women as victims, a portrayal which marginalises agency and the reality of everyday life.
>
> (1997: 252)

Determining the difference between forced and voluntary migration is a similarly flawed ambition I argue, as the context of migration in an individual's life can be the only real determinant and as Bridget Anderson argues: 'It must be recognised that ideas about the precise point on this continuum where labour can be described as "forced" is a *political* decision' (2006: 26, italics in the original). Padam Simkhada similarly writes that there is little value in trying to separate forced from voluntary movement in the case of many trafficked women whose life course has never been theirs to choose (2008: 244).

Invoking trafficking as a crime, it can be argued, is a powerful way of advocating for the rights of migrants and as Catherine Dauvergne writes 'more than refugees the victims of trafficking trouble the insider–outsider dichotomy of migration law. Faced with the victims of trafficking, some of the righteous indignation that defends prosperous borders crumbles away' (2008: 69). The problem for these victims allowed entry to the state, is that they are obliged to remain 'victims' and to act accordingly. Dauvergne goes on to the point out that policies aimed at controlling migration will always fail and 'the not-really-global crackdown on illegal migration has improved the market for trafficking and smuggling enterprises' (ibid.: 72). The trafficking discourse, which argues for the entry of some migrants based on what they have suffered, is an essentially pragmatic one and connects to the so-called 'victim discourse' on sex work and trafficking. Such discourses can take a moral view of the activities and decisions of women and men that negates their agency and their humanity. Perhaps more importantly, focusing on victims separates their situation and disempowerment from the more uncomfortable realities of globalisation. Larrissa Sandy writes: 'The moral value of the word "slavery" legitimates interventionist impulses that simultaneously author the saving redeemers (often urban, middle-class and educated) as agents and sex workers as trafficked "victims" (often poor and uneducated rural women)' (Kempadoo 1999: 228 and Doezema 2001: 29, both cited in Sandy 2007: 196). She continues:

> It is easier for the public to believe in the notion of 'sexual slavery' and the image of the 'sex slave' than to acknowledge that women consciously choose to migrate for prostitution. The idea resonates with assumptions about women's natural sexuality and vulnerability, but amplifies this myth by associating passivity and submission with developing countries, in global circuits of sex, commerce and travel.
> (Sandy 2007: 196)

By introducing the notion of 'force', people labelled as trafficked sex slaves or victims of forced marriage (usually assumed to be women), become free of blame or responsibility for their situation. While this discourse is usually based on the desire of liberal-minded people to challenge discourses of women as immoral or in the wrong, by moving straight to a label of 'victim', women become disempowered and disconnected from the circumstances that brought them into dangerous and demeaning relationships or trades. The social, political, economic and cultural injustices that resulted in their involvement with trafficking or forced marriage potentially become obscured by the end result of that oppression – the experience of force and violence.

The victim discourse, then, is a 'useful discourse' for governments seeking to control migration (and to emphasise its criminality), but who simultaneously wish to appear sympathetic to the plight of migrants. So a 'sex trafficking discourse' obscures the migration of women under a veil of criminality to 'reassert the role of the state in protecting borders (Berman 2003: 50). While allowing entry to a few, the discourse ultimately exacerbates the problems migrants face and supports the idea that migrants would be better off staying at home (Sharma 2003). Laura Agustin makes a similar point against the uncritical use of the victim label noting: 'The label migrant goes to poorer people who are conceived as workers with no other desires or projects, but when migrants are women who sell sex, they lose worker status and become "victims of trafficking"' (2007: 191). Na Young Lee has argued that the focus on trafficking represents a male ideology which ignores the other possible explanations for transnational prostitution that have meaning for women (Lee 2006b). The trafficking discourse only looks at the situation of women as and where trafficking is identified ignoring that the problems of women caught up in trafficking go beyond their experience of forced movement. As Sallie Yea's work shows trafficked women who have married GIs may be considered to have successfully escaped situations of forced sex work and traffickers but have achieved little agency and remain on the fringes of legality (Yea 2004: 191).

If marriage migrants, trafficked women and sex workers are to be considered as capable of acting with agency, it is useful to consider how they may exhibit that agency, to be able to resist and to act autonomously. Any consideration of resistance needs to consider the power structures that agents might wish to resist or transgress against. Doreen Massey's concept of 'power geometry' (1994) reminds us of the importance of understanding who initiates flows and movements of people and of who may be 'in charge' of the movement. The arguments in this book show that identifying who is 'in charge' and initiating cross-border marriage migration may be obscure as while women may be putting themselves forward for marriage, power may rest, or be shared, with brokers or other agents. Within families, the power of parents or community elders may be tempered by other adults or family members brought in to advocate for alternative objectives. As Massey writes: 'different social groups and different individuals, are placed in very distinct ways in relation to these flows and interconnections', the issue, therefore, is not just about who moves and who doesn't but their 'power *in relation to* the flows and movement' (Massey 1994: 149, italics in the original). The power geometry behind the negotiation and arrangement of cross-border marriages may be very complicated, not least as traditional patterns may be used by the actors to cover or disguise a modern logic to marriages veiled in traditional practices (Gallo 2005; Lu 2005; Wang 2007). This complexity may obscure the agency of the individual but may also provide opportunities for those near the base of power structures to play off the other actors and negotiate their own path between them.

Trafficking and forced marriage migration

People trafficking is linked to marriage migration through the assumed connection between marriage migration and sex work and also through forced marriage. Marriages are typically said to be forced when a family or community forces or obliges people to marry but also occurs when women are trafficked as brides. Forced marriage within transnational communities has been the focus of many studies, and particularly of reports by campaigning groups and agencies. In the UK and elsewhere, campaigns to end the practice of forced marriage have been launched by governments and non-governmental organisations and have been the focus of much media interest. As has already been discussed, much of the debate around forced marriage tends to treat it as separate from other forms of domestic abuse and violence and have focused on its cultural aspects. Separating forced marriage from domestic abuse more generally risks exoticising a form of abuse and of reifying it as something that happens 'elsewhere' and which can be seen as evidence of the barbarity of others. Lori Handrahan's work on the phenomenon of 'bride-knapping' makes the point that, like forced marriage, bride-knapping is an example of patriarchal systems which subjugate women. She argues: 'Feminists who engage in such research should not be side-tracked by cultural manifestations of patriarchy – however bizarre one particular act may seem, like kidnapping, but must focus on the dominant paradigm common to all women' (Handrahan 2004: 225). In my view, this point is pertinent to the study of forced marriage where the temptation has been to study it as somehow exotic and therefore separate from broader structures and systems which oppress and disempower. So-called 'honour killings' may be linked to forced marriage and are at the extreme end of the logic that links family and community honour, status or prestige to the behaviour of women. Such murders are not the product of community logics alone but of broader environments and systems that women themselves take part in and maintain. As Meeto and Mirza write (2007: 189), women may be agents in and perpetrators of honour killing and may have vested interest in maintaining 'honour' for economic reasons as well as social/cultural ones. None of this can ever excuse forced marriage or honour killing but serves to place these extreme types of domestic violence and abuse beyond strictly cultural explanations.

The literature reviewed for this book indicates that marriage migration is connected to people trafficking as there is evidence that women may either be trafficked across borders to be married and that trafficked women may be tricked by the promise of marriage into forced prostitution (Agustin 2006: 35). Padam Simkhada's research (2008) found that women from Nepal were tricked into the sex trade through the promise of marriage in India (8 women out of the 42 interviewed said they been deceived by the offer of marriage). Some of the women went through a marriage ceremony before becoming forced sex workers. There is also anecdotal evidence from South Korea and Taiwan that women have been trafficked into the country on the pretext of marriage. Doubtless the existence of legal migration routes through marriage opens the possibility of their exploitation by people traffickers and may lead to women living in servitude as wives and/or as sex workers. Cross-border marriage migration, I have argued, becomes linked to criminal activities as, because it represents one of the few ways migrants can legally cross borders, it gives people traffickers and promoters of the international sex trade a channel through which people – usually women – can be moved across borders. The effectiveness of criminal strategies is enhanced by the attitudes taken by immigration officials and by policy-makers who focus on determining the guilt or innocence of individuals rather than considering the broader context of migration (see Julia O'Connell Davidson's examples of how police and officials treat women who may have been trafficked – the chief question being to establish their status as 'innocent victims', 'guilty sex workers' or merely illegal entrants (O'Connell Davidson 2006: 15)). As Nandita Sharma writes: 'Border controls – and the moral panics that drive them – have very little to do with stopping the movement of people. Instead, they work to make those who do cross the line incredibly vulnerable'

(2003: 56). Rutvica Andrijasevic proposes that research should shift the focus from 'trafficking' to migration arguing that, 'there is a direct relationship between women's entering into trafficking systems and their search for ways in which to realise their migratory projects' (2007: 98). The victims of forced marriage and trafficking often find themselves in this bind – they are prevented from migrating to better their circumstances but if they are forced across borders or resort to criminal means to facilitate their crossing they are punished and usually deported.

The final section of this chapter will continue with the theme of how policy contributes to the vulnerability of women by focusing on domestic violence within cross-border marriages.

Dependency and domestic violence in cross-border marriages

In this final section, I will consider forms of abuse marriage migrants may face once married and living with their partners. While trying to avoid slipping into the 'victim discourse' and assuming cross-border marriage migrants are all victims, it is clear that many migrant women are more vulnerable to domestic violence and abuse than their citizen peers and that violence, when it happens, is likely to be more severe. The following section therefore, will look more closely at why this increased vulnerability occurs and at its consequences.

Palriwala and Uberoi (2005: viii–ix) argue that patrilocal kinship patterns (when women move to live with their husband on marriage) have always had three negative effects on women: (1) women lose inheritance rights to the land they have moved away from; (2) they lose bargaining power on becoming outsiders without local knowledge; and (3) they become vulnerable if marriage ends by widowhood or separation. These observations apply to women in cross-border marriages but are all the more acute for women without formal citizenship in their country of residence and who lack the capacity to participate fully in their new country. Across borders, women may be far from traditional forms of redress and mediation and far from the on-going relationships of reciprocity that govern more traditional forms of marriage exchange (Bourdieu 1977). Lu has described how these roles may be taken on by the brokers who arranged the marriages in the first place (2005: 291) but there is little chance of brokers providing much protection for brides facing severe difficulties. Migration, for the many who cannot access their full rights within the state, reduces their capacity to act independently, so should be seen as intrinsically a risk factor for domestic violence and intimate abuse. Menjivar and Salcido have suggested that 'immigrant–specific' conditions – of racism, limited language and cultural skills, reduced access to dignified jobs and an uncertain legal status, are factors that 'exacerbate the already vulnerable position – as dictated by class, gender and race – of immigrant women in domestic violence situations' (2002: 898). These factors, overlaying other systems of oppression, combine to increase the vulnerability of women in cross-border marriages and leave them few alternatives but to stay with abusive partners. Research with immigrant women in the US (Raj *et al*. 2004;Abraham 2005; Himelfarb Hurwitz *et al*. 2006; Fujiwara 2008) has shown how marginality and 'enforced dependence' can give a focus to the abuse experienced by women and that these factors are 'predictive of more severe intimate partner violence' (Raj and Silverman 2003: 436). Many women in cross-border marriages may be obliged to rely heavily on their husbands and/or their husbands' families to engage with official institutions and services. As migrants without full citizenship and until they have adequate language and cultural skills, their husbands or their husband's friends and family may need to help them fill in forms, make applications for change in status or otherwise deal with authorities and services. Women who have taken the brave step of migrating from their country of birth may feel extremely disempowered on arriving in their new homes, as they may be living in circumstances of total dependence on their new partners.

Migration shapes the experience of domestic violence for cross-border wives and in many countries the residency status of women who enter the country as wives is conditional on their remaining married to their husband for a specified period. The length of time differs from country to country – in the case of Taiwan, marriages must last three years for immigrants from countries other than Mainland China who must wait longer; in the UK currently for two years. This obviously makes leaving one's husband while immigration status is conditional extremely difficult and gives an abusive husband a powerful tool to use against a wife. Mei-Kuei Yu found, in qualitative research in Taiwan with women in cross-border marriages who were living in women's refuges, that husbands used their wives' dependence as a means of control and had prevented them from applying for legal status as a Taiwanese citizen. Violent husbands and their families were found to hold the woman's passport or Taiwanese ID for the purpose of preventing her leaving or applying for citizenship (Yu 2006). Similar findings are presented in Raj *et al*.'s qualitative research with abused women in the US who describe how husbands withheld their documents; refused to support applications to make their visas more permanent and used deportation as a threat against women and their children (Raj *et al.* 2004: 29–30). Earlier work on the specific effects of conditional immigration status on the incidence of domestic violence by Anderson (1993) and Narayan (1995) gives ample evidence and examples of how immigration policy itself can make women vulnerable to abuse. In the United States, the so-called H-4 visa, which allows holders of work permits to bring in spouses but which prevents them from working until their partners petition on their behalf, has been heavily criticised by activists working to prevent domestic violence in migrant communities (Raj *et al.* 2004; Abraham 2005). When women have children, the pressure on them to acquiesce to their husband's demands may be even greater and Ruri Ito (2005) describes the struggles women may have to stay in their country of migration and to maintain custody or even access to their children if they leave their husbands. Mei-Kuei Yu's research (2006) makes similar findings and notes that women's refuges in Taiwan (as in many countries where the fathers' custody of children is assumed) rarely accommodate children with their mothers.

Like immigrant women in general, women in cross-border marriages may experience language difficulties when they first arrive in their new homes. Lack of a common language inhibits communication between husband and wife and between the new wife and her husband's extended family who she might be expected to live with. Lack of language knowledge also increases the isolation of cross-border wives especially if they are living in rural areas where there may be few opportunities to make their own friends or meet with members of their ethnic community. Husbands, and sometimes the families of husbands, may not want their new wives to meet and socialise with others from their home country as they are anxious to ensure that the new wife learns how to live in her new home. In Taiwan, non-governmental organisations supporting women have produced material in the languages of many of the cross-border wives but apart from the problems of illiteracy in native language, the isolation of the most vulnerable women means they may not be able to access such information. Isolation is one of most significant features of many migrant women's experience (Abraham 2000) and they may have very little knowledge of services and opportunities that exist beyond their immediate social group. Work, as for most people, is an important way in which migrant women can expand their social horizons, make friends, improve their language skills and their knowledge of their new home but, the marginal position of migrants may mean that any employment they can get will be of low status or at least of lower status than they may have previously enjoyed (Liversage 2009). Abusive husbands have been found to use the isolation of their wives to control them and Margaret Abraham describes the tactics which may include 'limiting the woman's spatial mobility, not providing her with access to a bank account, creating all forms of financial dependency and preventing her from contacting friends and family, even to the point of locking her within her home' (2005: 440). Yang and Wang quote an Indonesian woman married in Taiwan describing a similar situation:

> My mother-in-law really doesn't like me because I don't yet have a child. It is not my fault. In order to control me they do not process the official identity papers for me. Although I have been here for 10 years, I am still an illegal resident, no legal identity.
>
> (Yang and Wang 2003: 172)

All of these tactics may be attempted in any abusive relationship but will be more powerful and effective methods of control when the woman is as distant from her own social networks as cross-border wives may be. Thus, it is the isolation of the migrant experience which works against the women's capacity to break free from abusive relationships rather than the migration experience itself. The issue of isolation is perhaps the most challenging of all the issues impacting on cross-border brides and other vulnerable migrants because, as well as it being a risk factor in itself, isolation and lack of social networks mean that services aiming to support vulnerable women may not know about them. Alvi *et al.*'s study of Hmong and Black women in the US (2008) demonstrates how promoting mental well-being and supportive social networks can reduce the risk of abuse in intimate partnerships. Their findings show, however, that while promoting resilience and a sense of self-efficacy can make women less likely to experience abuse and to escape it if it occurs, some of the minority women they studied still faced great problems in accessing help. They write:

> Hmong women may have been very aware of the level of supports available in the community to potentially help them, they may not have used them due to communication issues, fear of disclosure to authorities, or perceptions that disclosure may bring shame to the family.
>
> (Alvi *et al.* 2008: 62)

It remains, however, that some women are simply so isolated that they only become known to the authorities when they commit suicide, see Menjivar and Salcido whose research also records how women living with abuse are unlikely to contact services to ask for help and support or report the incidence of abuse (2002: 908–10).

Conclusion

This chapter set out to explore the two discourses on violence implied in van Walsum and Spijkboer's questions (2007) – that violence is the product of inherent gender differences *or* that violence is a result of a desire by the powerful (men, nation-states) to control the weak (women, migrants) using the experience of cross-border marriage migrants as an example. This chapter has attempted to address the complex and contentious issue of violence and coercion used against migrants in general and migrant women in particular. While never intending to underestimate the degree of physical violence, coercion and very real and debilitating force that is used against women through the migration process and through controls placed on them post-migration, this chapter has emphasised the continuing agency of migrants and the importance of placing their experience in the broad context of global migration, social and economic inequalities. I have argued against a focus on 'culture' and cultural practices as means of understanding violence against women and instead have argued that systems of patriarchy should be viewed more broadly. I have criticised the so-called 'victim discourse' which separates migrants into the deserving and the undeserving and have highlighted how policy can act contrarily to its explicit goals of protecting women by making women more vulnerable.

Marriage migrants are made vulnerable to violence and oppression because of the symbolic violence inherent in legislation and policy. Policy which is operationalised and normalised by a public that has been encouraged to accept the restriction of certain people's rights as unproblematic.

6
Transnational Marriage within South Asian Communities

The following three chapters will compare examples of cross-border marriage migration from across the globe. The focus throughout will be on how these marriages are negotiated by individual agents and communities acting within structures represented by international migration regimes as well as the structures imposed by social and cultural norms. This part of the book will also explore the notion of transnationalism as it relates to cross-border marriage. It is my view that cross-border marriages are both a consequence and an instigator of transnationalism. Marriages across borders can initiate cross-national connections and can represent the first steps in the creation of the international links necessary for transnational networks and structures. Cross-border marriages are also frequently made because of pre-existing, transnational connections. The literature review presented as Chapter 4 of this book has already introduced the concept of transnationalism and the following three chapters will consider whether and which cross-border marriages can be considered 'transnational'. In Chapter 4, I discussed theories of transnationalism and in the following section I will use a combination of Steve Vertovec's (1999), Michael Peter Smith's (2001) and Thomas Faist's (2000) definitions of transnationalism to analyse different forms of cross-border marriage. Following their work, I define transnational communities as those that possess a transnational social morphology and a shared sense of identity that crosses international borders. Such communities have a diasporic consciousness through their shared imagination of an original homeland represented by a (possibly loose) sense of cultural, traditional and/or religious authenticity. Such a community may reproduce itself through meaningful kinship ties and will be bound by ties of reciprocity that take advantage of the different resources, rights and entitlements accrued by the residency or citizenship statuses of its members. Some of these communities will be well established and institutionalised through formal channels of exchange, for example, businesses and agencies that service the community while others may be incipient communities that are little more than informal networks of friends and family acting together to further their transnational projects. This latter group may be 'transnational' even while they do not share a community identity and may be examples of the transnational 'circuits' described by Thomas Faist (2000).

These three chapters will focus on the processes of transnationalism as they relate to cross-border marriages but will emphasise that this is a study of *marriages* first and foremost. While these marriages may have a logic beyond or in addition to the union of two people, this study is essentially about intimate relationships between individuals. These chapters set out to investigate how the notion of transnationalism affects the processes and the outcomes of cross-border marriage, and to do this, Chapter 6 will focus on marriages that have a clear transnational logic using marriages within South Asian transnational communities as examples. Chapter 7 will consider cross-border marriages that are less obviously, or perhaps incipiently, transnational and the marriages discussed, mostly between the countries of East and Southeast Asia, are made between, rather than within, communities. Such marriages may be the result of transnational connections but are not necessarily *transnational* by Vertovec's definition. These marriages *may* represent the first steps in a migration process that leads to the enduring international relationships that are the hallmark of transnational communities, but I argue that cross-border marriage alone does not indicate transnationalism. In Chapter 8, I focus on marriages contracted within refugee communities as it is my contention that the relatively few accounts of refugee marriages describe a mix of transnational and non-transnational marriages. This mix, I argue, is interesting as it describes communities in flux and presents the development of transnational communities in process and through the magnifying lens of forced migration. Throughout I will attempt to differentiate between the different types of transnational entities that are sometimes 'subsumed under the heading of transnational social spaces' (Faist 2000: 190).

Cross-border marriages within South Asian communities

The marriage practices of transnational communities with their roots in South Asian countries have, I would argue, been the most studied and scrutinised of any such communities. This may be explained in part because of their presence throughout the countries of the developed world and because they make up a visible and distinct minority. In the UK, colonial and more recent history has meant that South Asian communities are considered almost archetypal migrants and as a homogenous group despite their diversity of origin, language, culture and migration history. It seems most countries have their archetypal migrants and the place the South Asian, and especially the Pakistani community, holds in the UK is similar to the place Turkish communities hold in Germany, Turks and Moroccans in the Netherlands and migrants from the Philippines in Japan and Taiwan. The academic research used here has attempted to get beneath these stereotypes and to find emic explanations for the continuation of intimate links between the transnational communities and the countries of origin. Many South Asian communities are truly, and indeed typically, transnational by the definitions used in this book and they exhibit and promote a shared sense of identity that crosses borders. Communities have also developed social and cultural structures and networks that support the practical projects and aspirations of their members across international borders. Such communities also have a diasporic consciousness that lends them a shared sense of religious and/or cultural authenticity. They reproduce themselves in accordance with meaningful kinship patterns and are bound by ties of reciprocity that take advantage of the different resources, rights and entitlements accrued by the residency or citizenship statuses of their members. Some of these communities are well established in multiple countries of residence; they participate fully and are well represented within local institutions.

As previously stated, I define transnational communities as those that share a transnational social morphology and a sense of identity. They share an imagination of an original homeland that in different ways guides their social practices and informs their relationship to their country of residence or settlement. This identification leads to the maintenance of links between the communities in the diaspora and with the country regarded as 'home' and may lead to the establishment of formal mechanisms such as banks, religious establishments and businesses that service community members in their various locations. Such structural links may enable the continuation of relationships between the countries of migration and 'home' as well as facilitate ties of reciprocity that may include the transfer of capital and further the migration aspirations of its members. The hallmark of transnational communities is their position within nation-states but also between them, and, as Katy Gardner suggests, members of transnational communities may be best represented as 'savvy cosmopolitans, maintaining bases in several places while keeping a constant eye on opportunities elsewhere' (Gardner 2006: 373).

This chapter will consider research on transnational communities, with a country of origin located in the South Asian sub-continent for the purpose of identifying the place of marriage in maintaining and developing transnational ties and consciousnesses. In using the phrase 'South Asian', I am aware of applying an 'outsiders' term that may have little meaning for community members themselves, some of whom might prefer the term 'Desi' (see Grewal 2008: 2). As an outsider to the community, however, I will use South Asia as a geographical, rather than a cultural term to refer to the Indian sub-continent and to the countries of Pakistan, India, Bangladesh, Nepal and Sri Lanka. I focus on transnational communities originating in South Asia firstly as they include some very well-established communities with a global reach. Rather than focus on just one community, such as the Jat Sikhs described by Nicola Mooney (2006) or the Malayali community described by Ester Gallo (2005, 2006), I have chosen to draw examples from across the Indian sub-continent as, while the groups discussed have significant differences in terms of culture and tradition, resources and aspirations, they share a colonial history that has had, and possibly continues to have, a strong influence on their migration patterns. I am conscious of the very important social and cultural differences within and between these groups and note, for example, Alison Shaw's work (2001), which describes the high degree of diversity in terms of caste, origin, socio-economic status and upbringing that is significant within an apparently identifiable group such as British Pakistanis.

The whole issue of who constitutes a 'group' is always a vexed one and one that is impossible to clarify from the outside – and even from the inside, it may be hard to decide who is 'one of one's own' (Charsley 2007: 1123). Studies of transnational communities (as studies of any group identified as 'other') are dogged by conflation and generalised assumptions that communities can be recognised, labelled and understood through their culture. Culture, and cultural difference, have an important symbolic role in the formation and delineation of group membership but the degree to which respect for the symbolic iteration of tradition really impacts on 'how things are done' varies. The study of transnational communities, and marriage migration in general, provides many powerful examples for how practice can be adapted to allow symbolic cultural order to be maintained. Academics still tend to reify and generalise culture and Ada Engebrigsten, for example, in her otherwise excellent article in my opinion over-emphasises the immutability of 'culturally patterned structures of kinship' (2007: 744) by emphasising kinship patterns of Tamil and Somali migrants in Norway to understand and compare the outcomes of the cross-border marriages of the two groups. Yuval-Davis, Anthias and Kofman (2002: 532) have cited Yeatman's (1992) observation that groups have an 'authoritative voice' if they can establish a distinct identity with the implication being that the more different they are, the more authentic. This view certainly seems to be held by many commentators whose focus on examples of extreme behaviours, such as honour killings or forms of religious fundamentalism, allows, or indeed encourages, extreme manifestations of culture and tradition to stand for wider community values.

All communities have divisions within them and the decision to embrace someone as one of the group may be guided by established markers such as commonality of religion, kinship or class but often comes down to personal issues and bonds of trust and friendship that make exceptions for some. Gerd Baumann's study differentiates between religion and culture – that the religion, Islam, may be in common but 'a marriage between, say, a Pashtun and a Punjabi, or a Bangladeshi and a Gujarati, would certainly be judged highly problematic, and considered a crossing of ethnic and *culture* boundaries that responsible parents should prevent at all costs' (Baumann 1996: 125, italics in the original). So in Baumann's study at least, 'a "mixed marriage" in Southall parlance may mean one that crosses a boundary of culture, however defined by the people concerned, or one that crosses a boundary of caste' (ibid.: 151). In another context, this echoes Dona and Berry's observation that 'The similarity between Guatemalans and Mexicans disappears, however, when discussing more intimate interactions such as marriage' (1999: 180–1) – these authors found these culturally similar communities were alike in some ways, but not alike enough to marry. In a contrary case, however, Gopalkrishnan and Babacan found that when intermarriage occurred between caste, religion or other sub-groups who shared an Indian heritage, communities found these marriages to be not ideal, but 'better than being married to a non-Indian' (2007: 515).

Zareena Grewal presents a picture of a South Asian transnational community (or a section of one) that shows how arguments about religion can 'lace intergenerational debates about marriage and identity'

(2008: 2–3). Grewal's ethnographic study is of second-generation Muslim American immigrants who are challenging their parents' views of appropriate marriage partners. The primary identification of the group she studies is as Muslims and they find their parents' concern with skin colour, among other racial and cultural properties, offensive. Grewal uses the experiences of Rashid, the son of Pakistani immigrants, to illustrate how religious views on marriage can challenge cultural ones. She writes:

> Many community members watch interracial couples with fear and wonder. They are curious to see how they will make their marriages work, and how (or whether) they will be able to preserve their respective cultures. The second generation, armed with a scripture-based moral authority, is increasingly defiant of its parents and its critics.
>
> (Grewal 2008: 19)

This transnational community is facing a challenge from the changing views of its younger generation – a challenge that Grewal argues comes from the political climate beyond as well as within the community that is forcing a re-negotiation of values relating to how 'proper' marriages are understood. This case provides an example of transnational communities adapting to local, as well as global, circumstances and perhaps has lessons for the Pakistani and other Muslim communities living in countries where Islam is the subject of renewed interest – and controversy. This work, describing marriages based on religious identity, is contrary to Gabriele Marranci's findings in Northern Ireland where, during three years research with Muslim communities she found examples of Muslims marrying non-Muslims but 'did not come across a single example of inter-ethnic marriage between Muslims' (Marranci 2006: 48). It is unclear what lessons this may have more widely but indicates that within Northern Ireland's Muslim community at least, shared adherence to Islam is not enough to bring ethnic groups together.

While attempting to justify my focus on 'South Asian' transnational marriages I argue that generalising about group behaviour is difficult if not impossible. It is still remarkably, and unfortunately, common in discussion of cross-border marriage. Elisabeth Beck-Gernsheim, in her review of transnational marriage, has noted how certain types of marriages – those of 'non-European, non-Christian origin' (Beck-Gernsheim 2007: 276) have been problematised. She argues that these migrant groups have been focused upon because, she claims, they share the practice of arranged marriage. We could debate whether arranged marriage is necessarily a non-Christian, non-European practice and the value judgement implied, but in my view a more important challenge to Beck-Gernsheim's work is her argument that arranged marriage is *the* key to understanding transnational communities in the West. I find myself most at odds with Beck-Gernsheim's work when she asserts, of cross-border marriage, that 'geographical distance, rather than posing a barrier, is a *prerequisite* for such a union' (ibid.: 277, italics in the original). Beck-Gernsheim's focus is broader than just South Asian transnational communities and she argues that the common practice (as she defines it) of arranged marriage whether within Turkish, Moroccan or other communities is the source of the 'problem'. While the benefits, material and otherwise, of migration are manifest, studies of transnationalism indicate that transnational communities are more than just practical and strategic entities and that they carry social and emotional value too. The studies discussed in this chapter describe how cross-border marriage in transnational communities is highly important in establishing and developing the links between communities of 'home' and communities of migration and argues that these marriages are more than simply ways to bring relatives across borders, or as Beck-Gernsheim puts it, that provide 'a special wedding present, the ticket to migration' (ibid.: 278). Some of these studies also contradict the assumption that transnational marriages necessarily represent an escape from poverty for the migrating spouse as they show that the same logic that brings a spouse from the 'home' country to the country of migration may also take a spouse from the developed world back to the country of community origin. Global migration is increasingly happening away from the traditional migration destinations of Western developed countries and is increasingly occurring between countries of the Global South. The migratory movements that happen away from countries of the developed world and between less developed countries receive little attention from researchers but are important nonetheless in the strategies of many individuals and groups.

To explore the significance and practice of cross-border marriage within this broad group of transnational communities, I will use the available literature to first consider how kin and family relationships are managed across borders; second, to consider the structural mechanisms that facilitate transnational interaction and finally I will consider the implications these transnational communities have for individuals, regarding the agency of migrants marrying across borders within transnational communities.

The transnational family, kin relationships and the 'purpose' of cross-border marriage

In transnational communities in which cross-border marriage is common, the formal citizenship status of the marriage partners is not necessarily of primary importance. As Roger Ballard has stated: 'All they are doing is making the same kind of choices, guided by the same kind of priorities as they would have done had they never migrated at all' (2004: 12). For some communities, marrying across borders is less concerned with the separation of a bride or groom from their family than with the continuation of community and family life within a different part of that same community. Family and kin connections may be the building blocks of some transnational communities but others may be based on other forms of shared identity. Maria Balzani's work with the Ahmadi sect (2006) describes how transnational marriages may be intra-ethnic or inter-ethnic but that the important thing is to be Ahmadi, something that denotes belonging as family membership may. In many transnational communities marriages between the different locations of the transnational community is one of the most important ties that hold communities together and this may be for reasons of maintaining family relationships or for furthering the broader transnational goals of the community. Nicola Mooney's study finds 'marriage is central to Jat migration: apparently traditional practices of arranged marriage are fully modern means of negotiating the boundaries of citizenship imposed by states' (2006: 389–90). She relates this finding, however, very closely to the specificities of the community she is studying and it is not a generalisation that can necessarily be extended to other South Asian community. In the Sylheti communities Katy Gardner has studied for many years, the migration required by cross-border marriages appears to be of secondary importance to a desire to maintain relationships and she suggest that cross-border marriage should be seen as part of 'continued projects of transnational *connections*' (Gardner 2006: 374, italics in original) by which marriage plays a role as a means and an organizer of labour whether or not marriages lead to physical relocation.

Studies of Pakistani communities often focus on the community concept of *Rishta* (or *Riste*) to understand community attitudes to cross-border marriage. *Rishta*, as defined by Alison Shaw and Katherine Charsley (2006: 407), means match, proposal or connection and combines notions of strategic advantage and emotional elements. Roger Ballard notes that *rishta* is more than just the transferring of a bride from one family to another but also 'sets up a network of affinal relationships between two corporate, extended families' (2004: 8 ff). Successfully matched couples enhance material opportunities, and may increase the personal bargaining power of particular individuals (ibid.: 9) and Shaw and Charsley (2006: 407) describe a good *rishta* as one that connects people who are well matched and who share "complementary' cultural and religious characteristics and 'appropriate' social distance'. Such traditional concepts underpin many marriages as they are arranged to benefit and connect families and groups as much as individuals. In a transnational context these concepts are even more important as marriages contribute greatly to the emotional labour involved in maintaining transnational relationships. The *rishta* or arranged marriage itself will be shown later in this chapter to be defined in quite flexible ways as different matches become more attractive and appropriate in the different settings of transnational communities.

Community relationships of any sort, transnational or not, need to be maintained and constantly renewed, and the greater the number and type of links and interrelationships between parts of the community, the easier this process of social upkeep may be. The need and desire to maintain and increase links within communities may be reflected in the role of marriage as a conduit for the further migration of community members. This may be increasingly important as family migration categories become some of the few avenues open for migration in certain countries. Carmen Voigt-Graf's study of South Asian communities in Australia demonstrates that future migration was a clear motivation for one of her male Punjabi Sikh informants to marry from India to Australia, eventhough in doing so, he was breaking the tradition of patrilocality (2005: 373). Voigt-Graf argues that the global reach of the Punjabi Sikh community provided opportunities to arrange marriages which would open up migration routes that the Kannadigas, more recent migrants mostly from Bangalore, did not enjoy and who continued to marry spouses from a geographically discreet area of South India. The third group in Voigt-Graf's study were the Indo-Fijians who were reluctant to arrange marriages outside Australia, leaving their co-ethnics still in Fiji, so had no option but to advertise for partners in the overseas Fijian press. Voigt-Graf's account of migration and marriage strategy is interesting as it demonstrates the differences in marriage patterns between groups of South Asian origin but its focus on the geography of matches implies that marriages are arranged solely for the purpose of migration. This may be a common stereotype, but according to many in-depth studies, it is not the full story and ignores other possible factors that have influence on these marriage patterns.

Arranged marriages are often cast in opposition to 'love matches' – but this is clearly not a view shared by many members of communities where arranged marriages are common. Narayan Gopalkrishnan and Hurriyet Babacan, for example, dryly observe that: 'Some young people held the view, contrary to Western belief, that it is possible for men and women in arranged marriages to be happy and satisfied' (2007: 518) and they are not alone in making this observation. Nancy Netting's study (2006) of young people of Indian heritage in Canada, shows how there is not necessarily any clear separation between an arranged or a love marriage. Her research shows how young people 'see advantages and disadvantages of both systems, wavering back and forth as their circumstances evolve' (Netting 2006: 131). The study describes patterns of marriage arrangement in which matches were initially arranged by family but which the potential bride 'reconstructed her arranged marriage into a love-match' by establishing contact by telephone and experiencing a period of courtship more typical of so-called love matches. Others in the study found their own partners but were careful to only form relationships with individuals who would be acceptable to the community and with whom a marriage could be 'arranged' if the relationship became serious (ibid.: 137–9). Arranged marriages are also often conflated with forced marriage and are assumed to imply genetic risk when made between close kin, and cultural incompatibility if they are made between people who have grown up in different countries (Shaw 2006, 2009). Alison Shaw describes how many in the West unfairly view arranged marriages as a 'denial of individual autonomy and emotion' (Shaw 2006: 210) even though research in communities where arranged marriage is the norm, such as Nancy Netting's cited above, presents a more nuanced view of the practice. Shaw's work argues that the 'stereotypical distinction between arranged and love marriages obscures the role of love and romance even within conventionally arranged marriages' (Shaw 2006: 217) and reminds us that the conventions involved in arranging a marriage are themselves romantic and as wedded to an ideal of a love match as any other kind of marriage.

Nicola Mooney argues that the Jat Sikh marriages she studies encapsulate the ideals and aspirations of the community as a whole and have a highly symbolic role within communities (2006). These marriages, Mooney argues, have the pragmatic goal of maximising socio-economic advantage but which are nevertheless concerned with the emotional goals of maintaining community across international boundaries. These Jat Sikh marriages, like most others described within South Asian transnational communities (Mand 2005; Sheel 2005; Kalpagam 2005;

Charsley 2006; Wise and Velayutham 2008), raise the symbolic capital of the group as a whole by publicly demonstrating the continuing adherence to traditional values even in transnational settings. Rajana Sheel's work (2005) on Indian transnational marriages in Canada shows traditional rituals and practices becoming even more important (and expensive) in the diaspora. She writes:

> The increased sense of ethnic identity among different groups within the Indian community prompted them not only to seek spouses from within the socially approved pool of eligible brides and grooms but also necessitated the fulfilment of the demands and expectations of traditional marriage ceremonies and the attendant custom of dowry.
>
> (2005: 340)

Here, the transnational community seems to be trying almost too hard to maintain the symbolic value of marriages, or alternatively to re-shape transnational marriages in ways that are judged appropriate. Amanda Wise and Selvaraj Velayutham's (2008) discussion of their own marriage, against tradition in that it was not arranged by the community and was between a Tamil man and an Australian woman, provides a further example of how following the 'rules' of marriage and respecting the symbolic value of marriage ceremonies and practices can make marriage acceptable and proper in the eyes of the community. Ester Gallo (2005) also describes 'unorthodox' marriages, between Malayali women and non-Malayali men, which although unusual, are legitimated by the family and which allow the migrant to return to visit her family as a successful and respectable migrant.

These examples show how marriages within transnational communities can be both traditional and modern, as marrying in culturally recognisable ways but in transnational settings, confirms Charsley and Shaw's assertion that 'marriage emerges as an important means of producing and transforming transnational networks, while marriage practices and dynamics are themselves transformed in the process' (2006: 331).

The symbolism of transnational relationships may continue after marriage through shared participation in family events such as other marriages (for example Mand 2005) as well as in more material ways through financial and other remittances. Many studies refer to the importance of financial remittances from the transnational community back to the country of origin (Gallo 2005, 2006; Engebrigsten 2007) and Carmen Voigt-Graf refers to the symbolic value of these remittances as well as their practical value. The Indian migrant groups she studied in Australia do not generally have relatives who rely on material support so 'the primary purpose and value of remittances is not financial but symbolic, in the sense that remittances express transnational kinship solidarity' (2005: 379). The non-migrant family members send goods and information in return to reciprocate this solidarity.

Katy Gardner has written persuasively about transnational communities as communities based on care and on the maintenance of caring obligations across borders. Her work describes the pain of separation experienced when members of close family were in different places – 'they gave the impression that being physically close to those they loved was the single most important factor in their relative happiness' (Gardner 2006: 382). Caring obligations could either mean women migrated or stayed at home and some of the women Gardner interviewed had only left Bangladesh to live abroad with their husbands when their caring obligations, for in-laws or for other relatives, had come to an end. As with the women in Ester Gallo's research (2006), some of Gardner's informants had been separated from their children because of the transnational logics of the communities they belonged to and care arrangements for community members is shown to separate people from their loved ones as well as bring them together. Ada Engebrigsten (2007), in her study of Tamil and Somali migrants in Norway, highlights the caring responsibilities of the partners as a potential source of tension. She found that both husband and wife may want to remit money to their families but that problems arose when deciding which natal family to support. She argues that in the case of Tamil marriages, generally made between close family members, there was less tension as support for the wife's family was also support for the husband's. In the case of the Somali marriages, however, conflict was more likely as partners rarely had family in common (Engebrigsten 2007: 731). Migrant women, as transnational carers, play very significant roles in their communities which, as Gardner has noted, contradicts the assumption of female dependency on their male relatives who would clearly be unable to function in their economic and public roles without the domestic and emotional labour women provide (Gardner 2006: 376). This globalisation and glocalisation of intimacies in which 'local cultures pick up and usually transform the many features of personal life displayed across the globe' (Plummer 2003: 120), are a feature of transnationalism and these global intimacies demonstrate 'a global transformation of personal relationships' (ibid.: 122). Caring in many western countries is a devalued activity and has become 'formalized and officially labelled' rather than a 'cultural ideal' (Gardner 2006: 384). Paul Hoggett has described this phenomenon as 'the cultural devaluation of care' which devalues what is seen as women's work as well as undermines the rights of those who need ongoing care and support (Hoggett 2001: 44).

Women living in countries of resettlement who choose husbands from their transnational communities 'back home' may be looking for a closer match to their own career aspirations or worldview than simply an ethnic or cultural match. Maria Balzani's work (2006) shows women from the Ahmadi sect with British citizenship are more likely to choose a spouse from the UK or Canada than from Pakistan (the homeland of the sect). In contrast, while she found British citizen Ahmadi men to be more likely to marry a Pakistani wife (Balzani 2006: 353). The reasons for this gender preference are hypothesised by Balzani as relating to the desire of women to choose a partner who shares cultural and career aspirations while men choose partners who bring with them traditional and cultural resources and who represent supposed cultural authenticity. Expectations of what marriage will mean and the reasons for marrying are gender-specific and these differ in non-migrant populations as much as in migrant ones. Roger Ballard (2004) has described some of the ways in which gender may affect the timing and choice of marriage partners and argues that ethnic group and cultural practice affect when and how men and women are encouraged to marry. Ballard writes that where cousin marriage is the norm, men may face less pressure to achieve, as 'their educational and professional achievements will have much less impact on their marriageability' (2004: 24). In the same paper, Ballard writes that while men, unlike women, may be allowed a certain period to 'sow wild oats' before settling down, an excessive attachment to someone considered an unsuitable marriage partner (typically a non-Pakistani British girlfriend) may result in their being taken to Pakistan for an arranged marriage.

This section has discussed the importance of marriage in the management of kin and family strategies in transnational families and has attempted to demonstrate the different ways marriage may be used within transnational communities to further individual or collective goals. The next section will consider how structures – presented by policy, family and community institutions impact upon marriages contracted across borders.

Structural mechanisms that facilitate, or impede, transnational interaction

John Lievens (1999) argues that choosing a spouse from the country of origin (or heritage) is an indicator of the 'strength of network connections' within a transnational community and that 'Marriages across national borders require intense contacts and a feeling of commitment of migrants with non-migrants' (ibid.: 724). His paper offers little evidence of how contacts are maintained within the Turkish and Moroccan transnational communities he studies or of how 'feelings of commitment' can be measured. This is not necessarily to disagree with the sentiment of Lievens' work but to point out that the research reviewed here shows that marriages are contracted within transnational communities that have very different degrees of contact and levels of commitment. Some transnational communities have very strong, intimate ties that reach across borders but others rely on structural rather than personal connections. In these cases, it may be impersonal brokers that provide the means of making transnational marriage matches rather than closely connected people. By whatever means marriages are actually made, their arrangement is clearly an extremely important activity for the families involved as not only is the future well-being of their children at stake, but the family's standing in the community and possibly the continuity of the community itself are at issue.

Kalpagam (2005: 191) refers to a 1980s film about a transnational marriage that went wrong which was still being referred to by her research participants nearly twenty years later – this may give some indication of the concern that exists to match marriage partners carefully and to minimise risk for the partners and for their communities. The Tamil Brahman communities Kalpagam describes have developed complex and formal structures to help them make suitable matches. These include the institutionalised networks that circulate the horoscopes used in matchmaking via temples, the internet or through the commercial networks that have become more important than personal networks (ibid.: 197). Matchmaking services have themselves become businesses to meet the demand for matches between India and the Tamil Brahman migrant communities in the US and Canada. These networks may be used to make the initial selection which will then be followed up by consultations with astrologers and finally with personal contact. In Kalpagam's view, these matchmaking strategies represent the 'acquisition and deployment of symbolic capital for the reproduction of class *habitus*' (ibid.: 192, italics in the original) and that the underlying logic of these marriages, to maintain and enhance the group's symbolic capital, has allowed and justified changes in marriage practices from the traditional kin-based system to a class- and status-based system.

The sophisticated structures developed by this community demonstrate the important role transnational marriage has in maintaining and advancing community goals. The fact that matchmaking is increasingly professionalised may indicate that the personal networks more traditionally used no longer have the global reach to successfully connect the aspirational individuals looking for particular skills and resources. Research shows how symbolically important weddings are but also how traditions can be adapted and Kalpagam describes the sophisticated way the calculation of an appropriate wife was managed. She writes: 'Marriage preferences in diasporic marriages appear to be shaped by considerations of the durability of the migration and the nature of the boy's employment as well as the girls' attainment' (2005: 193). This, she argues, meant that male migrants with longer-term residency status and higher salary contracts were looking for a homemaker (who would not be expected to be economically active) while those holding more temporary visas and statuses were looking for a wife with qualifications. The implication is that these wives would be able to contribute in economic terms but Kalpagam notes that the short-term visas of their husbands did not extend permission to work to spouses.

This last example may indicate that marriage preferences are not entirely rational (at least not in economic terms), but have a social meaning that may be complex and may appear counter-intuitive from the outside. Not all transnational communities are as institutionally organised as the wealthy and technologically sophisticated Tamil Brahmans Kalpagam describes and Kanwal Mand's research with Sikh transnational communities in East Africa and the Punjab demonstrates how rules governing marriage arrangements can be flexible and highly 'place'-dependent (Mand 2005). Mand describes how rules about caste endogamy, village endogamy and 'got' endogamy (whereby the partners should not share clan membership in the last four generations) could be relaxed. The marriage rules were maintained but 'subject to innovation and agency' (ibid.: 234).

The social structures that influence marriage choice in transnational communities are observable in some decisions to marry close kin and Alison Shaw's work (Shaw 2006) describes the 'positive social and cultural reasons for preferring a spouse from Pakistan' which may inform the expressed preference of some young British Pakistanis for a spouse drawn from close family from the homeland of Pakistan (ibid.: 216). The close-kin marriages in Britain are often assumed by majority commentators to represent an increased risk of congenital abnormality for any children as well as representing the maintenance of outmoded traditions that discriminate against women. Alison Shaw's (2009) exploration of the negotiation of genetic risk and of how it is perceived and managed challenges the orthodox view of cousin marriages as necessarily risky. Shaw's work presents a sophisticated picture of young British Pakistanis, and their families, choosing to marry close kin while fully aware of the potential genetic and cultural risks.

There is research that argues that, for some of the men, choosing transnational matches over marriage to local, more assertive cousins is linked to preserving gendered power differences. This debate links to the discussion in the next chapter of how images of the 'exotic' woman may make certain matches appear more attractive and the lure of the exotic, foreign wife over the known may have some bearing here too. Shaw describes, however, how British Pakistani women also wanted a husband from Pakistan whom they felt would be more likely to be faithful and respectful. In the words of Farhat,

> A man from Pakistan... knows how to talk respectfully to the elders, he knows his culture, he is more religious, less obsessed with money. Men from here, they are too forward, too confident in talking to women. A man from Pakistan, I don't think he would cheat on me.
>
> (Shaw 2006: 217)

Shaw's paper, along with many others (Mand 2005; Gallo 2005; Sheel 2005; Charsley 2006, 2007; Mooney 2006; Netting 2006; Gopalkrishnan and Babacan 2007; Grewal 2008) presents a picture of the structural frame of arranged marriage practice being adapted to allow more negotiation and to allow potential spouses more space to participate in the process of marriage arrangement and to express preference – whether that is for a marriage from 'back home' or from the transnational space.

The evidence from research challenges the popularly assumed binary relationship between arranged and 'love' marriages. The choice of marriage convention, and ultimately of marriage partner may rest on highly personal factors (as exemplified by the example of the woman who argued that because she liked football she would prefer a British match over a Pakistani one who would not understand this important part of her life (Charsley 2005: 96–7)). Such personal factors are filtered through an individual's *habitus* and a community's traditions – transnationalism can be argued to have multiplied the diversity of these factors without ever challenging the basic desire people have to marry in personally and socially meaningful ways.

Implications for individual agency across borders within transnational communities

Transnational communities may be very close knit and controlling of their members even when those members are spread across different countries and continents. It may be that the effort needed to maintain community identity when communities are cultural or ethnic minorities means that the migrant branches of transnational communities adhere more strictly to what they see as community and cultural norms. This self-consciousness may undermine the agency and opportunity for innovation of younger generations whose challenges to tradition may be seen as wholesale rejection of community norms rather than a plea for variation. In Gerd Baumann's study of communities in Southall, West London, Baumann notes how social norms have been created in transnational communities that may have more relevance to the social norms of an older generation and that 'the 'traditional' *Asian culture* which young Southallians have to assess is that which their parents construct for them' (Baumann 1996: 153, italics in the original). The inference is that the migrant parts of transnational communities can get left behind and cling to outmoded interpretations of tradition and practices through their efforts to demonstrate respect for tradition and cultural authenticity. As a result, they may enforce stricter rules in relation to important cultural markers, such as the behaviour of women and the contracting of suitable marriages, than may be the case in parts of the community that can afford to be less self-conscious about their traditions and more confident about adapting them. This observation about the conservative tendency of transnational and diaspora communities is also found in Roger Ballard's work. Ballard found that the 'pardeshis' living away from the Indian subcontinent found their privileged 'deshis' counterparts from Delhi and Islamabad were more Westernised than they were (Ballard 2004: 17, note 11). Christiane Timmerman, referring to Turkish communities in Belgium, argues that, while Turks in Belgium view potential marriage partners living in Turkey as more traditional and better behaved, they have not appreciated how these home communities have changed to become, in cultural terms, more like their Western counterparts (Timmerman *et al.* 2009: 134). The notion of the self-conscious transnational is challenged by Kanwal Mand's research participant's comment, however, who stated in response to a criticism of ceremonial marriage practice that 'we do these things in Africa, we have such traditions in Africa' (Mand 2005: 245) – claiming her own authenticity for a tradition rooted in the diaspora.

Katherine Charsley has argued that the transnational marriage migration she observes is best understood as a 'consequence of culturally-grounded dialogues on risk and how best it can be managed' (2007: 1117). This view challenges the purely strategic view of marriage as a way of negotiating borders and of circumventing restrictive migration policy and focuses instead on community and family decision-making strategies that minimise risk for their children and for the community more widely. Arranging the marriage of a child is always a risky business but arranging one within a transnational community brings its own special risks (for example, the risk of a visa being refused leaving a married child separated from their new spouse – see Charsley 2007: 1119). Charsley reminds us of the social nature of risk and that it is understood through 'cultural filters' (Adams 1995, cited by Charsley 2007: 1127) which determines how risk, and therefore trust, are calculated. This view of risk is affirmed by Meeto and Mirza (2007: 194) who see risk as malleable and socially constructed. Risk is therefore identified and managed variously in different social and temporal contexts. Charsley argues (2007), that in the Pakistani families she studies, 'risk' is identified and located with marriage outside the family so to mitigate the inevitable risk in contracting any marriage, it is best for marriages to be arranged within the known group where 'the family provides trusted referees in mutual kin to advise on the character of the proposed spouse and their family' (Charsley 2007: 1120). I have argued earlier (Chapter 3) that agency can be found in risky situations where making a change in one's life may be only possible by striking out from the known. It seems in the case of these Pakistani groups, families may be attempting to use the strategies they have available to them to minimise risk and to guide their (and their children's) decision-making through systems they have control, or at least influence, over. Arranging marriages within the known of the immediate family controls risks as far as possible and is a conservative, safety-first strategy. This observation turns the received wisdom of the inherent dangerousness of arranged marriages on its head.

Families are not always able to minimise risk for the younger generations as they marry overseas and Margaret Walton-Roberts (2004) has described marriages within Punjabi Sikh communities that allow very little agency for some women entering Canada as wives of Canadians of Punjabi origin. Walton-Roberts argues that the power imbalance created by the Canadian Indian prospective groom radically alters traditional practices as the match is not only about the migration prospects of the potential bride, but of her whole family as well. In addition, the imperatives of marriage across borders means that negotiation processes are speeded up, reducing the bride's family's chance of making an informed choice of match. According to Walton-Roberts: 'This transnational marriage process overwhelmingly favours the mobile male' (2004: 368), and the perceived desirability of a match to a foreign citizen, creates pressure on families and brides to accept matches that would otherwise have been rejected. The exogamous nature of these marriages also means that the bride travels without the support of her natal family. The desirability of a match in the developed world has also meant that the cost of arranging marriages has risen dramatically, again putting the prospective spouse in the country of origin at a disadvantage. Apocryphal stories also tell of men based in the West marrying, claiming the dowry traditionally paid to the husband and leaving the new bride with an empty promise of sending for her when a visa is obtained.

Traditional gender roles institutionalised by marriage traditions and practice may be reinforced rather than challenged by cross-border migration and Nicola Mooney argues that, in some cases 'family-class immigration may re-inscribe their subordination within gender paradigms' (Mooney 2006: 399). Ada Engebrigsten (2007) describes the strong social family pressure in support of the institution of marriage within the transnational Tamil community in Norway. Although she emphasises the pressure this places on the marriage partners to remain married, she also points out that the Tamil wives coming from Sri Lanka to marry in Norway bring resources of their own including their dowries, which gives them leverage and a certain bargaining power. The nature of Tamil marriage migration to Norway also means that the newly arrived wives may have male family members who can support them in negotiating their relationships with their husbands (Engebrigsten 2007: 740). The role of other family members in supporting and advocating for newly arrived migrants (often through culturally appropriate channels) is an important one which can increase the agency of the less powerful in transnational communities. Many transnational communities carry authority structures and hierarchies with them from the home country and, while these structures may work to maintain inequalities, they are also available to 'correct' the excesses and inappropriate behaviour of some community members. It may not be ideal that a migrant wife cannot argue her own case but, if she has a brother, a cousin or a sympathetic elderly relative who can balance the power of her in-laws or her husband, she may be able to re-negotiate community expectations of her or achieve a change in her situation without forcing a rupture in the community. Kanwal Mand's study of separated, divorced or widowed transnational Sikh women (2005) argues that the location of their own kin networks is essential in understanding women's experiences and opportunities for resistance and agency. Esther Gallo's research with Malayali women migrants to Italy (2005) describes a situation in which women use marriage across borders in a positive and active way despite those marriages being, ostensibly at least, in line with traditional practice. Migration and the resulting remittances are seen as important in marriage strategies as, by migrating prior to marriage, migrant women may earn their place in the local marriage market through their financial contributions. They may perhaps pay for building a house and for their own wedding arrangements. Gallo writes of marriages as 'a form of rehabilitation' for migrant women and also 'an important context in which they claim more equal gender relations in their family and the wider society' (Gallo 2005: 244–5).

Conclusion

The chapter has looked at studies of South Asian transnational communities and at their various marriage practices. The evidence presented here shows people marrying in accordance with the three categories John Eekelaar and Mavis Maclean (2004) have proposed to explain why people marry: for pragmatic, conventional and internal reasons. In transnational communities, marriage decisions are often made with reference to a far wider constituency of interest than other marriages may be. These marriages may be seen to represent the community and may be interrogated to test their fit for the community at large as well as for the individuals involved. Transnational marriages may also carry the weight and expectations of family members beyond the immediate couple who have hopes that the marriage will indirectly improve their material or symbolic standing in the community and outside. All of that acknowledged, transnational marriages have the potential to bring people together in emotionally fulfilling ways that promote and are promoted by a supportive community.

Families and communities are sites in which individual and collective agency is negotiated and enacted and the studies reviewed here indicate some of the ways this may happen. Tradition can be used to argue for greater freedom of choice in marriage and can be used to put pressure on individuals to encourage, oblige or force them to conform. The intimate scale of many of studies allows analysis to get beyond the stereotypes of arranged marriages and of the marriages of 'other' communities – so often lumped together as South Asians. There are clearly great differences in how the many communities that can be included under the category 'South Asian' view marriage and these differences impact on the agency of individuals. Recognition of these differences humanises discussion of transnational marriage and hopefully encourages a less stigmatising view of people who make choices that are different from the norms of majority communities. Studies that focus on South Asian communities or other multi-generational migrant communities reflect on just one manifestation of transnationalism and it may be that other social groups will become transnational based not on ethnic and family ties but on ties of religion, interest, experience or any other shared identity. It is hoped that the studies reviewed here have demonstrated that while transnational marriage has an important and culturally highly-charged place in the shaping and maintaining of transnational communities, cross-border marriage is not necessarily the stagnant and unbending site of tradition it is sometimes assumed to be. Many of those most closely involved in these marriages have found creative and imaginative ways to get the best from the opportunity transnational marriage presents and while marriage is always a risky business, many have found ways to use their culture and their traditions to moderate and mitigate those risks.

Cross-border marriages do not only occur between the transnational communities discussed in this chapter and the next chapters will show the place of marriage in the migration trajectories of individuals and of communities who may become properly 'transnational' in the future.

7
Cross-Border Marriages within East Asia

This chapter follows on from Chapter 6 as an exploration of a particular type of cross-border marriage migration. Chapter 6 considered marriages that may be considered transnational according to definitions employed in this book. They are made within communities that are linked across international borders by practical, emotional and symbolic ties and in this, markedly contrast with the marriages described in this chapter. Here, the subject of the chapter is cross-border marriages between ethnic and cultural groups. These marriages are made by individuals or networks rather than within communities and in contrast to transnational marriages, the partners may have little practical knowledge of the lives and expectations of their new spouses. Marriages within East Asia will be used as a sample to explore not least as there has been a great deal of research done in the area from a variety of perspectives and these marriages hold an important place in the national imaginations of the host countries as to what migration is and who migrants are. The importance of these marriage within the context of this book, however, is that I argue these marriages are not transnational – cross-national but not transnational. I argue further that some of them may be developing transnational sensibilities and logics, but that, as they stand, they cannot be considered transnational by accepted definitions.

Inter-cultural marriages, sometimes known as 'mixed marriages' are becoming more and more common across the world through processes of globalisation and as global travel for leisure, education and employment increases. The internet and social networking sites have enabled intimate relationships to develop over geographical distance which may or may not result in migration or in partnerships being formed. Whether or not these contacts ever become formalised, the possibility of forming relationships with people from across the world has become open to many people in the developed and the developing world. Travel for work, education and employment is also more commonplace and, particularly in the developed economies, increasing ethnic diversity means that people with backgrounds in different countries meet in their everyday lives. As previously stated, this book is concerned with the marriages and long-term partnerships made between people of different citizenship statuses, it is not a study of marriages between members of different ethnic groups *per se* but rather a study of marriages between people considered 'different' by virtue of their immigration statuses and identified as such by the governments of the countries where they live. Such marriages include therefore, people of the same ethnic group but who have different migration histories, as well as people born in different countries and from different ethnic groups whose families and wider communities have had no previous connection.

This chapter will focus on cross-border marriages migrants, chiefly in East Asia, who have migrated, or made their residence permanent, through marriage to a citizen or long-term resident of a country that they have little or no previous familial or cultural connection to. I distinguish them from migrants in the partnerships discussed in the previous chapter as they have not travelled as part of an identifiable transnational community. I include, for example, women who have married spouses met via the internet (for example, the Russian women described by Ericka Johnson 2007) and who move to live in countries in which they have no previous connection; I also include women travelling to marry husbands they have arranged to marry through brokering agencies (for example, Wang 2007) plus women and men who originally travelled for work but who subsequently married citizens of their country of residence (Rodriguez Garcia 2006; Faier 2007).

Some of these marriages have been considered 'mail-order' marriages and problematised as such while others, for example, the marriages described between professional immigrant women and Danish men (Liversage 2009), have attracted less critical attention. All of these marriages are, at least in their early stages, subject to immigration controls that put pressure on them and tend to make the migrant party in the relationship dependent on their citizen spouse. The story of many of the marriages described in the literature is of women (and outside established transnational communities marriage migration is predominantly a story of women's migration), trying to establish themselves in their countries of settlement through working, where possible, and through building meaningful social support networks. For some, these networks are based upon connections with their new families and with their new friends in their locality, some of whom may share similar migration experiences, while others may look back to their natal countries for continuing support, possibly encouraging the migration of friends and family from home. As the literature shows, the potential for forming social networks varies from situation to situation and may be affected by popular attitudes to migrants, positive and negative, and by where – in rural or in urban, traditional or more modern settings – the migrants live. The chance to meet and form friendships with their ethnic compatriots may also be extremely limited in countries that have generally ethnically homogenous populations and where cultural difference is not embraced or valued. Being incorporated, as they often are, within the families of citizens, it may be expected that cross-border marriage migrants would have opportunities to participate and interact with the social structures of the ethnic or cultural majority community but the studies presented here show how the interaction of these migrants in society is still shaped by both social attitudes and, importantly, by the immigration rules that continue to affect their lives after migration.

Intermarriage, or marriage between people from different community or ethnic backgrounds, has often been used as a measure of the degree to which minority ethnic groups have become integrated, or assimilated, into the majority population. This idea of intermarriage as a measure of integration stems from the work of Milton Gordon (1964) and continues to be used by some writers (Rodriguez Garcia 2006; Roer-Strier and Ben Ezra 2006; Beck-Gernsheim 2007; Hidalgo and Bankston 2008; and challenged by others, Hwang *et al.* 1997; Song 2009). Gordon's argument is that as minority groups become more integrated, they will be less likely to favour long-term partnerships from their own ethnic or minority group and will instead form partnerships with the majority populations. Jutta Lauth Bacas (2002) argues that 'intermarriage . . . is a strong and effective mechanism for turning a stranger into "one of us"' (ibid.: 5) and marriage undeniably brings cross-border brides into the mainstream of communities – whether this represents 'integration' is a much bigger question. As Kathryn Robinson writes of marriage migrants: 'Here they are introduced in the most remote regions into Australian households, giving birth to Australian citizens' (1996: 54). Certainly marriage brings women into close contact with majority ethnic families but contact alone does not mean they will become integrated or assimilated or that they won't seek to develop ethnic-based transnational communities in the future.

Hidalgo and Bankston (2008) use Gordon's ideas as a predictive theory assuming that as minorities become assimilated there will be more intermarriage. This argument is underpinned by the assumption that integration is marked by assimilation by which the differences in groups are ironed out post-migration and implies that minority groups that maintain a distinct cultural or ethnic identity cannot be considered integrated. Elisabeth Beck-Gernsheim writes that 'mixed marriages' are 'widely considered to be a benchmark for integration' (2007: 272) but while it can be argued that marriage into the majority community may afford special insights into life in the country of settlement (as Gopalkrishnan and Babacan 2007: 515–16 have observed), such marriages do not necessarily grant acceptance or ensure a migrant a sense of belonging. Studies discussed in the previous chapter show how earlier generations of settled migrants married partners from majority communities (Ballard 2004) but that when they had the chance to bring in partners from their kin networks from their homelands, they preferred to return to more traditional patterns of in-group marriage. There seems to be little evidence that there is an inevitable trend towards intermarriage but that migrant communities marry in ways that match their evolving personal and community priorities. Dan Rodriguez Garcia cites work that argues, with Gordon, that assimilation is the 'final destination' of migrant integration but he argues for a more subtle understanding of the 'multifaceted nature of integration and assimilation processes' (2006: 406). Similarly, Dorit Roer-Strier and Dina Ben Ezra's study of marriages between Western women and Palestinian men (2006) argues for a view of 'acculturation' as a two-way process that does not affect the migrant partner alone, but also partners who belong to the majority community. All these studies support Miri Song's argument that links between intermarriage and integration need to reassessed and reappraised (2009).

This rest of this chapter will review literature relating to cross-border marriage migration relating specifically to countries of East Asia where research on marriages between migrants and minority ethnic groups and majority populations is particularly rich. As referred to earlier (Chapter 4), the academic literature tends to separate out marriages made *within* ethnic communities from marriages *between* ethnicities and *between* citizen populations and migrants. I aim to challenge this simple dichotomy by arguing that the ethnicity of the partners is not necessarily as meaningful as the transnational aspirations of marriages and their meanings for the individuals themselves. Migration to Japan, South Korea and Taiwan in particular makes an interesting case to study as they share a history of this type of cross-border marriage migration that has been studied in-depth over a long period. These countries have developed economies with significantly greater GDPs compared with neighbouring countries, for example, China and Southeast Asian countries such as Vietnam, Thailand and the Philippines. The economic differences between these countries sets up a logic for migration that is reinforced by social changes in Japan, South Korea and Taiwan that have led to 'shortages' of local women prepared to marry local men. This chapter will consider the literature relating to cross-border marriage migration in the region and describes how structural limitations and opportunities have interacted with the aspirations of women motivated to migrate and settle abroad for reasons related to their personal and family situations. These marriages, then, have features in common with the transnational marriages described in Chapter 6 and perhaps show how transnational relationships and communities can develop. To compare the marriages I have categorised as transnational and non-transnational, this chapter will divide the literature reviewed into the same thematic headings as used in Chapter 6. Therefore, after first introducing some of the patterns of migration and the demographic factors that have influenced cross-border marriage migration in East Asia through a description of the case of Taiwan, I will discuss the effect of kin and family relationships on the marriage migration patterns of women entering East Asian countries. Following that, I will consider the structural mechanisms that facilitate transnational interaction and will conclude by considering the implications of marriage migration outside transnational communities for the individual agency of migrants.

Patterns of cross-border marriage migration in East Asia

In East Asia, research has typically focused on cross-border marriages that are, at least in part, the consequence of regional economic imbalances that juxtapose the strong economies of Taiwan and South Korea, for example, with the less developed economies of China and Southeast Asia. Nicola Piper locates international marriage migration within the broader context of labour migration and argues that, in Japan at least, marriage is a way for women to break out of circular migration between home and country of employment (2003: 457). Marriage migration, conceptualised as a by-product of labour migration, is a valid way of studying the phenomenon but is only part of the story. Cross-border marriage may be motivated by a desire to improve the collective socio-economic situation of families and communities but is also a way of fulfilling personal ambitions. Given this complexity, it is helpful to look at cross-border marriage as both an end in itself as well as means to other ends – in other words, does one migrate to marry or marry to migrate? This question can equally be posed of marriages between ethnic groups but the focus on tradition and culture in such marriages tends to obscure the question. The reality in all cross-border marriages is somewhere between these two clear-cut choices and decisions are made after balancing the desire to marry and migrate with the perceived opportunities of both.

Pei-Chia Lan (2008) has argued that cross-border marriage migration should be linked to the cross-border migration of domestic workers and this is a strong strand within research on marriage migration in East Asia. Lan argues that the similarities between foreign brides and foreign maids is based on their place at the 'intersection of globalisation and nationalism' and that they represent 'a class specific solution to the alleged shortage of reproductive labour' (Lan 2008: 834). As elsewhere, 'Taiwanese working-class men seek cross-border marriages not just to end their bachelorhood: they also need the unpaid labour of foreign spouses to assist with agricultural production in farming households and the reproduction of the next generation' (ibid.: 840, citing Hsia 1997). Yu Kojima (2001) similarly links cross-border marriage to domestic work and views female marriage migrants as reproductive workers who take the roles more affluent women refuse. Marriages may represent many different types of labour, for example, economic, reproductive and sex work but as this is private work, set within a closed domestic context, it does not grant *citizenship* to women which in most states is rewarded for market-based economic activity (van Walsum and Spijkerboer 2007).

Bridget Anderson has observed that in acquiring domestic labour, families are buying 'personhood' (2000, 2006) and this is even more the case when that domestic labour is provided by a wife. Families may claim that they treat their domestic workers 'like daughters' but Anderson's work (2006: 15–16) describes how domestic workers are expected to *want* to serve their employers to earn a place in the family. Anderson explains this need for domestic workers to work *willingly* as a result of power imbalances and the uncomfortable nature of such power – especially when the power is wielded by one woman over another. She argues that 'the beastliness of power is clothed in the language of obligation, support and responsibility, rather than power and exploitation' (ibid.: 18) and is dressed in concern for the well-being of the worker. When it is a wife who is providing domestic labour, then the fact that such labour is free and unsullied by commercial exchange 'offers', according to Andrea Lauser, 'a higher moral value and social recognition' (2008: 102). In a similar way, paying for sexual services is separated in moral terms from the same services provided by a wife even when the relationship may be very similar. Pei-Chia Lan introduces a class discourse by arguing that in Taiwan, the labour needs of the working class are met by marriage, while the middle and upper classes employ migrant domestic workers to fill labour gaps (Lan 2008: 841, citing Wang 2001). This is undoubtedly the case for some marriages and domestic arrangements, but as noted throughout this volume, such generalised discourses can drown out accounts of marriages that have more personal and emotional foundations contributing to the stigma the people and families choosing these living arrangements face.

As women in these developing economies have moved away from rural areas to find work in the cities, disadvantaged rural men may have few local marriage prospects so may look abroad for wives (see, for example, the work of Lu 2005, Faier 2008: 637; Oum 2003, relating to Japan, Taiwan and South Korea). Delia Davin (2007) has reviewed some of the literature on cross-border marriage migration in East Asia and cites figures on cross-border marriage in Japan. She (along with Ito 2005) argues that before 1975, Japanese marriages to non-Japanese citizens were rare but usually between Japanese women and foreign men (she records that 75 per cent of all marriages to foreign nationals in Japan were between Japanese women and foreign men representing only 1 per cent of all marriages in Japan). By 2001, marriages between foreigners and Japanese citizens had reached 5 per cent of all marriages and had reversed in terms of gender with 80 per cent of marriages now between Japanese men and foreign women (Davin 2007: 93). In Taiwan, Tsay (2004) claims that in 2004 over 90 per cent of female migration into the country was through marriage migration and it has become a significant proportion of all marriages (discussed later).

Inter-cultural marriage in East Asia has clearly different causes than cross-border, inter-cultural marriage in other parts of the world but the effects on spouses migrating for the purpose of marriage may be similar. Cross-border marriage migrants moving into countries where they have few or no friends and no transnational community may be very isolated and may depend heavily on their new spouse as an intermediary to help them access local society. This dependence may lead to vulnerability to, or actual, abuse if marriage migrants do not know or cannot access their rights which, in any case, may be limited by the conditional nature of their residency status. The specific conditions in countries of the region obviously differ and local responses to cross-border marriage migration, the country of origin of cross-border migrants and the circumstances of their migration reflect the history and socio-economic features of the country. In the following section I will refer in more detail to the case of Taiwan in an attempt to demonstrate some of the salient features of migration in East Asia – many of which occur more broadly across the region.

Cross-border marriage migration: the case of Taiwan

In Taiwan, as in most industrialised countries, the government's response to increasing migration flows has been to restrict legal migration to a few possibilities – chiefly, specified types of labour migration and family reunion. The entry of marriage migrants into Taiwan as part of this second stream represents a significant inflow of people who are identifiable as minorities because of their physical characteristics and/or by their style of speech. They have been the focus of government statements, regulation and control as well as of media interest. There are many different terms used to describe the women who migrate and then marry or who migrate for the purpose of marriage and in Taiwan these include 'foreign spouses', 'new migrants', or 'foreign brides'.

The influx of foreign women as wives of Taiwanese men is partly the result of demographic and social change, specifically a trend away from marriage across the whole of Southeast and East Asia (Jones 2004). Gavin Jones argues that both men and women have been more reluctant to marry but that the trend has been particularly marked on the part of women. Some demographers have referred to a 'marriage squeeze' whereby men still prefer to marry a wife who is younger and less educated than themselves while at the same time, more women are becoming educated to secondary or tertiary level (Jones 2004: 105). The 'marriage squeeze' is assumed to be occurring in Taiwan as Taiwanese women are increasingly well educated and benefiting from their changing role in society and the family which allows them to participate more fully in the economy. Women from the countryside have left the poorer rural areas in large numbers to take advantage of the opportunities in the prosperous cities and this has affected their attitudes to marriage. So out-migration has contributed to the significant sex-ratio imbalance in the rural areas of Taiwan that have a high instance of cross-border marriage. In the rural areas of Japan, there has been a similar trend referred to in some areas as a 'bride drought' as local women have left rural areas to look for economic opportunities and husbands in urban centres (Faier 2007: 150) Lu (2005: 280) argues that before the mid-1990s, when brokering agencies became common, the main reason for Taiwanese men to look to China and Southeast Asia for wives was the lack of opportunity for them to find Taiwanese women to marry. Since the mid-1990s, she argues: Taiwanese men have looked to marry outside of Taiwan in preference to local women – partly, because of the advertisements placed by brokering agencies. For whatever their motivation, marriages between Taiwanese men and women from other countries represent a significant percentage of marriages in Taiwan. The peak year for cross-border marriages in Taiwan was 2003 when 15.9 per cent of all marriages were between Taiwanese men and foreign spouses. Since then the figures have reduced and in 2008 the numbers of cross-border marriages were 7 per cent of all marriages – the smallest number in the preceding ten-year period (figures from the Republic of China Ministry of the Interior, Department of Household Registration (2007); Ministry of the Interior, Department of Statistics (2008), cited in Yang *et al.* 2009). Male blue-collar workers and farmers have been most affected by changes in the local marriage market and, generally speaking, most cross-border marriages seem to be initiated by less economically successful men (Chen and Huang 2006). In Taiwan, we find examples of women's hypergamy being defined by their entrance into a stronger economy rather than into an economically advantageous position with their new husband and his family. Traditional Taiwanese society, like many other Chinese societies, places considerable importance on the forming of a family and on having descendants, and the possibility of choosing an intercultural, cross-border marriage has encouraged stigmatised men, including disabled men, to marry foreign women (ibid.). This may be an example of how the 'unmarriageables' in society, described in Chapter 4, may be able to find matches because of cross-border perceptions of what constitutes a hypergamous marriage. Most wives enter Taiwan from Mainland China and Southeast Asian countries such as Vietnam, Indonesia, the Philippines, and Cambodia. In the more traditional areas of Taiwan where many cross-border wives live, there is a strong expectation that they will have children, in particular a son or sons, who will carry on the family name. Taiwan, as a whole, has a very low birth rate and it has been assumed that cross-border brides will raise this rate and bring up a significant percentage of Taiwanese children (Yang and Schoonheim 2006). In 2003, 13.37 per cent of babies born had non-Taiwanese mothers, although this had reduced to 7 per cent in 2008 – a year in which the Taiwanese birth rate fell to a new low (figures cited in Yang *et al.* 2009). The Taiwanese state is investing in support for cross-border spouses which mostly takes the form of 'Immigration counselling' designed to encourage their integration into society.

Taiwan is moving towards a recognition of itself as a multicultural society – this is despite the fact that Taiwan has always been ethnically and culturally diverse. The different ethnic groups native to Taiwan, such as the aboriginal people and various other linguistically and culturally distinct groups, are now being acknowledged in policy and public life as are migrants who have settled in the last ten or twenty years. The 'imagined political community' (Anderson 1991) of Taiwan since the founding of the nation in 1949, stressed a mono-cultural 'Chinese' identity but movements to recognise Taiwan as an independent state distinct from the People's Republic of China have led Taiwan to reassess this imagination. The degree to which Taiwan is becoming a multicultural nation may be evidenced by the way it addresses the needs and aspirations of its largest settled migrant group – the cross-border marriage migrants.

The effect of kin and family relationships on migration

Family relationships have a powerful effect on a migrant's experience of migration whether they travel with, or to family. As Andrea Lauser writes: 'People who relocate carry with them not only their physical belongings but also their memories and people who stay behind are nevertheless involved in the experience of transnationalism, especially a kind of "emotional transnationalism"' (2008: 89). Emotional transnationalism may be key to understanding many of the migration movements described in this book as even travelling alone, many of the migration decisions observed and analysed in the literature are made in the light of the emotional responsibilities and priorities of the migrants. Many of the women described in this chapter migrate because of a desire to found a family or because they wish to support family they already have and in that, they are little different from the marriage migrants described in Chapter 6 who have migrated within transnational communities. There is, however, a crucial difference in the level of support and prior knowledge they may have about migration and what migration will entail.

Nancy Abelman, and Hyunhee Kim's (2005) work in South Korea presents a mother's attempts to find a wife for her farmer son whose marginal socio-economic position in the countryside is obscured by South Korea's GDP. South Korea's comparative affluence allowed this family to 'claim membership in that national community of relative prosperity . . . to sustain the possible fiction of the Filipina's presumed hypergamy' (Abelman and Kim 2005: 111). In this example, the mother was trying to maintain traditions and norms of the continuity of the Korean patrilineage in a globalised context.

Marriage is generally more than the simple joining of two people and the attitudes and behaviour of the husband's family can have a powerful effect on the experience of cross-border brides. In rural areas of Taiwan, the brides may be expected to join their husband's extended family who will often take on the responsibility of teaching the bride the family's language and culture and whose manner towards and expectation of the bride will be very significant in her early experience in Taiwan. While many of these brides may experience problems with their in-laws, women living in the cities alone with their new husbands may experience social isolation and greater difficulties in learning Mandarin Chinese. While many cross-border wives find economic security and freedom from the traditions and family responsibilities of their homes, migration may also result in a loss of status and security as women lose their independence and their sense of place in society. In common with other long-term migrants, they may experience the loss of familiar social worlds and their ability to keep in contact with their natal home will depend on the attitudes of their husband and his family. Women may find they have exchanged one set of traditional social roles for others that are just as difficult and limiting without the benefit of familiarity. During the first three years of marriage to Taiwanese citizens, for example, migrant spouses have no independent right to remain in the country and may find this enforced dependence on their partners very disempowering. Cross-border brides are in a marginal position in Taiwan as, until they gain citizenship and sufficient cultural competence to act independently, they are reliant for the majority of their day-to-day activities and needs on their husbands.

Suzuki (2005: 137) points out how women in cross-border marriages are often marginalised because their husbands too are marginalised and labelled as 'non-elite, divorced, unattractive, violent males'. Yung-Mei Yang and Hsui-Hung Wang's small sample of Taiwanese men married to migrant wives found that the husbands were older, less educated, less healthy, more likely to have disabilities than the average population and that 'They seemed to belong to a disadvantaged male group in Taiwan in terms of mate selection, whose marriages are mostly arranged by marriage agencies' (2003: 169). This research shows a reality that may underpin the stereotype but also indicates how international marriage agencies may just be a traditional means of arranging marriages that has simply shifted overseas. The negative stereotyping of husbands reflects on the wives who are stereotyped as poor and needy yet simultaneously scheming and calculating. These negative images of cross-border and especially of 'brokered' marriages put pressure on marriages and may contribute to the high incidence of violence reported in cross-border marriages – an issue discussed in Chapter 5.

Studies of the marriage patterns of women migrating from the Philippines are possibly the most numerous of all studies of marriage migrants to East Asia and many of them focus on how marriage migration meshes into the value system of the Philippines. Nobue Suzuki writes that marriage migration is seen as a 'good' way to migrate – 'Marriage is "safe" because spouses' legal status, unlike that of contract workers, is guaranteed for a longer term and can potentially become a permanent form of transnational relocation' (2005: 128). Marriage is seen as not only less risky but also more 'moral' and 'is consistent with gender and family ideologies and role assignments' (ibid.: 128). Nicola Piper confirms the idea of marriage migration being more respectable noting that the 'entertainment visas' many women travel on are linked to prostitution. She writes that 'when men return, they are often celebrated as heroes', whereas women are likely to be looked down upon. 'Marrying out, thus, can be a convenient way to escape such prejudices' (Piper 2003: 462). Converting migration from the dubious category of 'entertainer' into the respectable one of 'wife' allows women to repair a 'spoiled identity' (Goffman 1963) and to make moral sense of their choices.

Research studies emphasise the on-going importance for many cross-border marriage migrants of maintaining ties with the country of origin. These ties are often in the form of remittances and Lieba Faier's study shows how women were appreciative of husbands who allowed them to send money home and who allowed them to see their Filippina friends. She writes:

> When women asserted that they loved their husbands, they gestured to forms of intimacy and subjectivity that enabled the transnationalities of their lives. They suggested that love was not only a product of their migration to Japan but also of their ability to maintain their ties to the Philippines.
>
> (Faier 2007: 157)

Maintaining relationships and meeting financial responsibilities for family (often children) still in the Philippines was reported by Sallie Yea (2008), as one of the biggest problems arising between migrant Philippine women in South Korea and their GI husbands. Yea's research records a reluctance on the part of the American husbands to continue to support their wives' families in the Philippines that was often implicated in marriage breakdown. In the case studies Nobue Suzuki presents, family concerns feature heavily in the motivations of migrant women from the Philippines. An example is the case of the eldest daughter supporting her unappreciative family or the daughter whose status has grown through the remittances she has sent home. Suzuki's study also contrasts the comfortable lifestyle these women enjoy on visits to Philippines with their lives in Japan 'as an isolated urban housewife who is the sole caretaker of the home and a newborn and who receives virtually no help from her husband's female kin or younger family members' (Suzuki 2005: 136). Japanese husbands too may look forward to trips to the Philippines and fantasise about their new family there repaying remittances by looking after them in their old age (ibid.: 136).

Structural mechanisms that facilitate cross-border marriage migration

Commercial networks are very important in the facilitation of cross-border marriage migration in East Asia. These networks may operate with or without governmental sanction and Carol Freeman (2005), in relation to South Korea, has noted how the migration of Chinese women with Korean heritage started as a government strategy but became a commercial moneymaking business. Within China, Cindy Fan and Youqin Huang's work (1998) shows the importance of marriage migration as a family and/or community, economic strategy. In this case no borders are being crossed but the importance of brokers, kin and other social networks in facilitating marriages is made clear. As described by Fan and Huang, the motivation for marriage across distance is to maximise economic benefit in an environment in which movement, even within the nation is restricted for most people. In cases in which marriages are made across borders the same sort of brokering arrangements may come into play as, in the absence of a direct connection, go-betweens are necessary to arrange both the practical and the symbolic aspects of the marriage.

Cross-border marriages in Taiwan usually take two forms, that is marriages between individuals from different ethnicities and/or cultures and marriages brokered through ethnic ties. In a Taiwanese context, the different ethnic groups in the country may look to marry women from their own ethnicity living in other countries – an example of this is the Hakka ethnic minority in Taiwan looking to the Hakka communities in Indonesia for marriage partners. This raises interesting questions about the cultural compatibility of individuals who are generally considered to share an ethnic/cultural identity but who are from different parts of a loose ancestral diaspora which may or may not share common language, values and practices. Ethnicity may have a symbolic value and if migrants cannot successfully match local assumptions made based on their ethnicity, their failure may create further difficulties for them (see Freeman 2005, discussed in Chapter 10). Whether mediated by commercial institutions, personal or community ties, active channels negotiating between female migrant partners and grooms are indispensable (Wang and Chang 2002). Increasingly in Taiwan, third parties, in the form of introduction agents, may broker marriages and make arrangements that take on different cultural guises depending on the countries of origin of the potential marriage partners.

Unlike in other East Asian countries, Melody Lu argues that in Taiwan, despite the large number of migrant domestic and sex workers in the country, they rarely become wives. She writes that 'maids and prostitutes seldom become wives, despite ample opportunities for daily contact. When Taiwanese men look for wives, they have recourse to matchmakers and/or brokers' (Lu 2005: 281). Lu's detailed work on marriage brokerage identifies three types of matchmakers and brokers namely institutional brokering companies, individual entrepreneur brokers and networks of women already married to Taiwan who act as matchmakers (ibid.: 282–93). This last category may show the beginnings of properly transnational communities and sensibilities as individuals are not just arranging marriages but are also building relationships and networks of reciprocity that both support families back in countries of origin *and* support the transnational projects of women already migrated. According to Lu, the motivation for migrant women to engage in matchmaking is not just financial: 'It is a way to be able to renew her ties with her natal kin, both by physically visiting her home and by bringing her relatives to Taiwan' (ibid.: 288). Hongzen Wang (2007) focuses on what he describes as 'commodified marriages' arranged by commercial agencies between Vietnam and Taiwan. He describes how these agencies arrange marriages in ways that reflect traditional matchmaking processes thereby lending the marriages a traditional authenticity that is valued by the Taiwanese families looking for a suitable wife and daughter-in-law. In Wang's view, the traditional nature of these arrangements is superficial, as although they may mimic traditional exchange of money and gifts, they do not make the reciprocal social and family connections that are the hallmark of traditional Chinese arranged marriage.

Wang writes: 'The social logic behind the traditionally arranged marriage and the commodified transnationally arranged marriage is very different. The former aims to create and develop bilateral social relationships between two families while the latter aims to have a quick market exchange' (2007: 716).

Studies show that marriage migrants into East Asian countries often have experience as labour migrants and may have some experience of the countries they marry into. Nicola Piper has argued that for many, marriage presents a way for migrant workers to end the cycle of visa application and the uncertainties of repeat migration (Piper 2003: 459). It is also a mistake to imagine that cross-border marriage migrants are necessarily drawn from the poorest socio-economic strata, this is also true of migrants in general. It has been noted earlier that marriage migrants are often better educated than the men they marry (see Thai 2008; Thai 2005 for Vietnamese examples) and many Filippina brides marrying overseas, for example, come from middle-class families and already enjoy comfortable lifestyles but who aspire to a different sort of life. The migration route of many women from the Philippines into marriages in Japan or South Korea is through the entertainment industry in clubs or in 'hostess' bars. Work in these clubs may or not include providing sexual services but certainly includes providing emotional labour through convincing customers of their affections. The women described by Lieba Faier in Japan (2007) drew on their perceived innate nature as loving and romantic people and emphasised that their marriages had been positive choices between boyfriends in the Philippines and customers at the club. Similarly, Sallie Yea (2004) describes marriage as a clear strategy (or tactic) to continue to live away from home but one that contained real emotion and desire to find a husband who they loved and who really loved them. 'For these Filipinas, migration, then, is an advancement strategy with opportunities to form relationships and possible marry GIs enhanced by their positioning as transnational migrant entertainers' (Yea 2004: 184).

Implications for individual agency in marriage migration outside transnational communities

I argued earlier, in Chapter 5, that stereotypes including those of cross-border marriage migrants can have very negative effects on the well-being of the families caricatured. In countries of East Asia, marriage migrants from poorer countries are often assumed, or accused, of marrying to escape poverty and to gain access to the economic benefits of living in a richer country (i.e. of pursuing strategic marriages). In reference to Japan, Ruri Ito writes that Filipinas are associated with 'prostitution, immoral women, illegal workers with expired visa, barefoot children, unstable political system etc.' (2005: 64). Yung-Mei Yang and Hsui-Hung Wang cite media representations linking the cross-border marriages to fraud, prostitution and to 'runaway brides' who abandon their husbands as soon as they gain entry to the country. 'Thus, Indonesian women in transnational marriages are a stigmatized, special culture group, especially those believing in Islam or having darker skin colour, who are often called "barbarians" to their faces' (Yang and Wang 2003: 171). Yang and Wang's work also argues that the commercial brokering arrangements that often support cross-border marriage migration further stigmatised wives as they may be perceived to have been 'sold' by their families supporting a negative view of their home countries as backward (ibid.: 170). Carol Freeman (2005), in her work on cross-border marriages in South Korea, similarly argues that women marrying into Korea (who in her study were from China but of Korean ethnicity) were represented as either 'powerless victims of a government-sanctioned form of trafficking in women or...as heartless opportunists who actively exploit the South Korean men they marry' (2005: 81). These two stereotypes, as abused or abuser, underestimate and misrecognise (McNay 2000), the agency of women in participating and taking advantage of the opportunities presented by cross-border marriage migration. Hye-Kyung Lee's work, however, describes cases of women forced into prostitution in South Korea having been brought to the country as marriage migrants so perhaps at least one side of this stereotype has some grounding in recent events (Lee 2006a).

Melody Lu (2005), as we have seen, has described various forms of marriage brokerage that facilitate marriages between Taiwanese men and Vietnamese women. Her nuanced description of these agencies and networks emphasises that women who use them, or who are used by them, are able to exhibit different degrees of agency and she states that 'women are not faceless commodities, but active agents in making their life choices' (Lu 2005: 289). Sallie Yea provides further examples of women contracting cross-border marriages in conditions of very limited choice and considerable duress but who still act with agency. Yea's work describes women working in the South Korean entertainment industry who use marriage to American GIs as a means of negotiating exit from their contracts and improving the economic and social situation of themselves and their families in the Philippines. Yea writes of marriage being an 'advancement strategy' (2004: 184) but one that is undermined by the stigma of being a woman from the Philippines in South Korea which severely restricts women's opportunities for acting with agency. Yea quotes Cohen (2003) who has described some marriages as analogous to an on-going form of prostitution with a marriage visa and onward migration as the reward. The weighing up of risks and possibilities described in both Lu's and Yea's papers is similar to the calculations transnational families may make and the space for women to act with agency is circumscribed by an assumption that migration, despite its risks, offers valuable life chances for the families and dependants of migrants as well as for those migrating.

Nicola Constable's work with migrant women from the Philippines in relationships or seeking relationships with men from outside the Philippines is based on long-term ethnographic work and has studied marriage and migration strategies in the light of lived experience and legal and political structures. She writes of the twin goals of many Filipina migration strategies as economic and social advancement but also that 'marriage in itself [is] an important goal and status' (Constable 2003: 167). For some women, marriage overseas was a response to being 'too old' or otherwise undesirable in the local marriage market (see discussion in Chapter 4). In this way seeking a spouse overseas demonstrates the agency of women in acting positively to change their life chances – as Constable puts it: 'Labor and marriage migration allow women an opportunity to create new marital subjectivities and to pursue opportunities that seem unavailable in their homelands' (2003: 176). For the women Constable studied, marriage migration allows women to act with agency even if the outcomes of their decisions post-marriage may be unclear and potentially risky – this is something as true for marriages within cultural and ethnic groups as it is for marriages between cultural and ethnic groups. Yea's study demonstrates a collective sense of agency among Filippina women in South Korean clubs who had established running away from a contract as an entertainer as an almost routinised process thus sharing experience and reducing risk. Yea's informants followed the path taken by others who ran away from their employment to depend on boyfriends or fiancés who might either buy them out of their employment contracts and/or financially support them (Yea 2004: 183). Marriage was the stated goal of many of these women as marriage alone could free them from their contingent immigration status. Marriage equalled personal security, legitimacy and legality through a GI spouse visa affording them legality in Korea and also chance to live in the US (ibid.: 192).

Cross-border marriage migrants, once in their country of settlement are often stigmatised for being at the very least 'alien' within countries that have strong traditions of ethnic endogamy (see Oum 2003: 435, in relation to South Korea) and discriminatory stereotypes of women are common throughout East Asian countries. Lieba Faier's work (2007, 2008) describes some of the strategies the Filippina marriage migrants she studies use in Japan to gain a sense of agency and to re-establish their own sense of worth and self-esteem in the face of negative stereotypes. Faier describes their moral rhetoric of love for their husbands which they used to counter assumptions made about their motivations in marriage (see also Suzuki 2000: 435, on how women present themselves as good wives and mothers to counter the pervasive stereotype of them as bad girls, entertainers and whores). Faier argues that this rhetoric is connected to the strongly held religious beliefs of the Catholic Filipinas and that 'if one believes marriage to be a sacrament and a life commitment based on love, one has little choice but to try to find a way to love one's spouse' (Faier 2007: 156). For these women the sense that they actively chose their husbands out of love and who were good 'catches' (who they love) was an expression of their agency. Through this rhetoric, they were 'claiming a sense of humanity, countering the stigma associated with their work in bars and articulating a sense of themselves as cosmopolitan, modern, and moral women who possessed an emotional interiority' (ibid.: 149).

A second tactic Lieba Faier identifies in her work with wives from the Philippines in Japan was the real or imagined tactic of 'running away' from a bad marriage. Running away from marriages put the women into 'extradomestic spaces' at 'interstices of marriage and immigration laws' (Faier 2008: 644) where the women had to live clandestinely but were free from the restrictions of living with their Japanese families. 'They lived in communities of Filipina women, freely sent money home to their families in the Philippines, and, unlike their married lives, did not have husbands or mothers-in-law telling them what to do' (ibid.: 644). The less positive side to this situation was that they led uncertain, frightening lives outside the law, as living away from their husbands they couldn't renew their visa, were vulnerable to abuse, and may be stigmatised even by their own community who saw them as foolish for making a poor marriage choice. Hongzen Wang (2007) describes the similarly liminal situation of Vietnamese marriage migrants in Taiwan who find a limited form of agency on the occasions they can spend free time away from their husbands and families. Wang argues that it is the very liminality of these women's position in relation to Taiwanese society that allows them a private space and a limited form of citizenship, away from their families and 'unhinged from the scripted roles like mother, father or daughter' (Wang 2007: 713). For the Vietnamese brides in Taiwan, their 'private space' is to be found in the 'public spaces' of parks, squares, Vietnamese restaurants and the government-sponsored integration classes. Here they can find a marginal form of citizenship and agency in spaces that are more Vietnamese than Taiwanese. Further, the brides' cultural and social separation can be turned to an advantage as if the brides felt they had been effectively 'bought' by their husbands, they were freed from their own and local social norms and thus allowed to threaten to leave their husbands and behave in ways which would be sanctioned were they more integrated into the mainstream of the community.

In many ways the objectives of marriage migrants make a close fit with the cultures they marry into. We have already seen how the desire of migrants from the Philippines in Japan to form a 'moral' and enduring marriage should match the desire of their husbands for social acceptable marriages. Yung-Mei Yang and Hsui-Hung Wang's study of the marriages of Indonesian women in Taiwan indicates that both parties emphasised the importance of children and wanted to have a similar number of children (Yang and Wang 2003: 173). In this study the wives' views of gender and family roles conformed to Taiwanese expectations but were also seen as a way of helping their natal family at home.

Marriages between migrant women and citizen men are often stereotyped, as discussed in more detail in Chapter 5 and possibly as a result, there may be a great deal of pressure placed on women, and their relationships, to conform to social norms and ideas of what a *proper* marriage is like. As a result, women may be able to use this social pressure as a bargaining chip as by threatening to leave or divorce a husband, they may be able to change the behaviour of their husbands. Research in Taiwan, South Korea and Japan has all pointed to the power women can gain by threatening to break social conventions. Hongzen Wang has described how the Vietnamese women in his study may feel freed from their own social constraints against divorcing or abandoning their husbands because of the way the marriages were arranged and husbands risk losing not only a wife but a substantial financial investment as well as a great deal of 'face' (Wang 2007: 719–20). Carol Freeman (2005) found the Chinese wives in her study had a similarly strong bargaining position in threatening to divorce their South Korean husbands and likewise, the Philippine wives of Japanese men adopted strategies of leaving their husbands until they had undertaken to change their ways (Faier 2007, 2008). These tactics on the part of women are clearly high-risk but demonstrate ways in which women can and do use what leverage they have to improve their situations.

Research on cross-border marriage migration includes many accounts of the positive nature of relationships between migrant wives and their in-laws. Ruri Ito, for example, notes the importance of making connections with in-laws and that 'family ties with the in-laws constitute one of the scarce resources for migrant women' (Ito 2005: 62). Ito provides example of how Thai women married to Japanese men were able to make use of their husband's family's willingness to provide childcare allowing them to work. Cultural adaptation is also not a one-way thing and Lisa Faier records how the citizen husbands of foreign brides have to adapt to the food their wives cook and to different ways of life (Faier 2007: 155). Migrant women have been successful in developing formal self-help and advocacy groups (described in Japan by Ito 2005: 64; Suzuki 2000: 435–6) as well as the loose, informal groups described by Wang in Taiwan (2007). In Ito's example, self-help groups have worked to counter the stereotyping of foreign wives in Japan, promoting their language and culture and a positive sense of bi-culturality for their children. Women's groups have advocated for women in disputes with Japanese citizens, for example, in paternity cases, and have supported economic cooperation between migrant women (Ito 2005: 63–5). This last function of migrant-run support groups has allowed them to start small businesses in which women can work flexibly and combine their economic activities with their domestic responsibilities. Suzuki describes the charity work carried out by a group of women from the Philippines in Japan which she describes as being a truly transnational event with the women in Japan acting in concert to support and engage with issues back in their country of origin (Suzuki 2000).

Conclusion

In this chapter, I have argued that kinship and family relationships are important drivers and motivators of marriage migration in East Asia but that, unlike the cross-border marriages made within more developed transnational communities described in the previous chapter, families are rarely involved in the actual process of migration. Within transnational communities, family members may be involved throughout the arrangement of both the marriage itself and the migration. There may be a pool of practical knowledge available to migrants both before and after they arrive in their new country of settlement. For many marriage migrants, such practical help and information may be lacking and migrants may have to rely on their personal resources, the resources of their husband and his family and possibly support from other women in a similar situation. Ruri Ito's work argues that in Japan, migrant women's rights are very clearly linked to their position within families and are much reduced if, for whatever reason, they no longer live within that family. I argue that one of the important lessons from this chapter and Chapter 6 is that in transnational networks and communities, cross-border marriage migrants may travel across borders but they may not travel away from their communities. This is in contrast to cross-border marriages that are non-transnational which separate migrant spouses from their home communities. The literature discussed here from Japan and elsewhere shows how migrants so separated may work to renew and rebuild a sense of community and in doing so, assert a transnational sensibility.

8
Marriage within Refugee Communities
Some examples of transnational and non-transnational marriages

This chapter is the third chapter in this book to explore the notion of transnationalism in cross-border marriages. Chapter 6 considered marriages within South Asian transnational communities and Chapter 7 considered cross-border marriages in East Asia that I consider to be non-transnational or possibly pre-transnational. This chapter will explore marriages within refugee communities as, I argue, these marriages demonstrate how the two types of cross-border marriage, transnational and non-transnational, can provide opportunities for migrants to exhibit their personal and collective agency in negotiating the structures of policy and politics. Marriage within refugee communities represents a relatively unexplored field and the evidence presented here is slight, in comparison to the welter of research in relation to the other marriages discussed. Despite this, I argue that research in this field presents an opportunity to study marriages within communities that are just beginning to establish a collective identity and may be informative about how transnational consciousnesses develop and the potential role of cross-border marriage in that development.

Research with refugees provides another example of how cross-border marriage may play a significant role in the establishment of transnational communities and the maintenance of links between countries of settlement and countries of origin. Marriages not only strengthen and maintain communities but may also be important in rebuilding communities and identities shattered by conflict and war. Marriage may be significant for its facility to open up channels of migration which may offer a means of escape or protection for family members. I will argue that cross-border marriages may have an important place in the strategies and tactics employed by refugees and asylum seekers who may use marriage to reunite family members and/or to bring them to safety. Marriage may be important as a means of meeting short-term goals, of establishing rights to enter and to remain, as well as the long-term goals of family formation, cultural continuity and the maintenance of tradition and identity. My own research (Williams 2004, 2006) indicated that marriage, as a rite of passage, is particularly important for refugees who seek a sense of belonging in exile and, for some, marriage is an essential means of establishing oneself as a full member of the community. This research will be referred to in this chapter, along with other research material. It is my contention that refugee communities provide examples of how migrants marry, following both transnational and non-transnational logics. They may marry to strengthen their connection to countries of settlement – and thus have features in common with the marriages described in Chapter 7 – but refugees may also marry to build and maintain cultural identity and as such, their marriages may have more in common with the transnational marriages described in Chapter 6.

In this chapter I will first make some general points about forced migration and suggest some important features of refugee transnationalism. I will go on to discuss the significance of marriage for individual refugees and their communities. As in earlier chapters, I will attempt to demonstrate how structure and agency may impact upon cross-border marriage choices in these communities and will try to differentiate the impact of power structures represented by community and policy from the action of individual, personal agency.

Forced migration and refugee transnationalism

I am aware, first, that using the word 'refugee' to describe transnational communities with a history of forced migration may be problematic for some groups who do not wish to identify themselves as victims of 'force'. The word 'refugee' also has various connotations and is sometimes conflated with stigmatised (and legally and spatially specific) labels such as 'asylum seeker'. Here I use the phrase refugee to refer to groups and individuals who see their migration as having been 'forced' and do not restrict the meaning to the legalistic definitions operated by the UNHCR and state entities – here, if groups consider themselves to have been forced into exile, then they are refugees. I concur with Roger Zetter (1991) that labels, such as refugee, can impose identities on individuals and groups and so shape and limit their agency. Exile and displacement carry a powerful legacy, however (see Suvin 2005), and I argue that the manner of migration and its on-going emotional impact give marriages within refugee communities a special significance and carry obligations to the communities left behind as well as shaping aspirations for a new life in countries of settlement.

To my knowledge, little research has focused explicitly on marriage within refugee communities (an important exception being Grabska forthcoming) but the importance of marriage to these communities is referred to by many writers. I have chosen to devote a chapter to the issue of cross-border marriage in refugee communities as it is my contention that they provide an interesting counterpoint to the more common explorations of marriage between and within communities and provide a picture of cross-border marriage within communities in flux. Roger Ballard (2006: 7) observes that marrying, and marrying appropriately, may be an integral part of belonging in any social group, refugee or otherwise, and mark entrance into a new stage in the life course and usually confer independence and adulthood. The transnational communities of refugees can support refugees throughout their migration – in fleeing their country of origin, in negotiating borders and in establishing themselves in the countries of settlement (Williams 2006). Like other transnational entities, refugee transnational networks can support the development and maintenance of cultural and traditional identities and may be especially important for many refugee groups who have lost their homeland to war and conflict. Transnational communities and networks can provide a sense of belonging and may be the repository of cultural and social heritage. Marriage, with all its assumption of social and cultural reproduction, may play a key role in symbolically and practically demonstrating that the group goes on – despite the efforts of others to destroy it.

Refugee transnational networks and communities (I consider networks to be the more functional precursors to transnational communities which aim to meet a wider range of social and cultural needs), may use cross-border marriage in very different ways. I argue that refugee transnationalism is always shaped by the fact that migration – especially for the first generations – has *force* as an underlying factor. This follows Sherrell and Hyndman's view of refugee transnationalism which argues that it 'differs markedly from that of other immigrant classes because refugees are *forced* to leave their homes, often with little notice' (Sherrell and Hyndman 2006: 9). These migrant communities developed out of necessity rather than choice so have at their heart a loss of homeland and possibly a longing for a righting or wrongs, for recovery and for restitution.

Maintaining the role of cultural and traditional symbols, such as language and ritual, may be even more important for refugee communities than for transnational communities of migrants defined more generally. Some refugees may feel that cultural authenticity is only possible in exile from countries where language and practice may be banned or repressed, so they may be motivated by a desire to re-establish, or indeed re-imagine, what was lost in their home countries. Other refugee communities may not have had a 'homeland' for long periods of time (examples being Palestinians and other groups who have lived for several generations in refugee camps and have been prevented from returning home) so may find their first chance to live culturally authentic lives on establishing home in exile. Louisa Schein's study (1998) of incipient transnational relationships proposes that the developing transnational links between Hmong refugees, originally from Laos now living in the US, is based at least in part on romanticised views of homeland. She argues that a presumed shared historical identity is used by the migrant group as a link back to their past and by the 'homeland' group as an asset to make the best of. For the Chinese Miao (groups sharing an ancestry with the Hmong originally from Laos), marriages may have very different meanings than for the homesick American Hmong and the links these marriages offer have other advantages unconnected to the transnational projects of the Americans.

> If Miao peasants represented an object of nostalgic longing for urban American Hmong, the latter likewise have come to represent a focal point for the desires of Chinese Miao who seek to circumvent the limits imposed upon them by a Chinese national plan that allocates to them only sacrifice and patient labour.
>
> (Schein 1998: 304)

Many refugees have had direct experience of violence and of human rights abuses that may leave them emotionally scarred. Extreme experiences can have very powerful and long-term effects on individuals and these may affect refugees' lives and their relationships. Paul Hoggett refers to how extreme experience may result in shame and/or guilt that can reduce a person's capacity to act reflexively as 'To think about and try to make sense of what has happened to them threatens to destroy their residual experience of self' (2001: 42). The long-term psychological effect of war and exile may undermine an individual's capacity to develop intimate relationships thus necessarily affecting their marriage opportunities. A further, but related, characteristic of refugee communities concerns their ability to act together in cohesive ways. Many refugees flee their countries because conflict and political repression have destroyed or undermined community bonds leaving uncertainty as to who can be trusted. The destruction of social cohesion and solidarity is a common strategy of governments and other groups engaged in campaigns of persecution and the use of extreme forms of violence, such as torture and campaigns of rape, are designed to break down the cohesiveness of communities. Long periods of conflict and war force people to make choices, perhaps to collaborate or to take sides, which may be interpreted as betrayal by others in their group. Communities may also be disrupted by the sense of resentment felt by those who were unable to flee or who chose to stay; this may be mirrored by a sense of regret on the part of those who left. Neither group, those at home (or nearer to home) and those in exile, may ever be able to fully understand the long-term effects such choices have on their community or on their individual or collective sense of self. These processes of community disruption and the consequent breakdown of trust have been attested to by the articles in the edited volume by Daniel and Knudsen (1995) as well as by other authorities (for example, Summerfield 2002). Mistrust within communities cannot be shed overnight so obviously carries over into the countries of exile. The re-establishment of relationships that include marriages is deeply affected by this community rupture and individuals and families may have difficulties establishing their suitability for marriage. Refugees who have many family members also living in exile may be able to use relatives to vouch for their reliability but many refugees who do not migrate with or to family members, may find it hard to establish themselves as trustworthy potential suitors.

As well as being distinguished by possible diasporic consciousnesses, refugee communities may be in the process of development. Some members of communities will be established in countries of exile, perhaps into a second generation, while others are more recent arrivals. Yet others will only be making their way towards new homes or be seeking safety within or near their country of origin. Refugee communities may have well-established networks in some countries that can support the further migration of group members still in the homeland but, as with any other group, it may be difficult to distinguish who belongs within the group and who does not. These differences may be particularly acute with refugee groups where political difference and factionalism may have driven the forced migration. Kunz proposed the concept of 'vintages' of refugees to explain what he called the associative patterns of forced migrants. He writes:

> While the refugee of today leaves, the refugee of tomorrow endeavours to stall off further advance by working in retreat for a compromise. As the political situation ripens for each, they will leave the country as distinct 'vintages' each usually convinced of the moral and political rightness of his actions and implicitly or openly blaming those who departed earlier or stayed on.
>
> (Kunz 1973: 137)

Kunz goes on to describe how 'to the outsider the immigrant's "vintage" may be imperceptible, but for the refugee himself, the date of his departure from his homeland signifies the bona fide of his political credo' (ibid.: 137). An individual's 'vintage' may go some way to explain who a refugee will naturally be drawn to and who they will avoid within their own national or ethnic group and this distinction between individuals, though often ignored by academics and policy-makers, may have a great bearing on who refugees choose to associate with. The importance of these different 'vintages' may be more or less important to refugees depending on many factors, but it does explain why at least some refugees express derogatory sentiments about groups who, to an outsider at least, should be allies.

Forced migration may be a particularly powerful catalyst for social change as not only are families broken up, but war, persecution and exile can destroy the economic and political basis for societies. Seeking refuge outside one's homeland often means that social hierarchies and structures become meaningless, or seriously impaired, virtually overnight. Life in refugee camps, for example, favours certain groups of people, typically young men (Turner 1999), who are able to transgress traditional social norms and take advantage of the lack of established power structures. Over time, forced migration may lead to the development of multiple community sites where transnational communities can develop and participate in the renegotiation of group social norms. Resettled communities may have a powerful effect on determining the social norms and values of the communities remaining at home, or at least nearer to home, and the interplay between communities that are based in geographically different places but which all refer back to a shared homeland, results in change *and* conservatism. The existence of transnational sites may have a radical effect on the expectations and sense of the possible for those remaining in or nearby the homeland and some of these effects have been described by Katarzyna Grabska in her work in the Sudan and in predominantly Sudanese refugee camps in Kenya (forthcoming). Hung Cam Thai's studies of refugee communities, (2005, 2008) observed the dynamics of marriages between the established Vietnamese transnational communities living in the West and their homeland. Louisa Schein has similarly described the effect of US citizens of Hmong descent returning to their ancestral homes 'seeking them [women] out for flirtation, entertainment, accompaniment, sexual trysts, mistresshood and marriage' (2005: 54). Schein describes the effects these visits by Hmong men from transnational communities have on the local population who see them as highly significant in opening up new possibilities for whole families as well as individuals. These studies indicate the enduring importance of marriage from country of origin or heritage both to the migrant parts of transnational communities and to those 'at home'.

Stephen Lubkeman's work with the Machaze of Mozambique has shown how forced migration can push migrants to adopt longer-term life choices in exile than might have been the case had return home been an option. Lubkeman (2000) writes that war meant that Machaze men stayed in South Africa for extended periods and so began to establish a 'total social life' in South Africa. This didn't mean they cut themselves off completely from their homes and family in Mozambique, but meant that they built full lives in exile – which included marriages with local women. These marriages were often polygamous, something not against Machaze tradition, but which had powerful effects on their families left behind because of the way transnationalism changed the shape polygamy took. First wives, rather than gaining the traditional benefit of the labour of these new wives, found their resources, in terms of remittances, reduced and their power in the family undermined.

My own work with refugees has also shown how the existence of transnational communities provides new marital opportunities both inside and outside the country of origin and these options will be considered further in this chapter. These marriages reflect social and cultural gendered assumptions in that different opportunities are open to men and women. In addition, changing notions of what is and is not acceptable within groups affect men and women in different ways at different times. Forced migration challenges gender norms in multiple ways – war and persecution may mean that women take on more active and public roles in the absence of men while at the same time the political and economic disruption inherent in conflict situations necessitates change as the 'old ways' lose their cultural logic and power. Women may become overt targets of violence especially as inter-ethnic war and conflict are often directed at undermining the honour of communities and therefore the honour of women. Conflict and flight undermine or destroy structures that protect vulnerable people and the lawlessness of countries at war and often of refugee camps, can be particularly dangerous for women (as well as for the young and the elderly). Displacement considered as temporary by individuals and communities may be enough to result in social upheaval lasting years and may bring about social change that is never reversed. More permanent forms of displacement – which include resettlement in countries of refuge – lead to major reconfigurations of social norms and traditions. This is not to say that displacement leads to a rejection of the past, quite often the reverse, but to argue that different logics come into play. Madawi Al-Rasheed, in her study of the experience of Iraqi women in exile, considers gender to be central to understanding their everyday lives stating that 'As women, their experience of exile is shaped by their gender, a factor which, in general, determines their position not only in their country of origin but also in the host society' (1993: 89). In Al Rasheed's study, exile is seen to have a significant impact on marriages which are traditionally understood to confer security and status. Al-Rasheed's research argues that the women in her study found marriage could no longer confer either security or status in exile, something that led them to question their understanding of marriage. My research, however, indicated that married women, especially those with their husbands or male relatives were more able to act with personal agency. Compared to single women from the same ethnic groups, married women had more latitude to move about and to make friends and networks. Some of the young Kurdish men from Iraq in the study, who became very well connected and who had a great deal of useful advice and information to share, spoke of their problems in helping single women, as being seen to show too much interest in them would undermine their own and the women's reputation in the group. Being married, therefore, opened up resources not available to single women.

Marriage for many, if not most, social groups is a marker of passage from youth to adulthood and on to full, group membership. Oivind Fuglerud (1999: 95–116) devotes a chapter of his book to a discussion of how marriage and marital status affect the lives of Tamil refugees in Norway. He describes how the expectation of providing dowries and of making good matches has a powerful effect on the day-to-day lives of refugees. He describes unmarried men as being bound by social marginality and that within the Tamil group 'the main internal, interactional boundary ... is not one of political affiliation or regional origin but the one between married and unmarried men' (Fuglerud 1999: 105). Marriage makes men full members of Tamil society and it is through 'a properly arranged marriage that...his "value" is set' (1999: 107). Unmarried people are, in this sense a liminal group, their social standing is unclear in the eyes of their community and their future uncertain. The majority of the participants in my ethnographic research were young, single, male refugees from cultures where marriage is the norm and where the choice of marriage partner is as much a community choice as a personal one. Becoming realistic, and/or fatalistic, about their future marriage prospects came to these young men along with the realisation that past assumptions were no longer valid in their new home and that most dearly held expectations were unlikely to become realities. Marriage was described by some of the participants in my study, as a community event and as confirming their position in the world of transnational networks and of 'home'. Others were reluctant to involve their community and described marriage as a more personal decision. During my fieldwork, two of the participants got married, one with the involvement of the transnational network and one without. Most of the other participants had discussed their potential marriages and some saw marriage as a way of furthering community goals and were prepared to leave their families to choose their spouse. Others were more concerned to find a partner themselves – whom they would choose and who would, in some sense, make their lives respectable and complete (Williams 2004).

The symbolic value of marriage within refugee communities should not be under-estimated. Marriage which conforms to traditional patterns and customs signifies the wholeness and correctness of society. Research also indicates that the attitudes of refugee communities to the choice of marriage partners may change over time with recent refugees marrying to protect vulnerable family members or to establish themselves in their country of settlement while more established refugees may choose spouses with a view to developing transnational and diasporic identities. In both these cases, marriage may be between group members living in the country of origin or living in countries of settlement. Marriage is also a marker of establishment in a given society and may signify an *arrival* not just into the adult world, but also into society. Participants in my research often spoke of their hopes for marriage in terms of it being the real beginning of their lives in the West after the frustrations of waiting for asylum decisions were over. Marriage represented a normalisation that contrasted with the chaotic nature of life as an asylum seeker and the power of marriage to mend and heal was demonstrated by the community insistence that one participant who had experienced serious mental health problems should marry so that he might be cured. Throughout fieldwork the subject of marriage was high on some personal agenda and unlike many Western young people of similar age, it was generally seen as an absolute necessity and an essential part of everyone's life. One participant, for example, told me that 'Everything will be alright for me when I am married.' Finding a wife, however, was no easy matter and was a vexed subject with different people expressing, clear, though divergent, views about who would make a good wife. The degree of freedom these young refugee men would allow and expect of a wife varied, as it does in any group and for some it was essential that their wife shared their Muslim faith, by conversion or birth. Some participants had known before they left home who they were to marry and the preparation for bringing the bride to live with them had informed their choices since they had been in the UK. Others had given up the woman whom they had expected to marry and my field notes record how some participants made the decision to tell women who they were virtually betrothed to that they should not wait for their return and that they should consider themselves free to find new partners. One participant, D, described his girlfriend in very affectionate terms and clearly had not fallen out of love with her but told her before he left Baghdad to find someone else before it was 'too late for her'. Other participants had been married before they left home and some divorced their wives before they left; others still expected to be reunited with them. The majority, however, had either been actively looking for partners for themselves or had been speculating on the possibility in the future.

So far this chapter has made some general points about the effect of forced migration on marriage hopes and aspirations. In the following sections I will develop these themes to look more deeply at the subject by first addressing the nature of refugee marriages and arguing that marriages in refugee communities have elements in common with both the transnational and non-transnational marriages described in Chapters 6 and 7.

What do refugee marriages look like?

I have argued that cross-border marriages within refugee community groups may be both transnational and non-transnational. Those that are transnational are marriages that are made within an established community and which follow traditional logics, to some extent. As in previous chapters, I argue that 'traditional' does not mean unchanging, but it implies that transnational marriages are those that are recognised and accepted by the community as being appropriate and valid. Being transnational, these marriages also involve the crossing of borders and join individuals who have, at least at some stage of their lives, have been citizens of different countries. Marriages in refugee communities for the purpose of this book include marriages that have much in common with the transnational marriages discussed in Chapter 6 and may be arranged along traditional and socially meaningful lives by families and communities. Some of these marriages may be made for the express purpose of bringing relatives still living, and possibly in danger, in the homeland to the safety of countries of migration or may be made between different countries where transnational networks and communities exist.

Al-Sharmani (2006) reminds us that, just as the majority of refugees live outside the developed world, so marriage migration is not just from the less developed world to developed economies but occurs within the Global South as well. I also argue further that 'refugee marriages' should include marriages that have more in common with the non-transnational marriages described in Chapter 7 and which result from relationships made post-migration which may be inter-cultural and/or inter-ethnic. These last marriages may or may not be considered acceptable and appropriate within transnational communities and are also heavily scrutinised by policy-makers and immigration officials in the countries of settlement. Where marriages are made between citizens and asylum seekers, who have yet to regularise their status, many countries, for example, the UK and Denmark, have imposed strict regulations as they are often viewed, and stereotyped, as being purely strategic arrangements made to circumvent immigration control. A further possible category of refugee marriage may be the category sometimes referred to as 'war' or 'military brides' in which soldiers posted overseas marry local women. It can be supposed that some of the Vietnamese women who married American GIs during the Vietnam War were also refugees and that the chaos in their homeland may have had a bearing on their decision to marry.

Katarzyna Grabska's work on marriages in Sudanese refugee communities has a double focus – on the refugee camps where marriages happen, but also on the transnational communities that are driving the marriages in the camps. Grabska views marriage as a part of the renegotiation of culture post exile – that marriage represents 'a way of managing social marginalisation and loss of masculinity in one place (resettlement society) through re-establishing oneself "back home" through local marriage' (Grabska forthcoming). Grabska describes how the Sudanese young men now returning to Sudan, or at least to the refugee camps in Kenya, have been living in exile in the US, Canada and the Australia in marginal positions that afford them little opportunity for social or economic advancement. Their perception is that they need to get married to be able to enter full, adult society and become respectable men in their community. In refugee communities, ethnic identity may be very important and Grabska's informants tell 'stories of the family pressure to marry Sudanese girls from Africa in order to keep the connection to "home"' (forthcoming). The importance of making these matches is such, that as the bride price of young girls in the camps has become higher, men from the West, who may have already been sending home more than they can really afford, take out loans and borrow money from friends in order to maintain their image as success stories. Grabska's work places the importance of marrying at home alongside the other livelihood strategies of the refugees she studies and places marriage strategies alongside remittance as ways in which kinship relationships are maintained across distance. Marrying back home was also a way to find a wife in communities where 'appropriate' women were few and where those women available were typified as being 'either too old or "too free and too open"' (Grabska forthcoming).

The gender mix of refugee communities is likely to be heavily influenced by locality. While global refugee movements are evenly divided between the sexes, male refugees are often over-represented as migrants to countries with developed economies. In countries operating quota systems for refugee applications, for example, the US and Australia, women may be represented more equally but where refugees arrive spontaneously (for example, throughout Europe), forced migration is skewed in gender terms towards male refugees who for social and practical reasons, may seek refuge ahead of women in their communities. Refugee settlement in developed countries does not accurately reflect true refugee movements as the bulk of any mass refugee flow will stop at the first place of safety, for example, across borders and in designated refugee camps. In such camps, normal age and sex distributions may be expected but younger men may be under-represented where there is on-going conflict. Families, and especially the better-connected ones, may be able to seek refuge together and different refugee producing situations present different opportunities and constraints on movement. Emergencies, such as the wars in Chile and the former Yugoslavia; the humanitarian disaster of the Vietnamese 'boat people' and the eviction of South Asians from Uganda, allowed some families to migrate as groups while many other refugees from conflict zones in Africa and Asia have come singly and have been mostly male. Refugee transnational communities may develop from these often male-dominated beginnings possibly encouraged by official programmes including those supporting family reunification. Such programmes belong within Eleonore Kofman's categories of family migration (2004: 246–8), as the migration of the immediate family of refugees is seen as the 'primary migrant' reuniting with their dependent family members.

Some of these family reunification programmes are based on marriage with the first pioneer generation of refugees bringing their wives, and occasionally husbands, into the country of settlement. Family reunification programmes only come into play after immigration status such as refugee, settled or citizen status has been achieved and in many, if not most countries this can take a long time. The asylum determination process is a long one across the world and unless refugees are held in immigration detention, an increasingly common condition, young men are likely to form relationships with women from the local population. Here I am reminded of Katherine Charsley comment in relation to the marriage and migration patterns of the Pakistani community where 'In the early years of "pioneer" male migration to Britain, many cultural norms were relaxed. These were often restored once large numbers of women and children started coming to join their husbands' (Charsley 2005: 93). The pioneer generation's relationships, whether in refugee or voluntary migrant populations, are clearly formed for predictable, human and emotional reasons but are often suspected or even assumed to be merely strategic relationships to advance the migration goals of the migrants involved. There may be an element of the strategic about relationships and marriages between asylum seekers or migrants with irregular status and I have myself been told by refugees that if their asylum claim is refused, they will 'marry an English girl'. In reality, such marriages are not easy to arrange and may not result in the granting of settlement status anyway. Throughout this book I argue that marriage is always motivated by a combination of emotional and practical factors and that marriages which offer personal or economic advancement are no less genuine than those based on Giddens' 'pure relationship' (1992). It can be argued that policies that restrict migration and settlement to a few narrow channels have themselves undermined the free choice of partners by appearing to favour certain types of domestic arrangements and have made the commodification and strategic logic to marriage more attractive.

As transnational communities mature, the possibility of arranging marriages within a group becomes greater and marriages may be arranged with the assistance of family members in many of the ways described in Chapter 6. For refugee communities, however, the nature of the original migration may place extra pressure on some settled refugees to marry and support the migration of individuals in difficult and/or dangerous positions in the home country. The social disruption of forced migration may also make some members of refugee communities particularly interested in the public demonstration of their commitment to traditional forms of hierarchy and social structure. Getting married in a socially approved and validated way may be a particularly powerful way to demonstrate one's position in the community and thus confirm that a proper order has been restored after the chaos and ignominy of forced migration.

Marriage within community, then, may have an important role in restoring order to refugee communities and may have a role in balancing the sex ratio as well. Transnationalism, as we have seen, is about social groupings and communities living across borders but is also about having roots in different countries that allow the community to take advantage of what nation-states have to offer. There is evidence of transnational refugee communities based in different countries of the European Union taking advantage of the differences in regulations in different countries through secondary migration designed to further community goals. Cross-border marriage may have a role to play in such movements as has been shown by the example of would-be marriage migrants moving from Denmark to Sweden (across the so-called 'love bridge') to avoid the tight (some would say draconian) restrictions placed on marriage migration (*The Times* 2004). The effect on migration of these different regulations and restrictions confirms Annie Phizacklea's point that 'that migratory "choices" are circumscribed by factors not subject to manipulation by individuals such as immigration policy and the administration of immigration rules' (1998: 25). The UK has also placed tighter conditions on marriage migration raising the age of marriage visa applications from overseas to 21 years old (UK Borders Agency 2008). As well as restricting and placing extra conditions on marriage within transnational communities refugee or otherwise, restrictions have also been placed on the opportunities for migrants who have not yet become permanent residents to marry. At present, in the UK, temporary migrants have to apply for permission (through a 'Certificate of Approval') before they can marry (UK Borders Agency 2009). This requirement has created many problems for couples wishing to marry but who are prevented from marriage by immigration rules. The motivation for these restrictions and controls is explicitly to prevent circumvention of immigration controls on certain groups of migrants – chiefly those who are waiting for decisions on their cases or who are fighting efforts to be removed. Preventing them from marrying assumes that their relationships are fraudulent and based only on a desire to evade return to their country of origin. Marriage, it is assumed, will allow them to appeal to stay on the human rights grounds of having established a 'private life' and families in the UK. At this point, the categories of refugee and migrant blur and according to the asylum determination process, if migrants' refugee claims have failed they should be safe to return to their country of origin where they can apply to return to the UK on a marriage visa. The asylum determination process is far from infallible, however, and many asylum claimants whose cases have been rejected, have good reason to fear return to their country. In addition, family reunification visas are not guaranteed if they do return and apply from their countries of origin so it is understandable that migrants may prefer to stay in their country of asylum rather than risk returning home to take a chance on a successful visa application.

To summarise, I argue that the cross-border marriages of refugees may exhibit similar features to those in transnational *and* in non-transnational communities. At early stages in the development of transnational communities, marriage migration typically involves the migration of women from the 'home' community to marry men living abroad while other marriages in refugee communities may place men as the marriage migrants if they marry citizen women in their country of asylum. This potentially makes an interesting contrast to the generally female movement of non-citizen partners crossing borders to marry citizens as described in Chapter 7. Having provided a background to cross-border marriage in refugee communities and having argued for why these marriages may fall into both categories of transnational and non-transnational marriage I will continue this discussion using the same section topics as employed in both Chapters 6 and 7.

The effect of community, kin and family attitudes and marriage migration within refugee communities

Many refugees come from societies in which marriages are normally arranged, or at least facilitated by members of extended families. Potential spouses identified would be recommended and their suitability checked to some degree. In exile and with families and social structures ruptured, a person's history may not be known and an individual may have no one to help find a match and support their case for being a suitable match themselves. Where families are able to help make a match, the social dislocation inherent in seeking refuge may mean that the generations may have very different priorities in marriage choice. As Grabska's research shows (forthcoming), the high demand for marriageable women in communities where men outnumber women (as is the case in some exile communities), the choice of marriage partner is all the more fraught and parents and families may be reluctant to allow their daughters to marry until they are confident of having found the best possible match. Young people with established status in Western countries, however, may find themselves in the enviable position of having a choice of many prospective spouses from the country of origin anxious to marry into a country of safety. There is currently little research available on such marriages but research by Thai (2008), Grabska (forthcoming) and Schein (2005) all suggest that in marriages between refugees in developed countries and their country of origin, marriages are likely to be between younger women and older men. Such men are established in exile and are more able to prove their fitness to marry in cultural terms *and* be able to meet the family migration requirements of the immigration regimes in their countries of settlement.

Social conventions in exile inevitably diverge from the norms respected in countries of origin and the norms of gender roles are necessarily affected by the changes. Refugee women may complain that they do not get the respect they would have done had they been at home and Madawi Al-Rasheed's study of Iraqi women records their complaints that being married no longer confers respect. She quotes a woman living in London who states that 'The fact that my husband is not with me makes people feel they can interfere in my life and tell me what to do. Although I am married, I don't seem to enjoy the respectable status of a married woman' (Al-Rasheed 1993: 100). We may speculate that the lack of respect she enjoys is due to her position as a married woman without a husband present to guarantee her status but also that the agency and power marriage would confer back in Iraq are just not recognised in exile. In the male-dominated world of exile, the sources of agency women might have had at home may be eroded because they lack male 'champions' (for example, husbands, brothers or sons) and also because they may not be as visible as their male economically and socially active counterparts. Even though women migrants often find work more easily than men (though probably work of lower status than they had previously) and may become the breadwinners and heads of single-parent households in exile, they may find they lack a socially recognised voice once they become separated from their extended, multi-generational families who would traditionally argue their case. Being without a husband, then, may leave women isolated but finding a husband for daughters may be equally problematic especially if women seeking husbands and men seeking wives have no suitably respected male family members to 'sponsor' a culturally appropriate match.

As discussed in relation to the transnational communities from South Asia (see Chapter 6), communities living away from countries of origin may experience an insecurity that leads them to seek and to prove their 'cultural authenticity'. As cultural authenticity is so often judged by the behaviour and virtue of women, the burden of demonstrating respectability often falls disproportionately on them. Pessar and Mahler have made this point, stating that minority groups may 'invest the weight of the ethnic community's morality and social status in their daughters' sexuality' (2001: 18) and that a similar logic may lead men to look to their 'home' country for chaste brides. Grabska's work shows young men from the US holding strong opinions about who would make a good wife with the preference being for village girls over girls from camps in Kenya and Uganda. She quotes a prospective groom: 'These girls have their minds and they will not be good wives. They will want to control the men. Whereas the girls in the village they know their place, they will follow what the husband tells them' (Grabska forthcoming). Women's value thus becomes connected not only to their ethnicity but also to their place of upbringing. This discourse leads to women from ethnic communities being held as morally superior to women from the country of migration. Dima Abdulrahim (1993) shows how expectations of migrant (in this case, Palestinian) women were defined in opposition to perceptions of German women. The Arab women were perceived as modest in contrast to German women who were seen as promiscuous. The problem for the women involved is that with 'virtue' held in such high regard and carrying such weight for the community, transgression from the ideal of the moral and virtuous woman has a far reaching impact with any individual's indiscretion threatening the community's collective identity. The result is that marriages may become more 'traditional' in exile with women marrying younger and having less choice of partners so 'Marriage was turned into a measure to prevent the corruption of women' (Abdulrahim 1993: 73).

While refugee transnational communities do undoubtedly assist in the arrangement of marriages between settled community members and both aspirant migrants and new arrivals, Richard Staring's (1998) study of attempts to arrange marriage in the Turkish community in the Netherlands (made up of a mixture of refugees and labour migrants) shows how arranging marriage is by no means a simple process. Staring finds settled migrants to be extremely choosy about who they would consider as matches and that they were unwilling to allow their daughters to marry undocumented 'tourists' – it seems these migrants share many of the assumptions majority communities make about the unreliability of migrant husbands who may be seeking a passport or visa more than a wife. Staring focuses on the case of Erol, who was a divorcee with a child and who did not have strong contacts with migrants from his home area:

> Erol was keenly aware of the distrust that exists among legal Turkish migrants which makes them reluctant to allow their daughters to marry their undocumented compatriots. These parents fear – not always unjustly – that the suitor is motivated only by the prospect of a residence permit.
>
> (Staring 1998: 229–30)

The transnational community was not prepared to help Erol make a match so he tried to find a Dutch citizen outside the Turkish community – unsuccessfully as it turned out. Richard Staring's work shows how difficult it may be to obtain help and support from the transnational community as the general suspicion within it means that undocumented migrants seeking support but who are not well connected, may have to pay a very high cost literally and metaphorically to gain support.

Individual agency of refugees and cross-border marriage migration

It was noted earlier how war may have a disproportionate effect on women if they become the embodiment of nation, clan, or group. Their behaviour may become increasingly scrutinised, ironically matching the efforts of the group's adversaries who may be focusing attacks on women to demoralise their enemy. Pressure from within and without the group may combine to result in the reduction of freedom and agency of women. Cawo Mohammed Abdi has argued that in Somalia, and in the transnational Somali communities, civil war and the breakdown of the state has resulted in a 'reconfiguration or re-Islamization, which entails the invention of a new Islamic tradition in the Somali context' (Abdi 2007: 186) that 'further consolidates patriarchy and exacerbates women's subordination' (ibid.: 183). Abdi identifies the particular circumstances of refugee camps as catalysts for what she refers to the 're-imagination' of Somali women and draws on Eric Hobsbawm's notion of the invention of tradition (Hobsbawm and Ranger 1983) to explain the process. Liisa Malkki (1995) has described how new understandings of identity become forged in exile and which, in her example, has altered the identity of the thousands of Hutu refugees from Burundi in Tanzania. William Maley (1998: 20) similarly argues that the national identity the Taliban sought to enforce upon Afghanistan had its roots in an ideal interpretation of village life fostered in refugee camps by individuals with no experience of life outside those camps. Exile and displacement lead to a loss of certainty in modes of behaviour and in social expectations. It disrupts the 'habitus' (Bourdieu 1977) of an individual and of their immediate social group. The traumatic birth of refugee transnational communities carries these processes on into countries of resettlement in ways that may not happen in transnational communities based on voluntary, or at least more planned, migration. When these 'inventions of tradition' happen, it is often women and their opportunities for agency that suffer. This view should not be assumed to apply everywhere and individual women and men may develop their own particular understandings of nationalistic and/or ethnic identity that open up opportunities to demonstrate their individual agency. Al-Sharmani's work provides an example of the refugee experience leading to an increase in the agency of women through the case of Zahra whose personal history and background informed her view of women's roles as central to both the transnational projects of the Somali ethnic group in Somalia and in the West through their role as educators of the next generation (Al-Sharmani 2006: 70–1).

In Katarzyna Grabska's study of marriages made in refugee camps, the high monetary value placed on eligible girls has led to significant numbers of girls and young women being threatened with forced marriage in the camps. The institutional structure of the camp, however, offered a way out for these women who could appeal to the camp authorities to avoid forced marriage thus gaining them a source of support not traditionally open to young Sudanese and, in this case, Nuer women (Grabska forthcoming). At the same time, Grabska argues that it is the low status of women, their exaggeratedly high financial value combined with the a-social nature of camp that allows or even promotes the incidence of forced marriage. Money and hard-nosed financial calculation have become important in the calculation of bride price in the refugee camps Grabska has studied and are a product of the changes to traditional practice that result from forced migration. The devaluing of traditional forms of exchange has occurred partly because of the demands of camp life but also because the transnational nature of these marriages makes traditional payment for wives in cattle no long feasible. Cash, being easily consumable, is lost to a woman who is not satisfied with her marriage while cattle, the traditional form of exchange, was a good that remained with the wife and could be returned if she wanted to leave her husband. At the same time, Katarzyna Grabska finds women expecting marriage to a Western-based husband to not only offer them the independence of a married woman but also respect for having married a Western-based man. Grabska quotes a prospective wife thus: 'I will have a title and will be respected in society, especially because my husband is in the US' (Grabska forthcoming). In a resettlement context, marrying a husband from the homeland is considered to have advantages for the women in Timmerman's study who reportedly view the fact that their husband's family will remain in Turkey as an advantage. In this way young Western-raised women may be able to start their married life free from control and interference from the Turkish in-laws. This observation has implications for refugee transnational marriages where migration may involve the partner only and not his or her family members. This may leave the migrating spouse lonely and isolated but may promote social change as the influence of the homeland culture is diluted.

Mulki Al-Sharmani (2006) describes how a Somali woman traditionally becomes part of her husband's clan through exogamous marriage, yet retained a connection to her father's clan. Somali traditions have always been strongly patriarchal but 'women historically enjoyed diffused power through their roles within their families as favourite wives, bearers of sons, mothers-in-law, and peace brokers among warring clans that exchange wives to put an end to conflict' (2006: 58). She goes on to argue that as clan systems changed under colonialism, women's power eroded too as men were better able to access urban economy. In a refugee context, Somali women seem to be able to regain and increase their agency as their position as mothers gives them certain advantages. Mulki Al-Sharmani found that women in Somali transnational communities played four central roles in supporting and interacting with transnational communities. First, their relocation with their children achieved legal security which could be built on and which provided livelihoods and secure economic and social resources for the family. In addition, their role as agents of socialisation and education and as 'caretakers of this social capital' (2006: 68) guaranteed the continuation and reproduction of the community. Al-Sharmani's research with Somali women in Cairo presents a picture of highly motivated and strategic agents working to make the best of their chances for themselves and their children. The women in Al-Sharmani's study also used relocation to Cairo as a means of 'managing' their marriages by either dissolving them or forcing their husbands to take more responsibility for the family. The final way in which Somali women used their position in Cairo was to enhance their standing in the transnational community as a whole by increasing their relative standard of living by becoming 'middle class' in Cairo (2006: 57–8). These relocations do not appear to be arranged collectively and seem to be carried out on the women's own volition. These women are taking advantage of their own personal resources, no doubt augmented by informal contacts between friends and family and, according to Al-Sharmani, their transnational relocations are not supported or dictated by the transnational community more generally.

Conclusion

This chapter has attempted to highlight research carried out on marriage in refugee communities and has tried to place it within wider discussions of refugee transnationalism and diaspora. I have argued that marriage not only has a central place in the development of refugee transnational communities but also that it is important in the more personal, as opposed to collective, strategies of refugees. In this way the study of refugee cross-border marriage shows similarities with both the properly transnational marriages discussed in Chapter 6 and with the non-transnational and incipiently transnational marriages discussed in Chapter 7. In my view, marriage in refugee communities has been inadequately studied and research in this field has much to add to the understanding of communities in flux and in the process of re-establishing a sense of identity after experiencing the dislocation and social upheaval of war, persecution and exile.

9
Migration Regimes and Policy Implications

This chapter will attempt to analyse the effect of policy on how and why marriage migration takes place. Many policies relating to cross-border marriage migration have the objectives of controlling flows of migrants and channelling and shaping migration according to the norms of the country of settlement. I will begin my discussion, however, by considering the impact of policy in the countries of origin and on how they promote or constrain marriage migration. Following that, will look more closely at policy in the countries of settlement – which has been far more heavily researched. My focus will be on identifying the underpinnings of policy and I will look in detail at how conceptions of citizenship impact on the lived experience of marriage migrants. A common theme in work on marriage migration is how policies act to restrict the agency of migrants even while policy-makers may have the publicly stated aim of protecting migrants from those wishing to take advantage of them – be they smugglers and traffickers or unscrupulous family members. This chapter attempts to provide an overview of how policy impacts upon marriage migrants both positively and negatively.

The lives and opportunities of migrants both once in countries of settlement and as they plan their migration are affected in complex and intimate ways by legislation and policy. These mechanisms are themselves the product of national ideologies and reflect how a country sees itself and its population, its relationship to other countries and to citizens of those other countries. Immigration policy affects how, and if, people can migrate and as it opens doors for some, it closes down opportunity for others. Migration policy often has unintended consequences (Castles 2007a) as migrants, as innovative agents, interpret and take advantage of policies enacted with agendas other than their own in mind. This is as true of the policies of the migrants' countries of

162

origin as it is in destination countries. Policy in the natal country may affect how migrants cross borders in instrumental ways, through reciprocal labour agreements, for example, but also because they shape and reflect a national imagination of migration. Additionally, political and economic power structures and imbalances in countries of origin may promote or indeed compel the migration of certain groups of citizens. Likewise, traditions of migration may provide incentive, motivation and practical support for men and women considering migration as a life option. Once in the country of migration, the opportunities and entitlements of migrants are shaped by how they are classified in relation to the citizen population and by the degree of autonomy and security they may enjoy within the state. The lived experience of migrants living with their citizen partners as spouses will be discussed in more detail in Chapter 10 but the way in which legislation and policies shape social processes and agency will be introduced here.

Migration regimes globally are influenced by, and often based upon, ideologies of control. Global immigration policies control, or seek to control who enters the country; the conditions they enter under; who has access to the resources of the state and how migrants should interact and participate in the state. The state may expect migrants to 'earn' their residency status through adherence to local norms and, as Aihwa Ong has argued (2003), citizenship and belonging are conferred by practices beyond the state, as well by its overt policies. Migrants may be expected to formally commit themselves to the state by, for example, swearing allegiance but such overt declarations neither guarantee social participation and acceptance nor deny it. The expectations that any given state has of migrants settled within its borders or arriving at its gates are enacted and made concrete by its immigration and social policies. Policy may set the tone and represent the official line on how migrants interact with wider society, but policy is always shaped by public attitudes and by how policies are operationalised within society. Policy is reinforced, undermined and negotiated by the public, by service providers and officials and in this respect, the experience of marriage migrants is the same as that of any other migrant. Marriage migrants, in many cases, have families or communities who can interpret and possibly ameliorate the effects of policy. They may be able to cushion the effects of restrictive policy but, as we shall see, not all families have the best interests of their migrant members at heart and may use policy for their own purposes. Clearly, the personal resources of migrants – measured by their language and other cultural skills as well as by the number and type of connections migrants have within the country of migration, will affect how proactive they are able to be. Here the presence or absence of established transnational connections may be crucial as new migrants learn how to live in their new homes.

This chapter will attempt to place the cross-border marriage migrant within a context of the multiple migration regimes that shape not only the migrant's movement but also the migrant's relationship to the state of birth as well as the state of settlement. I will explore how policy and national ideologies are interconnected and argue that social and employment policy, as it affects migrants, continues to be gendered in ways that disadvantage women migrants. My main aim in this chapter is to describe how the extrinsic, structural features of migration and policy regimes interact with the intrinsic characteristics of migrants who bring with them personal and social resources that determine their agency in the face of structural control. I will begin by discussing how policy in the home countries of migrants may affect their means of migration and their motivation for migration. I will then develop the theme of how national ideology and policy can form a 'feedback loop' by which national imaginations, stereotypes and public representations reinforce and are reinforced by the design and implementation of policy. I will draw on academic literature that shows how migration regimes have influenced changes in how marriages are contracted and arranged and how marriage practices have evolved and altered in response to changes in law and regulation. Further, I will discuss how national policy may impact on the married life of migrants post-migration and demonstrate how the contingent and temporary nature of the residency status granted through marriage affects migrants and their families.

Policy at home and abroad – its effects on marriage migration

The Philippines provides a well-documented example of a country with an economy that is highly dependent on its migratory workforce. Patricia Pessar and Sarah Mahler (2001: 8) have described migration from the Philippines as being 'gender-induced and sculpted' with the state encouraging and supporting men and women to migrate through highly gender-differentiated streams as part of a clear national economic strategy. As Pauline Gardiner Barber describes (2000), male workers from the Philippines have been leaving home to work as labourers and seafarers for many years. Since the mid-1990s, however, women have travelled in greater numbers than men with the majority of them (according to Gardiner Barber 2000: 400), migrating as domestic workers. Migration has long been a strategy promoted and encouraged by the Philippine state and this fact influences citizens of the Philippines to see migration as a solution to their financial problems. Regardless of their often advanced skills and education, however, they may be obliged to adapt their aspirations to the narrow openings available to them thus contributing to the stereotypes common in the countries they migrate to. Gardiner Barber's study focuses on Philippine women working in Canada as domestic workers while other studies show Philippine women working as entertainers or domestic workers in Australia, Spain, Italy, Japan and South Korea (Constable 2003; MacKay 2003; Pe-Pua 2003; Roces 2003; Yea 2004, 2008; Suzuki 2005; Faier 2007, 2008; Lauser 2008). It is unlikely that either of these positions matches the aspirations of the women who fill them but they represent ways that many Philippine women can realise their migration dreams. Gardiner Barber argues that just as Philippine women in Japan are commonly assumed to be 'entertainers' so ' "Filipina" is becoming negatively coloured by the demeaned class and status connotations accorded paid domestic labour' (2000: 400). Across the world the 'market value' and thus the migratory capacity, of women from some countries rests upon stereotypes of their assumed domesticity which has become a tradable commodity. Ester Gallo's work (2006) with Malayali migrants from Kerala living in Italy similarly shows how some migrant women are perceived as good domestic workers while their husbands, who migrate to join them, have to reconstruct their masculinity into a 'feminized' domestic form to become acceptable. These examples show the lived experience of policies allowing migration through the narrow category of domestic work being shaped by the public. These beneficiaries of the migrants' labour, influence and mould the public identities of migrants in ways that suit their, rather than the migrants', needs.

Saskia Sassen's work (2000) describes how women become involved in migration circuits voluntarily or involuntarily but that women may also be key actors in promoting and facilitating their own migration and the migration of others. Policies on migration, be they encouraging inward or outward population movement, are defined primarily by the national economic priorities of the state and are based on the assumption that immigrants will generate wealth through their labour. Emigrants are assumed to remit and to return home with money or with useful skills. Women's role in these national strategies are largely overlooked but, Sassen argues it is the 'invisible work of women producing food and other necessities' working as a 'feminized offshore proletariat' that has subsidised low wages and financed the 'modernized sector' (2000: 508). Sassen uses the example of tourism and the sex trade which often goes along with it, to show how the economic development strategies of some countries, lead to female migration (ibid.: 519) and, in turn, to marriage migration. Tomoko Nakamatsu's work (2003) provides a further example of how marriage migration is linked to broader globalised business connections. Nakamatsu describes the interlinking of marriage broking businesses with the more general business trends that took Japanese business people abroad. She argues that the origin of such businesses was in part demand-driven but was also a product of the agency of women prepared to marry across borders.

Migration is thus driven by economic logics but, as has been argued throughout, it is important not to underestimate the role of personal and emotional aspirations in motivating and shaping migration patterns. Both Nicole Constable (2003) and Andrea Lauser (2008) stress the role of gendered inequalities in the Philippines in motivating women to seek cross-border relationships. Both cite the effects of the ban on divorce in the Philippines which encourages women to migrate not only to avoid the consequences of bad marriages but also to legally divorce their Philippine husbands in another country. Constable's work shows how social norms and policies in the Philippines create an environment in which women 'creatively negotiate transnational terrain in order to obtain divorce or annulment, meet new prospective partners, and achieve the desired goal of marriage' (Constable 2003: 163). In other countries, poverty may be the predominant motivation for looking for marriage across borders and studies based in Vietnam indicate that it is a lack of other economic opportunity that makes marriage abroad attractive. Lack of economic alternatives does not necessarily mean that women are 'poor' by local standards, however, but that the opportunities presented to them at home do not match their aspirations or ambition. Hung Cam Thai's work (2008) shows that it may not be absolute poverty that forces women to migrate but rather poverty of opportunity that induces them to look overseas. Thai describes the case of Thu, who is well educated and relatively affluent but seeks a husband overseas because she felt that in the Mekong Delta she was unlikely to meet 'someone who would permit her the autonomy that most village women would *not* expect after marriage' (Thai 2008: 57, italics in the original). Thai describes women who have above average standards of living in their home country and who are considering and entering into marriage with men of Vietnamese origin living the United States. These women, in terms of disposal income, have much more comfortable and affluent lives than their potential husbands. In this, these Vietnamese women are similar to the Philippine women described by Suzuki (2005) who leave financial and social security to pursue their ambitions and dreams overseas.

The role of policy in defining marriage

I argue that accepted gendered roles, assumed as natural in any country, impact upon the opportunities men and women have for migration and on how they migrate. I argue further that there is a 'feedback loop' between dominant national ideology and policy whereby policy interacts with public attitudes on any given topic and in doing so increases public awareness and scrutiny – possibly resulting in demands for policy change. This feedback between public opinion and policy can be seen in action in the UK where marriages within some settled migrant communities have come under increasing scrutiny. It is beyond the scope of this book to provide the kind of in-depth analysis of how public discourses and policy interact, but the following discussion is intended to give an indication of how this operates. This section will first look at how policy restricting cross-border marriages in the UK may have changed the marriage patterns between the UK and Pakistan but will go on to consider how the definitions of what constitutes a 'proper marriage' used by countries of settlement can have powerful effects on who enters the country on marriage visas. I will also discuss how discourses around 'sham' marriage can similarly shape the way marriages are contracted

Pakistani men coming to the UK have outnumbered female marriage migrants from Pakistan since 1997, and marriage has presented an opportunity to continue the migration projects of Pakistani families prevented from bringing in relatives through other avenues such as labour migration (Ballard 2004: 11). Shaw and Charsley report that more than 10,000 Pakistani nationals gained visas to join marriage partners in the UK during 2000 (2006: 405) and point out that the majority of these marriages were consanguineous. They argue that transnational, consanguineous and especially first cousin marriages, are now more common in the contemporary Pakistani diaspora than was the case in older generations and is more common in migrant communities than in Pakistan itself. Shaw and Charsley argue that it is the opportunities presented by UK policy on family and marriage migration that have altered marriage patterns rather than any cultural logic. Marriage patterns in Pakistani transnational communities have changed in response to immigration control but also to the transnational logic of communities which now seem to favour marriage between close kin to maximise the 'safety' of the marriage for the partners as well as to maximise the transnational utility of marriages. Roger Ballard similar argues that the different marriage rules imposed by UK immigration policies have led to different types of marriage migration (Ballard 2004: 7) – an opinion echoed by Katy Gardner who reflects how the 'spirit of strategic pragmatism' continues to influence transnational marriage as families manoeuvre through policy fields (2006: 386).

In every society some marriages are condemned as unacceptable and improper while others are considered 'normal, wholesome marriages which almost everyone agrees are a necessary foundation of a stable and equitable social order.' (Ballard 2006: 4) Such marriages are the archetypal marriages of any given polity or community against which 'other' marriages are judged. In some countries the definition of what can be considered 'normal and wholesome', and therefore acceptable according to marriage migration criteria, has expanded to include same-sex partnerships and may permit non-citizen fiancées to join their partners. The definition of what kind of relationships can represent 'genuine', long-term committed relationships remains at the behest of the polity, informed to a greater or lesser degree by the public. 'Society' therefore claims the right to judge which relationships represent family formation according to local norms which will therefore, be recognised as genuine. The sentiment of the partners themselves is only relevant, and tested, as far as it relates to the state's priorities. The state may refuse the entry of people in long-term, committed relationships which are as significant as marriages for the partners, if they are not recognised as such by the state's definitions. So the definition of what I refer to as a like-marital union, is in the gift of the nation-state, and the degree to which different relationships are legally recognised and which, therefore confer rights, depends on local laws. Couples in relationships not recognised by the states they wish to live in may have the chance to regularise their relationships by the local norms but equally may be effectively prevented from continuing that relationship.

The recognition of same-sex relationships as an acceptable form of cross-border marriage migration in some countries (for example, Australia, Parkinson 1994: 503–4, and some countries in the EU, see Elman 2000) demonstrates how states can and do expand their view of what marriage is and can be. This expansion does not necessarily mean that categories become broader, however, as while same-sex partnerships may become acceptable, other types of marriages may no longer be recognised. Polygamous marriages are no longer considered to be genuine marriages warranting the reunion of separated partners in most countries of settlement (see Parkinson 1994: 496–504, for a detailed discussion of the treatment of polygamous marriage in Australian law). There has also been a narrowing of definitions of acceptable marriage with several countries (for example, Denmark and the UK) raising the age at which cross-border marriages can be contracted. In these cases, concern for the rights of women has been used as justification for preventing migration. The assumption being that polygamous marriages are necessarily bad for women and that increasing the minimum age for marriage for some women (non-citizen women) will protect them from forced marriage even while it limits their right to family life (as established by Article 16 of the Universal Declaration of Human Rights or Article 8 of the UK Human Rights Act). These examples show clearly how policy is used to impose local cultural norms on migrants wishing to marry across borders and how the marriages of migrants are subject to controls not necessarily applied to citizens wishing to marry.

The assumption that some marriages are 'strategic' and little more than cynical ways to evade migration restrictions has been another focus of analysis. Marriage is often assumed to be a way for migrants with temporary, or no legal, status to maintain and strengthen their position in their country of settlement. Marriage is the only route to naturalisation for some migrants who may have been resident in their country of settlement for many years. Nicola Piper (2003: 459) has described how marriage to Japanese men is seen by migrant women, whose residence is based on temporary work permits, as a welcome end to the cycle of reapplication for work visas that complicates migrants' lives and works against them becoming truly integrated. Melody Lu (2005) similarly points out how in Taiwan, the most significant group of foreign men marrying Taiwanese women are Thai men who also represent the largest number of migrant labourers – this may be a coincidence but may indicate the desire of these men to be free of regular visa renewals as well as a desire to settle with Taiwanese women. Cross-border marriages, especially in the eyes of immigration policy-makers, are understood as being strategic paper exercises contracted to evade immigration controls (see Staring 1998; Herman 2006; Wray 2006, for examples and discussion). These writers all refer to the dominance of this cynical view of cross-border marriages in the popular imagination but all argue that it is heavily overstated and that marriage is a far from simple way of evading immigration controls.

Cynicism about cross-border marriage is reflected in the frequent claims of 'sham marriage' in relation to marriages involving non-citizens. Academic research on these marriages is limited, quite likely because of the problems inherent in defining what is after all a subjective judgement – as Helena Wray pithily reminds us that 'if marriage is a social construct, then so must be its negative, the sham marriage' (2006: 319). Her work on marriages of convenience, as defined by UK legislation, demonstrates admirably how 'marriages of convenience' are defined by policy-makers and implementers whose decisions may represent a form of 'moral-gatekeeping' (ibid.: 312) as officials search for the spouse who matches *their* personal criteria of a suitable spouse rather than criteria relevant to the prospective partners. Research available on marriages made for the purpose of legalising residency demonstrates the difficulties of arranging such marriages in the first place (Staring 1998) and indicates that few marriages have been proven to be 'sham' despite the intensive checks that immigration officers make on marriages (De Hart 2006a: 261). Foblets' work in Belgium shows how emphasis on 'sham' marriages works within an increasingly punitive system of immigration control and how 'by focusing too narrowly on potential abuses,...one tends to regard all marriages with foreigners as suspect' (Foblets and Vanheule 2006: 280). A further indication of the probable overestimation of 'sham' marriages can be drawn from Emma Herman's work (2006) on the role of personal networks in migration. Her analysis of data collected for the statistical bureau of the Commission of the European Communities in 2000 showed that, from more than 2,000 migrants to Spain and Italy, only seven mentioned marriage to a citizen or to someone with a residence permit as a way of entering the EU. In her discussion of possible explanations for the low instance of reporting marriage as an illegal strategy, she accepts that the differences in cultural perceptions of what represents a 'genuine' marriage may be a factor in the under-reporting of what to Western eyes might be 'sham' marriages. Nevertheless, Herman speculates that sham marriage may be 'simply less of a problem than many people thought' (2006: 210).

Research may provide little evidence to show that 'sham marriage' or 'marriage blanc' (a strategy of marrying a national to stay on in a country once one's visa has run out) is a common or a statistically significant practice but the *belief* that it is, has been used to argue for restricting family reunification policy more broadly. The real frequency of marriages of convenience or marriage for the explicit purpose of evading immigration control is hard to establish and deserves further research. It may be that it is more of a theoretical possibility than a real one. Certainly, migrants I have known have often told me that they will 'just marry someone' if they are unable to establish a right to remain any other way but these marriages may be much rarer than public discourse implies and may exist most commonly in the realm of myth and apocryphal story.

Potential marriage migrants to the EU have to demonstrate that their marriage fits local 'norms' by meeting criteria that include age, and often age difference, and are required to provide evidence that they can support themselves financially – these conditions may be particularly hard for refugees to meet (Kofman 2004: 255). Emma Herman, for example, writes that Dutch law as of 2005 requires anyone bringing in a spouse to earn 120 per cent of the minimum wage (2006: 196) – a high bar for many migrants to achieve. Individual EU countries have different criteria for family reunification and marriage migration which have led some couples to marry outside their country of residence, but within the EU, to avoid some of the more draconian regulations. Dan Rodriguez Garcia reports that Spanish legislation considers granting permission for marriage migration a 'concession rather than a fundamental right' and argues that bureaucratic process favours certain nationalities (e.g. Latin Americans) over other nationalities based on assumed social and cultural similarities (Rodriguez Garcia 2006: 428–9, note 6). Louise Ackers' work focuses on EU law, rather than the law of member states, writes that it considers the family as a 'functional, consensual and – importantly – stable "capsule" capable of responding to the emergence of dependency' (Ackers 2004: 384). The effect of this view of the family, as a driver of the economy, is that rights to family reunification are granted to support the economic productivity of the worker rather than to support the emotional or social well-being of individuals and groups.

Policy and the national ideologies and projects of states

Policy governing marriage migration is formed in response to legitimate state discourses of who belongs within any given state; how citizenship is attributed can be very telling in respect of establishing 'insiders' and 'outsiders'. Betty De Hart (2006b) has discussed how nationality has been attributed in cases of mixed marriage in the Netherlands where, until 1964 a Dutch woman marrying a foreign man automatically lost her Dutch citizenship. Until 1985, such a woman was not able to pass her Dutch citizenship on to her children. De Hart argues that the justification for the loss of citizenship for women boiled down four points: the need to protect the unity of the family under the assumed leadership of the husband; the legal complexity of a family bound by obligations based in more than one country; the idea that the women had made her choice through marrying a foreigner and, most importantly, that the women had made herself an alien and 'had left her own group and became a member of her husband's group' (De Hart 2006b: 55). A similar situation existed in the US at the start of the twentieth century where the 'single-identity theory of marriage' meant that migrant women would gain rights in the US but automatically lose their citizenship of birth (Calavita 2006: 114). It can be argued that there are echoes of the more extreme situation described in Kaufman and Williams' work which discusses how, during the Balkan wars, the children of rape victims were assumed to take ethnicity of their fathers ensuring that not only did minority women suffer the act and the humiliation of the original act of rape but that the community itself would be undermined by its women delivering the children of the victorious enemy (Kaufman and Williams 2004: 425).

Since 1985, citizenship law in the Netherlands has been reformed to allow greater options for dual nationality which have removed many of the gender inequalities previously inherent. Gendered inequalities remain, however, as while the children of Dutch men formally married to non-citizen women gain Dutch citizenship automatically, children born to Dutch fathers in unmarried mixed citizenship couples have to 'legally acknowledge, provide care for and raise the child for three years before they can pass on their nationality' (De Hart 2006b: 63). De Hart demonstrates how citizenship law in the Netherlands has been, and continues to be linked to a desire to 'protect the nation-state from "undesirable" migrants and mixed relationships' (2006b: 65). The Netherlands is by no means the only country to discriminate against women who marry out or their ethnic or national community (see also Breger 1998; Augustine-Adams 2002; and Oum 2003, for further examples), but this example shows how national policy can be shaped by changing national ideologies and that overarching concepts such as gender equality do not necessarily apply to migrants. As De Hart puts it: 'Women in general and women with a foreign husband were perceived as two separate classes' (2006b: 64).

Amy Elman (2000: 745) argues that rules regulating marriage and immigration lie at the heart of structures underpinning the modern state. Her argument is that challenging definitions of marriage and marriage-like relationships to, for example, allow same-sex relationships to be considered 'marriages' only serves to continue a view of family life that is based on the essentially unequal institution of marriage. Citizenship policies and national ideology are closely connected and, as a result, the ways in which migrants are positioned in relation to the state is informed by imaginaries and narrations of belonging that cut across gender, class and life cycle and which have contested, shifting boundaries and borders (Yuval-Davis *et al.* 2002: 521, see also Turner 2008). Linda Bosniak also argues that citizenship is a 'nationally situated and nationally framed project' (1998: 32), and that because of its focus on 'the nation', outsiders living in the state present a challenge for theorists of citizenship. Nandita Sharma likewise writes that: 'Concepts of citizenship... are the ideological cement that holds the repressive power of state practices in place' (2003: 62) and this observation applies very strongly to women who are already the subject of 'the current fetishization and devaluation of the figure of the alien' (Bosniak 1998: 31). Citizenship norms act very strongly on individuals who are cast as extraneous to the state and Pei-Chia Lan proposes that 'technologies' of citizenship and anti-citizenship that problematise certain individuals and groups can be identified. These technologies are operationalised through the strategies of the state, employers and husbands for example, and through the discourses adopted by non-citizens themselves (Lan 2008: 835).

Cross-border marriage migrants, as will be discussed in greater detail in Chapter 10, often find themselves in dependent positions if their residency status in their country of settlement is contingent on their continuing marriage. This situation, of having already separated from their natal homes while still being excluded from full participation in their new ones, can be seen as a form of liminality (Gennep 1960). Life in states of liminality makes citizenship, as described by Marshall's classic definition, impossible, if citizenship is 'a status bestowed on those who are full members of the community' (1992: 28–9). Marshall assumes citizens hold full legal status and rights to participate in the political, as well as economic, life of the country. By this definition, cross-border marriage migrants have clearly limited rights to citizenship. Citizenship, according to Ruth Lister, is about practice as well as status (1997), so in a discussion of liminal subjects, in this case cross-border marriage migrants, citizenship must be a negotiation of *process*, as *status* is often denied or is only a future possibility. Informal citizenship, argues Linda McDowell, carries 'an assumption of moral worth in which *de facto* as opposed to *de jure* rights of citizenship are defined as open to those who are deserving or who are capable of acting responsibly' (1999: 150, italics in the original). Citizenship can also be understood as 'a term that signifies belonging to and participation in a group or a community' (Plummer 2003: 50) so it can be drawn from a community sense of shared historical and/or social belonging whether or not that fits the national myth of the country of settlement. Citizenship, above all, is about being 'in place' however that place is defined, and as such, migration can lead to people feeling more or less 'in place' even as they travel. Moving from a place of origin where one has nationality but no freedom to express one's cultural, sexual or social identity, to a second country where legal citizenship has not been established, may nevertheless confer citizenship if a personal sense of freedom or belonging is established.

Many migrants may not be citizens in Marshall's sense of being both contributors to and beneficiaries of the state but migrants, especially those who place themselves within transnational communities, may experience a strong sense of citizenship even as they are deliberately excluded from the everyday life of the state. Citizenship for cross-border marriage migrants takes on different forms depending on immigration status, ethnicity, religious affiliation, class, professional status let alone personal circumstances but in considering the types of citizenship open to cross-border marriage migrants, it is important to remember that citizenship, especially legal citizenship, is generally linked to an individual's capacity for 'productive labour' (van Walsum and Spijkerboer 2007). Scholars have recognised that citizenship is a status generally bestowed on women by men (Lister 1997; Anderson 2000), either directly, through the attainment of economic or political value in ways recognised by masculine authority; or indirectly through association, for example, as a wife, daughter or mother. Rights to family reunion within the EU, for example, are in place to eliminate 'obstacles to the mobility of the worker' (European Community law, cited by Ackers 2004: 375) on the assumption that workers will operate more effectively if they have their family with them. In practice this means that entrants joining partners must show they will make a contribution and not be a 'burden on the public purse' (Ackers 2004: 377). Forms of temporary and conditional entry not only block citizenship but also emphasise its provisional nature (Kofman 2005: 456). Rights can be removed at the whim of the state and, as well as this being a disincentive for migrants to establish a home for themselves, it also throws doubt on the loyalty of migrants who are often accused of lacking commitment and willingness to integrate. So even while there has been a trend towards understanding citizenship as 'based more on personhood than membership of a national and bounded political community' (Kofman 2005: 454), there has been a simultaneous resurgence of the nation-state as an exclusionary device, especially in industrialised countries, through increased control over migration and a retreat from multiculturalism.

The 'problem' of the migrant woman

Women's assumed place within the family and domestic worlds puts further restrictions on their capacity to establish and enjoy 'citizenship' on their own terms. We have seen above how the granting of formal citizenship is usually connected to economic activity. Women's economic contribution is undervalued when made in domestic settings and through caring and reproductive labour. For Irene Gedalof, 'Women's association with that private sphere means that their access to the status of citizen ... is always problematic' (2007: 91), and she has described how the figure of the migrant woman is problematised. She writes:

> She is a problem defined by her linguistic isolation and limited awareness of cultural difference, and by her entanglement in the 'backward practices' of arranged marriage and gender subordination ... She stands, in her ignorant sameness, for the limits of difference that cannot be absorbed without shaking the stability of identity.
>
> (2007: 90)

Gedalof's study focuses on asylum seeking women arguing that 'current political discourse on migration and asylum problematises some families and some collective/ community understandings of "home" as things that need to be carefully managed if a broader, national sense of home and belonging is not to be compromised' (2007: 86). The idea of women as a conservative force in maintaining tradition is often assumed and Catherine Lloyd provides another example of the power of this view of women as maintainers of tradition which has resonance to today. She writes of colonial period Algeria that:

> The seclusion of women was identified as a major obstacle to the French conquest firstly because it meant that the family sphere was beyond their control and women as mothers and grandmothers could pass on alternative stories, helping to form a narrative of resistance.
>
> (Lloyd 2006: 454)

While women remain veiled or confined or assumed to be so, they may be perceived as challenging the state through their maintenance of difference and their apparent rejection of majority norms.

The degree to which the state and its policies can intrude and dictate behaviours and norms varies from state to state and is very much part of any state's 'contract' with its population. This contract between public and private freedoms is under constant negotiation but is often unspoken and therefore may be hard for outsiders, including migrants, to understand and negotiate. Ada Engebrigsten writes that the feminist movement in Norway, as in much of developed world, 'has demanded that the private domain should be a public concern' (2007: 733). This is justified in order that the vulnerable can be protected against the 'unregulated space' represented by the family, where different norms allow practices that could be criminal in any other setting. The role of the state in most countries is non-interventionist in relation to families and states are usually reluctant to intervene in the private realm of the family. This reluctance, however, usually only extends to the 'normal' majority of families while other families may be identified as warranting intervention for their own and the common good. In this vein, Bridget Anderson writes that 'As the home is imagined in opposition to the market, it is also imagined as a refuge from the state' but goes on 'Of course in practice this depends on the kinds of family and private life one is talking about – the families of the poor, and particularly of migrants are viewed as legitimate subjects of state control' (2006: 9). In relation to families where there is cross-border marriage, interesting differences between state attitudes to marriage between ethnic groups and within ethnic groups are thrown up. Marriages that bring a foreign, non-citizen member into a citizen family are usually seen as unproblematic and as deserving their right to privacy except when those families belong to ethnic communities. In such cases, as with the transnational marriages discussed here, relationships and marriages may become subject to much scrutiny.

The focus on the 'exotic', in this case represented by the transnational family, targets some families for official scrutiny but leaves the single person within a family subject to that family's norms and left without access to state protection or support. As feminist activists have long argued, the family can be a dangerous place for women as well as a source of protection. It seems an irony, therefore, that the state focuses its concerns on families where support for victimised family members may be available for a migrant member, but withdraws it from individuals within families who have no-one to turn to if a relationship turns abusive.

I argue that some families are considered as acceptable while others are problems (see Ada Engebrigtsen's 2007 comparison of attitudes to 'good' migrants – Tamils, as opposed to 'failed' migrants – Somalis), and this differentiation has consequences for how migrants are viewed by the state. The idea of the migrant as 'pollutant' within the body politic is not an uncommon one in the literature on migration and is developed notably by Liisa Malkki in her study of refugees in Tanzania (1995) This attitude to migrants was demonstrated starkly by a Taiwanese politician in 2006 (pers. comm.) who warned citizens that Vietnamese women could still be 'polluted' by Agent Orange as a legacy from the Vietnam War – making a direct connection between physical and social contamination. Sandra Buckley (1997) discusses a similar linkage made in the Japanese media in which migrant sex workers were associated with the spread of HIV and AIDS in Japan while downplaying the role of Japanese sex workers and their customers.

Gedalof argues that social policy 'takes the family (or at least some kinds of family) as a potential danger to border integrity by providing an entry point for difference' (2007: 84). The women described in Gedalof's work may be similar to those Eleonore Kofman had in mind when she wrote that legislation to limit citizenship 'has partly been directed toward women's roles in social reproduction and national identity and fears of rampant sexuality and breeding' (1999: 279). Dorit Roer-Strier and Dina Ben Ezra found in their review of studies of marriages between Western and non-Western partners, that these marriages were generally described as presenting problems for families and society and were even seen as a pathological (2006: 41–2). Their own work on marriages between Western women and Palestinian men emphasises the role of the state, arguing that it was unequal power relations between the states and intercultural families that 'especially in times of political conflict stand as additional obstacles to the cultural adaptation of intercultural families' (ibid.: 42). Their paper makes the important point that in times of conflict, the motives and loyalties of the Western women married to Palestinians were constantly doubted as they were seen to have an 'escape route' from the conflict should they choose to take it. In this scenario, the 'foreign' wives were assumed to lack commitment and threaten the integrity of the community but in very different ways to the asylum-seeking women described by Gedalof.

Related to the 'problem' posed by migrant women is the similar problem of marriages that may or may not be considered equal or comparable to marriage as it is locally understood. As already noted in relation to the identification of a 'sham' marriage, recognising an acceptable marriage is a function of not only establishing whether a marriage fits the norms represented by state policy but also making the subjective judgement as to whether such a marriage is a 'genuine' one based on often unspoken assumptions. Betty De Hart (2006a: 253) lists factors included in Dutch legislation intended to indicate when a marriage can be considered genuine for the purpose of entering the country. These indicators require that there must be 'matrimonial cohabitation', a shared contribution to marriage responsibilities, spouses must have met before marriage, be consistent about personal details and share a common language, no money other than a dowry can have been paid and neither partner can have a history of 'anomalies' in their residence or marriage history. This list presents a very prescriptive view of marriage that is essentially about the *contract* of marriage rather than about how the relationship is understood by the partners. Helena Wray argues that decision-makers judge whether a marriage conforms to what is typical in any country (of origin or settlement) and she writes: 'There is a strong tendency, therefore, towards accepting marriages that conform to the decision-makers' conception of how a genuine marriage, from a particular part of the world, would look' (Wray 2006: 311). As a result, marriages that are judged to be unorthodox, for example, those involving older or divorced women, may be unfairly refused. Wray concludes:

> An acceptable spouse may be a different creature to that of forty years ago but his or her contours remain the invisible mould against which certain applications are measured and found wanting. Their true defect may not be that their marriage is a sham but that they are unwanted and unwelcome immigrants.
>
> (ibid.: 311)

Studies of cross-border marriage beyond Europe show that some marriages are seen as conforming to established norms while others are problematised, treated as aberrant and as threatening to the nation-state. The nature of the problematisation depends on local norms and Gedalof's work, for example, demonstrates a European or possibly developed world concern for marriages that nurture difference within the heart of society. In other parts of the world there may be a similar anxiety about difference but anxiety may be located in concern for moral or even racial pollution rather than concern for cultural difference. Young Rae Oum describes a situation in South Korea where race influences perceptions of cross-border marriages. She records how marriages between Koreans and Westerners are privileged over other cross-border marriages. She writes:

> International couples in South Korea are polarised into two groups by their social standing and the western racial order. One would be

the predominantly Korean-Caucasian unions who are mostly middle class professionals, diplomats and entrepreneurs. The other would be the working class marriages between the locals and the 'imported brides', migrants workers and illegal residents originating from third world countries.

(Oum 2003: 436)

It is important to remember that mixed marriage or marriage resulting from migration does not necessarily result in discrimination. Many marriages that could be defined as cross-border – such as those between citizens of developed countries are not problematised and perceptions of class, for example, are important in determining how marriages will be judged.

Immigration policy, non-citizens and the vulnerability of marriage migrants

Nicola Piper has emphasised the importance of rights and citizenship for migrants making the point that without established and recognised rights, migrants are always vulnerable. She observes that: 'Marriage and migration are thus linked to citizenship and power relations that have evolved historically, and are created and sustained by the law' (2003: 464). For Piper and many other writers, the absence of rights or reliance on temporary and contingent rights is a significant way in which policy undermines the personal agency of cross-border marriage migrants and contributes to their vulnerability. Sundari Anitha's work on the effects of the UK policy of imposing a two-year wait on marriage migrants before granting independent rights, the so-called two-year rule, demonstrates how women can become destitute if they leave the violent partners who grant them rights (Anitha *et al.* 2008; Anitha 2008). They may find themselves within a category of 'No recourse to public funding' unless they remain with their husbands. Anitha describes how women who have experienced domestic violence and abuse can argue their case to remain in the country and to access state support but that few women are able to access these rights. She writes:

In reality, this means that women facing domestic violence within the two-year period or more, if their sponsor has not renewed their visa, face a stark 'choice' between living with life-threatening ongoing violence or facing destitution, namely lack of adequate accommodation or any means of subsistence if they leave, and deportation if they are unable to meet the stringent evidential requirements.

(2008: 18)

Describing a European context, Elenore Kofman reminds us that no EU state gives automatic rights to non-citizens and that the EU retains 'a high degree of sovereignty and discretion in terms of the conditions imposed on different categories of migrants and refugees' (2004: 253). This means that while international conventions on the right to family life are recognised by law, they have limited application as states effectively set their own standards. Louise Ackers (1998) highlights the distinction between independent and derived rights, i.e. those that are attributed to an individual and those that are granted because of an individual's relationship and connection to another. Ackers (1998: 314) suggests there are three tiers of rights relating to freedom of movement within the EU. These are full independent rights granting access to all state entitlements; derived entitlements as a spouse or a child that grant entitlement so long as the relationship remains and rights which allow free movement but withhold access to welfare services and which require the migrant to demonstrate that they will not become a 'burden' on the state. Beyond these categories, I would argue, are the non-EU citizens and other undocumented migrants who live as 'margizens' within the state but outside the protection of the state. In most countries that are the destinations of marriage migrants, non-citizen spouses enjoy derived entitlements by which their access to the state is granted exclusively by virtue of their continuing relationship to a marriage partner. As a result, if the relationship breaks down, they lose their entitlements in the state they live within. In some cases, this may lead to migrants becoming effectively stateless as they may have had to renounce their citizenship of birth prior to taking up the citizenship of their country of settlement. This has led to Vietnamese wives separated from their Taiwanese husbands becoming stateless and even to their children becoming stateless if their Taiwanese fathers fail to claim citizenship on their behalf. Even in the EU, where dual citizenship is the norm and mobility a watchword, long-term residency in an EU country as a non-citizen may not ensure entitlement to welfare benefits in the country of settlement while, at the same time, rights may have lapsed in the home country (Ackers 2004: 378).

The derived entitlements of marriage migrants leaves them living in circumstances that share similarities with domestic workers who, as Bridget Anderson has argued (2006), have little redress if their rights are violated, who may have little knowledge of the country they are living in and are vulnerable to abuse if their employers (or in this case their spouses) control their documents. Derived entitlement extends partial forms of citizenship to migrants which, as Roger Brubaker argues (cited in Schuster and Solomos 2002: 42), may 'trap them in an intermediate status'. I have argued earlier that this intermediate status may afford opportunity to employ some the 'weapons of the weak' described by Scott (1985), reminding us that they even these migrants may not be entirely without agency, but such agency can hardly equate to having recognised and protected rights to reside and participate in the society they live within. I would also argue that having rights is not the same as enjoying rights. Many migrants may indeed be eligible to receive welfare services from the state, but unless migrants are aware of their rights and the agencies responsible for providing these rights are committed to upholding these rights, eligibility is essentially meaningless. The failure of the state and others to inform migrants of their rights is an effective way of depriving them from rights whether intentionally or otherwise and this failure will be discussed further in the next chapter.

Conclusion

This chapter has aimed to show some of the 'unintended consequences' (Castles 2007a) of migration policy and to unravel which of the effects of policy are indeed consciously designed and which were not envisaged by policy-makers. It has been shown how migration results in the diminution of the human and social rights of migrants who may find themselves re-classified as being illegal aliens through no fault of their own. I have attempted to show that policies made by countries of origin and countries of settlement are constructed through the application of national imaginations of gender and gender roles, of marriage and indeed of citizenship. In my view, the individual migrant crossing borders for the purpose of marriage is hardly considered in the edifice of national regulations and policies, and when they are considered, they are likely to been seen as fitting one or other stereotype of 'the migrant' and treated accordingly.

10
Migrant Life/Married Life
Life as a cross-border marriage migrant

The life histories of women and men considering migration for the purpose of marriage naturally have a profound effect on their chance of finding foreign-national partners, on their potential for negotiating entry into their spouse's country of residence and on how such marriages are contracted. The Internet and other forms of global communication have radically altered the ways marriages are negotiated and arranged whether between ethnic groups or within them, and the use of agents of various types has increased and developed to take advantage of these opportunities. Academic studies of women in the Philippines who have contracted, or who wish to contract, marriages overseas describe their complex reasoning and some of the ways they seek to balance of the pros and cons of marriage and the realities of their own and their families' lives. Spouses who are citizens of the potential country of settlement are also shown, according to research, as weighing up the relative advantages of marriage with nationals of different countries. Potential spouses and their families in both countries of emigration and immigration may be involved in arranging and negotiating what, in their view, are suitable matches even though the information they are basing their opinions on may be sparse and unreliable. This chapter sets out to consider how the decision to marry across borders may come about and what the results of such marriages may be. As in previous chapters, the decisions migrants make are shown as being made by individuals able to act with differing degrees of agency and autonomy within the structural parameters set for them by families, communities and legislative frameworks.

Marriage migrants may have extremely variable knowledge about their new country of settlement – some will have already lived there, or indeed be living there while others may know very little about their proposed homes. Some migrants may have been misinformed about how they will live post-migration and may be quite unprepared for what they find on arrival. This may be because they have made assumptions about the living standards of their spouses (Thai 2008, 2005). Thai describes how the Vietnamese wives of US-based Vietnamese husbands may be unprepared for their husbands' low socio-economic status on arrival in the US, while others may find they have to work in occupations that they had hoped to leave by migrating away from home (see, for example, Mix and Piper 2003 who describe former sex workers finding themselves obliged to carry on working in the sex trade post-migration). Other migrants may expect to be better protected by the states they move to than is really the case and I will draw on research on the post-migration experiences of marriage migrants to demonstrate how social policy and social conditions in countries of settlement impact upon the lives of migrating brides and grooms. Experiences of dislocation and isolation will affect almost all migrants and in the case of migrant spouses, the period of dependency on the citizen-partner and new family members (a situation which some cases may last for years) may exacerbate already difficult situations. Restrictions on employment and on social welfare entitlements will negatively affect almost all marriage migrants regardless of how their marriages were contracted and should marriages break down, the non-citizen partner may become very vulnerable.

This chapter builds on earlier discussion of the tensions between the personal agency of women and men in cross-border marriages and the constraining factors that limit and shape that agency. The focus of this chapter will be on what happens after marriage and after migration. Are non-citizens married to citizens able to achieve or work towards their personal goals? Are their expectations met? How do they go about building lives in their country of settlement and what are the factors that promote or prevent their integration and participation in society at large and in their local communities? To answer these and other questions, this chapter will first look at what motivates cross-border marriage migration in the first place – enquiring into the different reasons men and women may have in choosing permanent migration as a partner of a citizen. The literature reviewed shows how, not only are expectations and motivations different between the citizen and the non-citizen partner, but that the treatment migrants receive and the obstacles they face depend on how they are viewed by the receiving society. Following this discussion I will consider the nature and degree of on-going contact with the home country and review evidence of how this impacts upon the lives of migrants in their countries of settlement. A third section will discuss the issue of citizenship and the dependency experienced by many migrant spouses that is recognised in the literature as a major cause of problems for cross-border marriage migrants. It will be argued that this dependency and lack of autonomy have serious negative effects for the dependent partner, but that they also undermine relationships and have broader negative effects. The final section will consider how and indeed whether, cross-border marriage migrants are able to achieve a sense of belonging and citizenship in their country of settlement.

Who marries across borders and why?

Throughout this book cross-border marriage has been defined very broadly – as marriages or permanent relationships between people with different formal citizenship statuses. This definition does not presuppose difference or similarity in ethnic or cultural background and it includes the marriages (or formalised relationships) of people already in the country of migration, but who do not hold citizen status of that country. The significant common point shared by these marriages is that the partners have different relationships to the state they live within with one being an 'insider' (at least formally) and the other an 'outsider'. There are important points that need to be made here that relate to the degree to which having formal citizenship actually grants an individual 'insider' status. As we have seen throughout this book, the meaning of citizenship varies dramatically from country to country and the ability to participate equally in society and to experience a sense of belonging is not something that comes from formal citizenship alone. That said, formal citizenship grants formal rights – to welfare entitlements, work, recognition, travel, etc. – and allows marriage migrants to claim rights as individuals rather than through their relationship to their citizen spouse.

   This broad view of what constitutes marriage migration means that there are many different explanations possible for why people choose to form permanent partnerships across borders. In relation to marriage within transnational families, Elisabeth Beck-Gernsheim (2007) has suggested three motivations for Western citizens to marry members of their transnational community living in the country of origin. These are loyalty and obligation, promise of upward mobility and shifting power balances in gender relations. Beck-Gernsheim elaborates on this third motivation arguing that '[the] choice of spouse becomes a vehicle for introducing new modes of gender relations; or conversely, for keeping them outside' (2007: 282). The argument being that women oppressed in the country of origin choose marriage in countries of the diaspora to free themselves of traditional patriarchies and gender norms while men in the diaspora choose women from home to maintain those norms. There is undoubtedly some power in this argument but it is based on a simplistic, culturalist discourse that makes dangerous assumptions about the motivations of 'others'. In my view, this argument does not leave sufficient room for an appreciation of the more personal reasons for marriage across borders that research reviewed for this book has described.

Hidalgo and Bankston (2008) have argued that a sense of familiarity between partners is a motivator for marriage and this observation can apply to all kinds of cross-border marriages whether between people who share an ethnic connection or who share common interests or experience. Hidalgo and Bankston's work relates to marriages between veterans of the Vietnam War and Vietnamese women and they argue that being a veteran of a war in a country leads to greater chance of intermarriage. They predict that a large number of marriages will take place as a direct result of conflict and from being stationed in a country on active service. Furthermore, they describe a 'delayed "military-bride" phenomenon' (2008: 179), defined as a greater propensity for veterans to marry from that country in later years. Sallie Yea's work (2004, 2008) has certainly shown that the existence of military 'camptowns' in South Korea led to many cross-border marriages and relationships but it remains to be seen how the present conflicts in Iraq and Afghanistan, for example, will affect future cross-border marriage patterns. This notion of familiarity, however, is an important one and familiarity may be represented by all kinds of shared interests and attributes. It is to the detriment of the body of research that, because of its focus on ethnic and cultural characteristics, other shared experiences are neglected. Commonality, for example, in terms of class and education, may be very important in bringing couples together but as these couples are less problematised, and fewer in number, they have not been the focus of much research (an exception being Rodriguez Garcia 2006: 403).

Jennifer Sanchez Taylor (2006) has written of the importance of marriage and sexual or gendered relationships matching a 'social ideal' that may be unspoken and highly individual. She applies this notion in relation to Western women in relationships with non-Western men arguing that these relationships grant women the social ideal of greater equality as the loss of power these men experience as migrants, is balanced by their inherent power as men (2006: 52). The social ideal represented by a 'proper marriage' has a powerful effect on who may be seen as a potential marriage partner and is shaped as much by romance, fantasy and desire as social and cultural norms. Nicole Constable uses the notion of 'cartographies of desire' to describe the role of fantasy and imaginings in relationships – important for both men and women in determining who may be acceptable as permanent partners. Constable records how

> Men's openly stated assumptions about the 'traditional' moral values and character of Asian women as well as their less openly expressed ideas about the erotic sexuality and women's assumptions about 'modern' outlooks, power, or attractiveness of Western and other foreign men are factors in their motivation to meet and marry.
>
> (Constable 2005a: 7)

Louisa Schein's work (2005) similarly demonstrates the role of imagination and fantasy in relationships, arguing that Chinese Miao women represented fantasy figures for Hmong refugees living in the US who looked to them as symbols of lost tradition and belonging but that relationships were temporary and not necessarily formalised by marriage. In Johnson's work with Russian women seeking husbands overseas (2007), both parties express a sense of grievance against previous and potential partners from their home countries – the women condemn Russian men as irresponsible and the American men reject Western women as unfeminine. Similarly Andrea Lauser (see also MacKay 2003: 30) describes women from the Philippines looking for marriage with Western men because they imagine them to be good husbands (i.e. romantic and good providers) in contrast to men in the Philippines, who are typified as having mistresses and where divorce is difficult (Lauser 2008: 88). For both sides, marrying across borders promises a way of finding partners that they believe, hope or assume will be more suitable for them than any they are likely to find at home. Inevitably, many in these partnerships will be disappointed.

Cross-border marriage migration happens through various different channels and processes. Women and men may be actively seeking matches abroad or may unintentionally find themselves in relationships that join citizens and non-citizens. Dan Rodriguez Garcia's (2006) research with bi-national Senegalese-Gambian-Spanish couples in Catalonia, for example, records a change in marriage patterns reflected in an increase, since the 1970s and 1980s, of marriages between Spanish women who have met their African partners through tourism rather than in Spain. Travel, for tourism, work or study along with a greater acceptance of cross-ethnic relationships increases the likelihood of cross-border marriages and partnerships. A further route to marriage across borders may be through the internationalisation of domestic work. Women's migration has long been linked to labour migration but Piper and Roces (2003a) have noted the reluctance on the part of commentators to see women migrants as not just workers *or* wives and mothers but combining both these roles. Since Piper and Roces' edited volume (2003b), the meshing of women's roles as workers as well as wives has been increasingly studied. Pei-Chia Lan's work, for example, links the migration of foreign brides and foreign maids through their shared place at the 'intersection of globalisation and nationalism' (2008: 833). Lan finds similarities between the desires of grooms and of their families and that 'Taiwanese working-class men seek cross-border marriages not just to end their bachelorhood: they also need the unpaid labour of foreign spouses to assist with agricultural production in farming households and the reproduction of the next generation' (2008: 840, citing Hsia 1997). Brides marrying into these families are marrying into a whole set of assumptions about the roles of wives as labourers, carers, reproducers as well as life partners. This work suggests that there are similarities between the working-class choice to marry a worker to provide labour and the middle- and upper-class choice to meet their labour needs by employing a migrant domestic worker with whom they have a less intimate and more 'disposable' relationship.

Hsui-Hua Shen provides another example of how the different roles of wives may play out through a study of families where the husband maintains a lover or a mistress as well as a wife. In Shen's examples, the wife's role in the 'international division of familial, sexual and emotional labour' (2005: 420), is to care and support the family at home, paid for by the husband who maintains his stake in the family through his financial input. The role of the mistress is more than just to provide sexual labour and researchers have noted the importance of emotional labour and intimacy in relationships whether or not they have a commercial basis. Graham Scambler (Scambler 2007: 1088) cites Gross' (2005: 286) reflections on the 'detraditionalization of intimacy' which recognise that intimacy and care can be bought in the same way that sex can. Foreign wives, in some circumstances, may be seen as embodying notions of womanhood and 'wifely-ness' by combining traditional roles of carer, mother, domestic labourer and intimate partner. Thus a wife may be obtained in much the same way as a domestic worker may be. The lived experience of such arrangements should not be condemned out of hand, however, and for women who share an expectation of the roles of a wife with her husband, such a marriage may allow her to travel, to improve her socio-economic conditions, to support her natal family through remittances and to enjoy security and a relatively self-governing married life.

The stereotyping of marriages, particularly those in which partners met through sex work, as merely a continuation of prostitution presents a very simplistic view of marriages based on the perceptions of those outside the marriages. Views, such as those cited in Cohen (2003), describing marriages between women working as bar-girls and tourists as 'Instead of prostituting themselves with many men, they prostitute themselves with only one man' (ibid.: 66) are commonly heard but deny the humanity of both the woman and the man in the relationship and tell us nothing of *their* hopes, dreams or expectations or of their lives together. This essentially male view of sex work, which decontextualises it from the rest of a women's life, should be contrasted with Larrissa Sandy's observation that 'Female labour migration for sex work is closely related to notions of filial duty and as a relatively high income earner, sex work is an integral part of this' (2007: 202). Undoubtedly, some marriages do oblige women to stay in the role of sexual labourer throughout their marriages but this may be the case whether or not the marriage came about from an initial commercial connection. The relationship between sex work and marriage or long-term relationship may be a close one but simply because a partnership came from commercial sex work, there should be no assumption that the relationship cannot be 'genuine' or that it is not significant for those within it.

This section has attempted to describe some of the drivers of marriage across borders. These include the transnational motivations described in greater detail in Chapter 6 and the effect of the various fantasies and assumptions made about men and women from certain countries and groups. The nexus between labour migration, especially domestic work, and marriage is also recognised as important in promoting and shaping the marriage opportunities of many. A further motivation for marriage across borders lies in the strategic value of marriage as a means of negotiating borders. This has been discussed in detail in Chapter 4 and it is an important explanation for why many men and women are prepared to take the inevitable risks of entering into marriage contracts. Such strategic marriages are difficult to identify in the literature and I have argued that their significance has been overestimated and have been co-opted into the rhetoric of immigration control with little substantive research to justify their ubiquity. Further, I argue that the original motivation for marriage is less significant in the understanding of marriages than the lived experience of that marriage. The subjective judgements as to why anyone marries or forms permanent relationships inevitably change through the life course and for this reason, the rest of this chapter will focus on that lived experience.

Continuing contact with country of birth

Throughout this book I have been at pains to emphasise the importance of family and caring responsibilities in motivating marriage across borders. These obligations to kin and country of birth clearly do not end on migration but it seems that continuing contact is not something necessarily anticipated by marriage partners. Sallie Yea (2004), for example, describes how the GI husbands of the women from the Philippines in South Korea generally assume that their wives are free from ties to their home country and husbands may not be prepared to accept responsibility for these family members nor be prepared to help their wives support family at home. Yea's work provides examples of marriages breaking down over the wife's continuing responsibilities either for children, siblings or older relatives. There can be no doubt that many women who marry across borders do so to meet their caring obligations and because they see marriage as a way of supporting those who depend on them back home. Conflict within marriages relating to family responsibilities may be very difficult for women who find themselves torn between loyalty to their new family and to their old one. The notion of transnational caring is becoming increasingly studied and the existence of ongoing interpersonal relationships across borders is an important signifier of transnationalism as opposed to uni-directional migration. Paul Hoggett quotes Susan Mendus (1993) on the multiple and conflicting roles of women and reflects on the 'unchosen nature to much of their moral life' characterised by contradictory social injunctions that result in women feeling that 'someone is always being let down, choices always seem to be between the lesser of competing evils' (Hoggett 2001: 45). This sense of conflicting obligations may be particularly debilitating for many cross-border marriage migrants whose caring responsibilities are multiple and complex as well as geographically spread. The provision of care is also culturally determined and migrant women may not only be dealing with disparate locations of care but also of divergent notions of what caring represents – as Martha Nussbaum writes: 'When we talk about love and care, we are talking both about emotions and about complex patterns of behaviour mediated not only by desire but also by habits and social norms' (2000: 264).

In marriages between people of different cultures and ethnic heritages, an accommodation needs to be made between the cultural expectations of the two partners, or indeed the two families. Jutta Lauth Bacas describes how Greek and German family members, linked by marriage, had different expectations of how that marriage would affect the family as a whole. Lauth Bacas shows how Greek families may feel they have 'lost out' as when a son marries a German woman, the Greek family doesn't gain the social advantages they might traditionally expect. German in-laws didn't feel obliged to their son-in-law's family and 'No German father of the bride feels obliged to lend money to the Greek groom for a surgery or a shop'(Lauth Bacas 2002: 9). In some cases, the couple may be able to balance their connection to the two countries but in many other cases the degree of connection to the country the couple is *not* resident in needs constant negotiation. Ewa Morokvasic has discussed the concept of mobility rather than simply migration between fixed points and argues that the care the Polish women she studies provide for their families is enabled by their migration away from home. She writes 'Their experience of migration thus becomes their lifestyle, their *leaving home* and going away, paradoxically a strategy of *staying at home*' (Morokvasic 2004: 7, italics in the original). Maintaining connection to a home country that is stigmatised as poor or backward may be particularly challenging but Carol Freeman found that the Chinese women she worked with in South Korea displayed an increasing sense of pride in their country of origin after some time as migrants (2005: 96). Perhaps they gain a sense of agency that allows them to reject the stereotypes of their country of origin and encourages their continuing allegiance and sense of identification with their natal country. For couples married within transnational communities or from the same country, maintaining a connection with home may be a given and may unite the couple who can reinforce each other's sense of identification with 'home'. Katy Gardner, however, writes of the challenges of maintaining caring relationships across distance and of the pain physical separation can cause whether or not that pain is shared and respected by those in the family (2006). Michael Peter Smith (2001) argues that theorists need to 'free' the everyday from conflation with the 'local' as the everyday of many migrants connects them to their home countries and other parts of their emotional worlds. Smith uses the example of Muslim communities who may identify community as existing on a global scale that is part of the everyday – 'physically absent but hardly spiritually distant...' (2001: 117). The notion of an everyday that is transnational is not restricted to Muslim communities, though for Muslims the concept of the global may have a more spiritual meaning than for other groups. Studies have demonstrated how global connections affect the day-to-day lives of migrants (Williams 2006). As for many migrants, their families and friends at home have an enduring and ever-present place in their daily lives. For migrants married to citizens of other countries, their relationships with their country of birth may be contentious but will always have an impact on how life is lived in the country of settlement.

Norms, expectations and 'value conflicts'

Once living in the country of migration, migrant spouses find themselves subject to the local policies described in Chapter 9. These policies set the tone for the interaction of migrant spouses with the general population. The attitudes of society in general are influenced by the citizenship policies of the state, and most spouses crossing borders experience a probationary period short of citizenship during which their connection to their citizen partners and families grants them their rights. In some cases this status will offer more security than their previous status as marriage may free migrants from the uncertainty of temporary, contract-based visas and may 'shorten the transition from contract worker to resident' (MacKay 2003: 45). Lisa Faier's work in Japan describes how spousal visas were temporary and could be granted from 6 months to three years – this meant that 'women faced considerable pressure to comply with their husband's and families' desires' and to behave in ways judged to be 'Japanese' (Faier 2007: 156). This pressure is contextualised by Nobue Suzuki's observation that in Japan, a 'legitimate' marriage marks a man's place in society and that the legitimacy of a match is reduced when wife is foreign (2005: 137) and especially when the wife is stigmatised by public assumptions about her past and respectability. Lisa Faier describes how the wives of Japanese men take trouble to establish their commitment to their marriage: they challenge Japanese stereotypes of them as selfish and greedy by explaining their lives in Japan as 'sacrifice' and that 'married women went to great lengths to demonstrate their selflessness.' (2007: 155). Elizabeth Mavroudi (2007) has argued that migration leads to new conceptions of national identity as well as to multiple identities which individuals may or may not be comfortable with. Mavroudi sees identities as constructions that are 'active and strategic, rather than "given"' (ibid.: 407), and in emphasising one facet of identity and downplaying another (as we see in the example of women from the Philippines in Japan), migrants may be able to increase their personal agency.

Thomas Cooke has argued that social constructions of gender roles have an important place in understanding the outcomes of migration and that scholars of migration should 'investigate how gender role beliefs mediate migration causes and consequences' (2005: 408). Cooke's observations, made in a study of the migration of same-sex couples, have important implications for the study of cross-border marriage migration more generally. The learning of new values and local constructions of an ideal woman and wife affects all the different stages of life that migrant women go through. Once they have come to terms with what is expected of them as wives, they may have to come to terms with what it means to be a mother in the new society. Many new experiences and value-conflict differences, which are faced by all first-time mothers, have cultural dimensions and even within transnational communities, shared values cannot be assumed. At least in transnational communities it is likely that a migrant spouse will be living among people who value the cultural traits they bring with them even if they may not wish to maintain them. Women's behaviour is generally scrutinised more closely than men's, and I note Martin Manalansan's argument that female migrant sexuality is an 'arena for the contestation of tradition, assimilation, and the travails of transnational migration' (2006: 233). This scrutiny constrains the ways in which women can position themselves within families as well as within society more broadly. Attitudes to tradition and to the homeland may also be seen as gendered and Maria Balzani's study of marriages (2006) shows that within the Ahmadi sect, women were more likely to choose a spouse from the UK or Canada than from Pakistan while the opposite was the case for men. She observes: 'British men are more likely to agree to marry a Pakistani wife and British women tend to be more concerned about finding spouses with common local cultural and career aspirations' (Balzani 2006: 353). The assumption being that men tend to opt for more traditional marriage partners than their female counterparts. This may well be the case, but giving too much weight to this argument without more research risks further stigmatising men as resistant to change in gender relationships.

A further challenge to relationships between citizens and non-citizens relates to cultural differences or 'value conflicts' around meanings of marriage and the gendered roles they presuppose. Marriage and intimate relationships reflect our personal *habitus* and our sense of the everyday to such an extent that individuals may not invest much thought into what they expect from such a relationship and how their expectations and assumptions may differ from their partners. Any differences in these assumptions may be seen in sharp relief as partnerships develop. Value conflicts may arise where wives and husbands have different views on gender roles and citizen husbands and their families may expect their wives to adhere to traditional gender roles which their wives may have hoped to have escaped by moving from their country of birth. This may be particularly acute in marriages in which the wife is expected to be a contributor of labour and services to the family as well as to her husband. Gender roles are to a great extent socially defined and research in Taiwan with women in intercultural marriages shows how the husbands' families, and sometimes the marriage brokers, actively instructed women on how to behave and be a good wife (Yu 2006). They were taught how to do housework, cooking and how to manage family life; they were not to have strong opinions and meeting their husband's and children's needs should be their whole life – that is to say, their own needs and aspirations were secondary to those of their Taiwanese family. Taiwanese men, in common with many others marrying across borders, hold certain received opinions about the women they marry – that they will be malleable and easy to control and the husbands may have unrealistic expectations of their behaviour as wives. Taiwanese families are not alone in this, and research in Japan (Ito 2005; Suzuki 2005; Faier 2007, 2008) shows that migrant wives are similarly expected to fit Japanese expectations of gender roles. Research shows women actively claiming respect for their individuality and humanity but having to do this through behaviours, such as duty and care, that meshed with Japanese ideas of proper womanhood and 'wifeliness'.

Jutta Lauth Bacas' study of Greek-German couples in Athens demonstrates how 'cultural differences were instrumental in expressing gender differences and different power claims' and cites Collet and Varro's (2000) argument that couples need to create 'a common everyday family culture' if they are to successfully bridge their cultural differences (Lauth Bacas 2002: 10). Lauth Bacas argues that bi-national marriages have more internal difficulties and conflicts than others but that in successful partnerships, the partners take on the role of gatekeeper to support each other and to acknowledge each other's differences. This role will clearly be easier to achieve when the partners' respective differences are valued and recognised which is not always the case when one partner's culture is seen as more of an embarrassment than a resource or an asset. Roger Ballard has argued, in relation to transnational marriages, that difficulties are 'better understood as the outcome of the micro-politics of interpersonal relationships within the spouses' immediate kinship networks than of the phenomenon of transnational marriage per se' (2004: 1). This important point applies as much to marriages between people who do not share ethnicity as to those who do share it. Dan Rodriguez Garcia's work with bi-national Senegalese/Gambian-Spanish couples argues that problems are often not from any 'clash of civilisation' but 'due more to socio-economic, situational and personal factors than cultural differences' and his work argues against 'culturalist explanations which favour processes of essentialisation' (Rodriguez Garcia 2006: 426). Rodriguez Garcia's evidence 'suggests that social class factors are more important than cultural origins in patterns of endogamy and exogamy, in the dynamics of living together and in the bringing up of children of mixed unions' (ibid.: 403). Ada Engebrigsten (2007) makes a slightly different point by arguing (following Elizabeth Bott's (1957) hypothesis) that close social networks are supportive for couples. Further, she draws on Kapferer's work (1973) that 'cross-linkage between wife's and husband's networks, and investment in the cross-links, are the most important features in order to understand role relationships' (2007: 738). Engebrigsten argues that the shared social investment represented by the interconnected networks that characterises Tamil marriages in Norway make them more stable than the marriages between Somali migrants whose marriages typically do not unite family and social networks.

Carol Freeman (2005) has described how the different cultural assumptions that may have drawn couples together at first, play out in the longer term. Freeman's point is that it is caricatures of certain ethnicities and nationalities that often lead people into relationships rather than the reality of those individuals. So the Russian woman who looks for a romantic and faithful American man is as likely to be disappointed as the Korean man who looks for a traditional and obedient village girl from Indonesia. Nicole Constable's case study shows how a marriage failed because the Chinese wife married for freedom and the US-based husband married in the hope of finding a submissive wife (Constable 2005b). The disjuncture between expectation and reality leads to the contradictory stereotypes of women recorded by Kathryn Robinson in Australia where, she argues, 'Filipinas have been constituted ... as meek, docile slaves, oriental beauties with shady pasts, passive and manipulable, but also grasping and predatory using marriage to jump immigration queues' (1996: 53). These examples of value conflicts may represent conflicts of purpose in seeking marriage in the first place but to some extent can be seen as the result of immigration controls that oblige migrants to clothe their desire to travel in different ways that reflect their limited migration options rather than their real desires.

Identity and belonging

Stephen Lubkeman's (2000) research on Mozambican (Machaze) refugees living in South Africa argues that relationships between Machaze refugees and South African citizens only became formalised by marriage contracts once refugees had come to the realisation that their 'temporary' migration had become permanent and that futures should be built in exile rather than back home. This suggests that the making permanent of relationships through marriage may mark a shift in attitude from expectation of life in the natal country to seeing a future in the new one. A positive decision to settle in one country or another may not be as stark a decision as Lubkeman's work suggests as the period of contingency or liminality experienced by many marriage migrants means that many years may pass before an intention to settle permanently becomes institutionalised through citizenship or permanent right to remain. Thus a husband leaving Pakistan to live with his British wife, or a woman from the Philippines marrying her Japanese boyfriend may be making a permanent commitment to family formation and to settlement away from home without having established the assurance of a secure legal status in that country of settlement. Even with the insecurity of contingent immigration status, migrant life may grant a sense of belonging in families and communities but for others, life as migrant means dislocation and isolation. Dan Rodriguez Garcia, for example, records migrants feeling they belong nowhere, neither 'here nor there' (2006: 424) and this sense of liminality, being no longer a member of the community of birth but not yet accepted within the country of migration, is a typical one. Yang and Wang's work (2003) refers to the physical adjustment which migrants have to make when they arrive in Taiwan. These problems, relating to food and customs, are likely to be shared by many marriage migrants coming to a country that they have no previous experience of, where they may be unfamiliar with the language and have few contacts, other than their husbands, to call on for support. Especially in cases in which marriage migrants' first experience of a country is after they are already married, their first weeks, months and possibly years may be marked by loneliness and isolation.

This sense of isolation may be exacerbated when marrying traditionally means marrying into another family. In the cases Katherine

Charsley (2005) describes, husbands are marrying into their wife's families, against tradition, and are unprepared for losing status, place in the family and the capacity to control how the family operates. Charsley records the heartache this may cause and how, even within ethnic communities, migrants may feel out of place and isolated. Anxiety about children growing up in a different culture is commonly recorded in the literature and Stephen Lubkeman's research participants expressed concern that their children, considered as Machaze children but born in South Africa may be "morally corrupted' by South Africa (2000: 61). This concern is manifested in encouraging children to relate to other Machazians and in fathers trying to influence children's marriage choices. Dan Rodriguez Garcia records the fears of Sengalese and Gambian fathers that their children, and especially their daughters, would (and were) growing up too Westernised in Catalonia. While the families wanted their children to grow up as Muslims, they found it difficult in a country in which 'Islam is looked down on socially'. One solution to this dilemma is described by Shuko Takeshita who describes how families living in Japan with Pakistani fathers and Japanese mothers left Japan for the Gulf States where they felt it would be easier to raise Muslim children (Takeshita 2007).

Studies also point to the importance of the mother in raising children and in setting the family's cultural tone. Rodriguez Garcia, for example, records fathers attributing the loss of the children's Senegalese or Gambian culture to the fact that the children spent more time with their Spanish mother (2006: 422). These fathers may hope to ultimately return to Africa, but the benefits of a Spanish education and of public health care, for example, keep them in Spain. As we have seen throughout this book, the 'normal' pattern in marriage migration globally (increasingly an imagined one) is for the mother to be the migrant party. Given that mothers are often assumed to be the nurturers and the maintainers of culture, it may be assumed that children growing up with migrant mothers will be more culturally in tune with their migrant parent's country of origin. This may well be the case with children growing up in transnational communities where the mother's culture is reinforced by family and community but where the culture of migrant wives is devalued, as it is in much of East Asia and beyond, it is unlikely that mothers will be able to bring their children up to be fluent in their language or in their culture. At present, there is little research on the issue of how children of mixed heritage relate to their heritage or on how that heritage *could* be passed on and valued. In my view, there is an urgent need for study as research that touches on this area generally indicates that women from stigmatised groups find it extremely difficult to pass on positive views of their culture with the result that children may grow up ashamed of their mother and of their heritage. Clearly, national attitudes to other countries and to the valuing of difference have a major effect on how mixed heritage is viewed. Some countries, for example Taiwan, have launched programmes to support multiculturalism and to counter the dominant nationalism based on ethnicity, but while a welcome beginning, 'foreign wives' in Taiwan are still under-valued.

Identity conflict and cultural misunderstandings are always likely to be issues in cross-cultural relationships but these conflicts also occur in marriages which are ostensibly intra-cultural. Carol Freeman's work with Chongsonjok women (women of Korean ethnicity from China) found that despite the Korean myth of cultural homogeneity that makes then attractive as wives for South Korean men, they don't fit in as expected. 'Readily identified by their style of dress, their patterns of speech and pronunciation, and their unfamiliarity with Korean linguistic and behavioural codes of politeness, Chongsonjok are for the most part unable to "pass" for South Koreans' (2005: 95). Their 'failure' to integrate within Korean society and their 'cultural incompetence', Freeman argues, are not forgiven as might be the case with people perceived as truly foreign. Again, the culture of migrants may simply become a problem recognised in countries where the population is relatively homogenous and where migrants have not established communities or a presence, except as a stereotype, in the national imagination. Gabrielle Fortune, found 'war brides' migrating to New Zealand after the Second World War experienced 'a lack of interest in their families and past affiliations' and as a result 'many war brides felt stripped of their identity' (2006: 588). Fortune's description of the war brides' experience could equally apply to many of today's marriage migrants: 'Being cut off from their own families and, more importantly, facing a life where the losses inherent in this separation were unaffirmed and unacknowledged, were common war bride experiences' (ibid.: 595).

Belonging, citizenship and the integration of migrant spouses

The literature relating to the integration of migrants is vast and it is beyond the scope of this book to summarise it. Within the literature, however, are studies that focus on integration defined as a sense of

'belonging' within the nation-state which adopt an informal definition of citizenship. Belonging, it is argued, offers individuals and groups
many of the benefits of citizenship, for example, the ability to participate in the life of the nation as an employee or a community member
even when citizen status has not been formally granted. The study of
citizenship

> recognises that the specific location of people in society – their
> group's membership and categorical definition by gender, nationality
> religion, ethnicity, 'race', ability, age or life-cycle stage – mediates the
> construction of their citizenship as 'different' and thus determines
> their access to entitlements and their capacity to exercise agency.
>   (Werbner and Yuval-Davis 1999: 5)

Cross-border marriage migrants may claim constructions of citizenship for themselves that are different from those imposed upon them
from society at large. Some transnational groups may be satisfied with
membership and participation within their own communities but other
migrants may want to participate alongside majority communities but
find their opportunities to do so are limited. The notion of belonging has been explored by Nira Yuval-Davis, Floya Anthias and Eleonore
Kofman who characterise it as a 'thick' form of citizenship that includes
emotional connections to place and community. These authors remind
us of the 'differential positionings from which belongings are imagined and narrated, in terms of gender, class, stage in the life cycle, etc.,
even in relation to the same community and to the same boundaries
and borders' (Yuval-Davis *et al.* 2002: 521). Imaginaries and narratives
of belonging, as they relate to gender, class and life-cycle are always
contested and have shifting boundaries and borders. By this definition,
belonging incorporates formal and informal citizenships (ibid.: 527),
and is fostered by a goal of inclusivity that is not always reflected in
policy. Linda Bosniak argues that 'the current fetishization and devaluation of the figure of the alien' (1998: 31) have fed into conceptions
of the national project that encourage the exclusion of aliens from citizenship despite a rhetoric of integration and inclusivity. Migrants are
fetishized and devalued in most countries of the world and migrant
families and migrants within families consequently suffer by having to
negotiate their own sense of belonging within the narrow constraints
imposed upon them.

Migrant women who are mothers make an interesting case study to
demonstrate how belonging and citizenship may play out in real life

and several studies describe and discuss how mothers may have to adapt their behaviour to fit the norms imposed upon them by society. I have already discussed how migrant mothers may not be able to employ their own cultural resources in the bringing up of children, where passing on their language and culture may be disapproved of and migrants mothers face criticism of their parenting skills. In Taiwan and Japan, migrant wives are accused of being unable to support their children at school and are blamed for the poor performance of their children (Yang and Wang 2003; Ito 2005). It is sometimes assumed that the children of migrant mothers do not do well at school but the data these assumptions are based on, is poor and may reflect prejudice in their collection. That said, the contested and devalued role of migrant mothers in the education of their children impacts upon the achievement of children. The problems of women who can't read the local language, for example, cause 'difficulties establishing communication with school teachers which creates much psychological pressure and frustration' (Ito 2005: 64–5). Racism within the school system is also likely to have an impact on the attainment of the children of migrants, but this has been less scrutinised than the capacity of migrant mothers to support their children. Ruri Ito recognises that schools have a significant role to play in the integration of migrant families but she argues that instead of challenging stereotypes, the school system 'participates in creating negative images of Filipino women migrants' (ibid.: 65). Young Rae Oum similarly recognises the role of racism in South Korea where the racially mixed children from working-class areas, including the mixed race US 'camptown' children, suffer more racism that middle-class children of mixed-heritage (Oum 2003: 436). For social integration to occur, there has to be more than a willingness of the migrant to fit in and participate. Institutions and policies have a part to play and the above discussion shows how the settled population may resist the participation of certain foreigners through a refusal to adapt to their needs. Ada Engebrigsten's work in Norway describes how economic integration is sometimes used to differentiate between 'good' and 'failed' migrants. Engebrigtsen argues that, in Norway, Tamils are seen as 'good' migrants while Somalis are considered to have 'failed' based on a judgement of their willingness to adapt to Norwegian society, and on perceptions of their cultural norms, kinship and gender practices (2007: 728). A contrary example comes from Pei-Chia Lan's work that describes how wives from mainland China who marry citizens of Taiwan are condemned for being 'too assimilatable' (Lan 2008: 838) and of representing a 'fifth column' whose loyalty and nationalism in Taiwan are doubted. These examples, of migrants being condemned for being both too different or too much the same demonstrate effectively how attitudes to foreigners differ from state to state and can foil the best attempts of migrants to fit into their new homes.

Problems and marriage breakdown

It is important to recognise that cross-border marriages do have a high rate of breakdown, which is hardly surprising given the pressure placed upon them through the social scrutiny they are subject to as well as because of problems that are intrinsic to each individual relationship. The following section will attempt to consider some of the challenges marriages between citizens and non-citizens are likely to face while trying to avoid stigmatising them further.

Within transnational communities, cross-border marriages are recognised as being 'risky' (Shaw and Charsley 2006; Charsley 2007) and that the process of arranging marriage can be understood as a way of reducing or at least managing those risks. Alison Shaw and Katherine Charsley (2006: 406) discuss the risks inherent in separation from natal family and there are many other risks too – of British women becoming 'immigration widows' (Menski 2002) if husbands are refused visas and unable to join their brides, of partners who are only interested in marriage for the purpose of migrating or of husbands only interested in a bride's dowry. Marriage within family, therefore can be seen as offering protection from at least some these risks (Charsley 2006: 1119–20). In a Chinese context, Min and Eades have made a similar observation – that 'marriages with outside wives are cheap but risky' (1995: 867), indicating that the involvement of family, or at least of locally known people, helps guarantee the success of a match. Kalpagam's work on marriages within Brahman Tamil communities between the US and India carry the risk of abandonment for the Indian women who marry an American-based Tamil but who never get invited to the US. She writes: 'Most of my informants were aware of the risks of American *varan* marriages, but were willing to take them' (2005: 206).

Chapter 5 discussed issues of dependence experienced by marriage migrants before they are able to gain independent rights and this period of dependency can cause great problems for marriage migrants. They may find themselves heavily reliant on their husbands – financially as well as socially, especially if they do not have access to sources of social support or good language and communication skills. David Griffiths has suggested that a further source of friction experienced in many cross-border marriages comes from their frequent dependence on welfare payments which creates problems in marriages and which can upset traditional gender roles. Griffiths quotes a Somali man who argues:

> One marriage is from social security, one marriage is from the women and the man. The important one is from the social security, because the marriage for the man is less respectable because he doesn't provide anything for her or the children…. So she's happy to marry to social security. And if you have a problem with your wife you will lose your benefit.
>
> (Griffiths 2002: 110)

This argument demonstrates how heavily enmeshed the private world of marriages can be with public policy perceived here as enforcing, in this case, British social norms. Ada Engebrigsten sees the relationship between welfare support and marriage slightly differently arguing that Somali women who separate from their husbands exchange dependence on a husband for dependence on welfare (2007: 742).

Within the EU, if marriage breaks down, the non-citizen partner may be obliged to return home with their children as they may not have established a right to state support and may not be able to manage to stay in the EU if they are left with neither financial support from a partner nor the support of a social network (Ackers 2004: 381–3). In these cases, a desire to be close to family may cause migration post-marriage breakdown. Ruri Ito (2005) describes the difficulties migrant mothers may face when their marriages fail and when children are born out of marriage. Ito's work demonstrates the importance of being recognised as having been a good wife if migrant women are to gain custody or at least access to their children (Ito 2005: 61). As right of residence is often connected to the success of marriages and custody rights in many countries are automatically granted to the father (especially if he is a citizen, and she is not), women may have extreme difficulties in remaining with their children after their marriages fail. This fact, added to their low social status in many countries, and the general view that they are poor mothers, can make staying with their children very difficult. Research from Taiwan and Japan shows how women may lose access to their children and may have to leave the country without them. There is also evidence that children from failed relationships may have to leave their country of birth and return with their mothers, losing contact with their fathers and in some cases becoming effectively stateless having neither the citizenship of their father *or* mother. Currently there are said to be about 3,000 children in Vietnam who were born in Taiwan but were brought back to their mother's country because their fathers did not want custody of them after divorce – the majority of them are girls (pers. comm., Hong Xoan Nguyen Thi). These children have been marginalized in both Taiwan and Vietnam and their rights to citizenship have not been recognised by either country.

When children are born in cross-border marriages, the problems for women in violent relationships increase and there are nearly always serious social sanctions against women who leave their husbands and children even when their personal safety is compromised. If women do manage to leave abusive husbands, these sanctions may affect migrant women particularly hard given their marginal position without family or community to support them and argue their case. Leaving the matrimonial home, may be a way wives can shame some husbands into treating them better (Faier 2008) but in violent situations, leaving home means women have to leave their children behind (in Taiwan, for example, refuges rarely take children as well as women, Yu 2006). Fleeing a violent relationship may leave them vulnerable and without rights of residence. In some circumstances, cross-border marriage migrants may have not only lost their right to reside in the country they had intended to live permanently, but also may have compromised their chances of re-integration into their country of origin and they may be forced to return to their country of origin to face shame and ignominy. Khatidja Chantler's work on services for minoritized women in the UK who are leaving violent partnerships argues that these services often privilege the achievement of public 'justice', that is identifying and punishing criminal actions over the provision of private 'care' for the victims of abuse (2006). Her argument does not excuse violence in any way but argues instead that appropriate care must recognize the interdependence of some communities as well as the independence of individuals. The point of comparison with Chantler's work and the experience of marriage migrants in other parts of the world is that this concern for 'justice' has little to do with the rights of the victim of the abuse. In Chantler's case, women are expected to cooperate in the public punishment of their abusive partners – something they may not wish to do because of the damage it will do to their family and community. In the cases described in Taiwan and Japan, migrant women who may have suffered abuse at the hands of their husbands are being punished further by been forced to return home and possibly by losing their children too. Such public 'justice' is not justice for the women concerned whose original abuse is compounded.

Conclusion

This chapter has attempted to describe and discuss some of the challenges that cross-border marriage migrants face once in countries of settlement. I have included a discussion of why migrants might wish to leave home to set up families abroad arguing that their situation in countries of origin and their imaginations of countries of migration have an important bearing on how they will find a partner and what expectations they might have of that partner. I have argued that migrants may enter into marriage contracts for very different reasons and while some marriages are undoubtedly the product of coercion and force, the majority are the product of positive decisions to further individual or community goals. The motivations that spouses have in establishing formal partnership may be very different, however, and I have argued that the migrant and the non-migrant citizen partner may hold very different views of marriage and enter into marriage with widely divergent expectations. These differences may only become obvious as the relationship develops but may cause problems for the partnership. These possible mismatches can include attitudes to continuing relationships with the migrant partner's home and natal family and, if there are children involved, a contested relationship between the spouses' homes and cultures may result in difficulties balancing caring and other commitments. Research shows that creative solutions to balancing responsibilities can be found but that, especially in countries where the homelands of the migrant partners are stereotyped as backward or inferior, maintaining contact and sense of pride can be difficult.

Sustaining a successful and happy marriage is a hard job at the best of times and cross-border marriages may be even harder to maintain than marriages between citizens – not least as they have to overcome public scrutiny and policies that enforce dependency and unequal relationships on the partners. Families, we have seen, adopt creative strategies to deal with these pressures but their capacity to self-direct and to find ways of living that are satisfactory and logical according to their own priorities are reduced by the structures of policy, responsibility and environment they must live within.

11
Conclusion and a Proposed Research Agenda

Introduction

In this final chapter, I will round up my argument and propose four themes that have come out of this study. First, I argue for the value of analysis of the balance of structure and agency in the lives of cross-border marriage migrants. Such an analysis reveals how the lives of many migrants are constrained by the structures of society, culture, family, gender roles and policy but emphasises that within those structures there remains space for individual agency. Second, comparing marriage migration globally is an important, if complex, task but one that places marriage migration within the human context of a search for love, companionship, family life and intimacy which can be lost when marriages in distinct communities or parts of the world are studied in isolation. Third, I argue that this study has implications for the study of transnationalism as it has placed marriage at the heart of transnational communities and networks and shown how marriage can play a role in all stages of transnational projects – from the first connections between communities to the maintenance of closely interwoven networks based on kinship or cultural commonality. Finally, this study has important implications for the study of gender – on gender roles and on how gendered assumptions affect the processes of migration. I have argued that attitudes to migrants and marriage migration across the globe are generally negative and that these attitudes are highly gendered and have undermined the capacity of women migrants to act as autonomous agents even when policy has been enacted ostensibly to promote their rights. This concluding chapter will explore these four themes further and concludes with recommendations for future research on cross-border marriage migration.

Structure and agency

I have argued that migration policy and some studies of marriage migration have reduced families and ethnic groups to ethnic and cultural stereotypes. Cultures and traditions are sometimes reduced to caricatures and migrants reduced to cultural proxies, presumed to be incapable of change or of self-reflection. This may be the result of the sloppy thinking and the 'cognitive miserliness' described by Jacqueline Bhabha (2007: 17) or of more sinister depictions of migrants as 'others' and as the malevolent strangers described in Irene Gedalof's work (2007). Many societies stereotype according to ethnic caricature and some societies have used their fascination with cultural and ethnic difference, to judge communities on the basis of behaviours seen as rigid markers of that difference. I have tried to challenge culturalist discourses that see social structures such as family, community and culture as having the overriding role in determining behaviour and have argued against the reduction of women and men to cultural ciphers. Such reductive thinking undermines the agency of women and men, negating their capacity to act while discriminatory policies may further limit their choices. The view of migrant women and men as merely victims or perpetrators of traditionally sanctioned abuse is, in my view, a form of violence in itself, but, worse still, permits and perpetuates actual violence within families and communities *and* by the state.

Throughout this book I have attempted to show how national and international migration regimes impose a powerful structure on cross-border marriage migrants. I have tried not to imply that the structure imposed by policy is the only determining factor in marriage nor that it is necessarily more significant than the structure imposed by family, tradition, community, culture, socio-economic or political position. I focus on policy here because its aim is often stated as being to protect the individual or the individual within the state. This often runs counter to the actual consequences of policy that we have seen leaves migrants, and especially women migrants, vulnerable to abuse and tied into relationships that are abusive and have gone wrong. Policy, I argue, should promote the agency of individuals but, as is often the case for policy in relation to migration, it often makes the weak weaker and limits their capacity to act with agency. The examples of agency displayed by migrants, and especially women migrants, in this book often oblige them to take significant risks that may be of dubious legality. Whether their activities can be called strategies is another issue that I have commented upon as the relative powerlessness of migrants shapes their actions as *tactics* (by the definition established by De Certeau 1984), rather than *strategy*. Migrants may find themselves criminalised for their attempts at acting with agency and the resulting stereotypes and their stigmatisation, as I argued in Chapter 5, can lead directly to abuse or at least set a scene in which abuse and actual violence is more likely. Policy structures isolate migrants and when violence occurs, their isolation and vulnerability mean that violence is likely to be severe and that its victims will have less recourse to redress or support.

I have argued throughout that cross-border marriage migrants face limits on their independent action from power structures external to them (in the shape of international migration regimes, for example) and internal to then – through their own personal *habitus* and the controls placed on their behaviour by socialisation, tradition, obligation, etc. Despite these limiting structures, migrants do cross borders and do form lasting intimate partnerships in their countries of settlement. Research discussed throughout this book shows how the drive of many to establish families and to carry out their caring obligations encourages them to take risks and act decisively to further their goals. In many of the examples described, we have seen it is the very complexity of structures that allows migrants to find a path through constraining factors. Through creativity and ingenuity, ways can be found to negotiate a border or to convince a sceptical family that a certain marriage is appropriate and in the best interests of all. Throughout migration studies the agency of migrants tends to go unrecognised and unseen as the low key and uncelebrated actions of successful migrants stay below the radar of many commentators. It takes close and careful studies involving migrants as research participants to identify possibly covert strategies and to tease out the important part of a narrative from more public expositions of motivation and process.

Part of the aim of this book has been to identify examples of cross-border marriage migrants' agency for the purpose of understanding how agency is promoted and how it is constrained. Structures can both promote and constrain agency and supportive social ties can act to support the self-determination of community members. Familial structures can also undermine capacity for independent action and the balance between community support and community control may be a fine one. What is clear is that agency is best promoted by allowing individuals to make choices that are in their own best interests. This is surely self-evident but in the research reviewed in this book there are many cases when, often a female migrant, sets out to cross a border for the very rational reasons of seeking personal or family betterment but is forced to make risky or dangerous 'choices', such as signing a contract to work as an entertainer or as a domestic worker or to become the wife of someone she knows little about. That women take these actions is surely a sign of their agency and of their determination to change their lives even while it may also be a sign of their powerlessness and lack of choice. The way such risks are perceived by others can also promote or negate agency as migrants who have taken a gamble on a marriage or on migration, may be punished when if it goes wrong. Even when the gamble pays off and settlement and family life are achieved, migrants may be accused of having transgressed social norms and codes of morality. In the cases discussed in this book, the devaluing of the agency of migrants, and especially of female migrants, is a powerful constraint on their agency.

Making a global study of cross-border marriage

Cross-border marriage migration is a highly significant stream of global migration but one that has been under-researched on a global scale. The complexity that such as study entails is no doubt one reason why this has not been attempted. The importance of studying cross-border marriage, however, lies at least in part in what it can tell us about patterns of relationships between the state, its citizens and the family. These relationships are clearly changing across the globe not least because of globalisation; migration for political, social and economic reasons; because of the low fertility rates in many countries; ageing populations and because of geographically dispersed families. Taken together, it is clear that 'From a sociological and anthropological perspective, international marriages can be regarded as a site where these contradictions between state and market are condensed' (Turner 2008: 53). With this in mind, it makes sense to study them at a global level.

The diversity of motivations and avenues for family migration makes global comparisons extremely difficult but studies focused at the local/national level and on specific groups inevitably emphasise the differences in migration patterns rather than the similarity. In can be argued that in some communities, 'migration' as in the crossing of national borders is not so important and as Roger Ballard has argued 'all they [cross-border spouses and their families] are doing is making the same kind of choices, guided by the same kind of priorities as they would have done had they never migrated at all' (2004: 12). Ballard is describing marriage within close transnational communities for whom re-location across borders may, in social and emotional terms, be a form of 'coming home' and no more significant than moving within a country's borders. For other groups, crossing the border is all important; it may be the sole motivation for the marriage and seen as something that will provide safety and security to more than just the marriage migrants. In both cases, however, the power of the nation-state can intervene in these personal and community projects and when seen from the perspective of international migration regimes, these marriages are categorised as one and the same.

Chapter 4 of this book showed the great variety possible in the manifestations of cross-border marriage migration and how the topic has already been studied from many disciplinary angles. Given that the institution of marriage and intimate relationships are fundamental to the organisation of so much human activity, it is unsurprising that marriage has been frequently studied – but possibly surprising that it has not been studied more. In the field of migration studies, forms of family migration have been far less closely examined than economic or forced migration for example. This is despite the common consensus that family migration – migration for family formation or reunification – is the most common motivation for crossing borders globally. The explanation for this, I believe, is that family and cross-border marriage migration has been subsumed within the discussion of other forms of migration and is only now becoming recognised as a distinct form of migration. Marriage migration within transnational communities was commonly viewed as the result of transnational logics rather than as itself being a driver of those logics. Marriage between culturally distinct groups is often seen as a mechanism for crossing borders and as a proxy for labour migration rather than as a goal and a motivation on its own account. These two marriage forms, discussed here through examples of marriages within South Asian communities (Chapter 6) and the migration of women to East Asian countries (Chapter 7), have been studied by researchers that have rarely shared insights. This is despite the many similarities that these marriages have when investigated as examples of human relationships and seen as motivated by human desires for companionship and security. Of course, these marriages are also entered into for many other reasons, but I argue that comparison reveals them to have far more in common than has so far been recognised in research. Whatever their divergence in the process of marriage contract and arrangement, these partnerships – the one group contracted within ethnic communities and the other group contracted between ethnic or cultural groups, take place within similarly structured spaces and result in experiences of separation and change. Both types of marriage migration result in migrants crossing borders of social and cultural familiarity and in starting lives that, while offering many potential opportunities, may present great challenges. Thus in marriages within community as much as in marriages between community, the agency of migrants is compromised by the structure of the immigration regimes they enter.

A key question to come out of this book's discussion of cross-border marriage migration is the degree to which marriage across borders represents a change in marriage patterns. Cross-border marriage, to the extent we see it in the twenty-first century, seems to be a new phenomenon – albeit one that has strong echoes with the migration of spouses who followed pioneering migrants in earlier times. Many people in the developed and the developing world look across the world to find intimate partners where previously they might only have looked in their immediate locality or in areas where they had family or other connections. Now, in a globalised world, many people see this 'local' area as one than crosses borders so it can be argued that marriage patterns are simply responding to the global reach of personal connections and opportunities. In short, marriage and family formation are the same as they ever were but the choice of partner is greater as is the opportunity available to those with assets that make them attractive in globalised marriage markets. In these circumstances, the study of marriage patterns should be less concerned with where intimate partners are, where they live and where they were born, but with how they are *connected*. If this is the case, and it is certainly my view that it is, then it is time policy-makers and opinion formers stopped treating marriage migrants as an aberrant group and accepted that their marriage choices are comparable to any other marriages which, as we know, have varied outcomes for the partners and which can be objectively judged as more or less equal.

Cross-border marriage migration challenges notions of what the institution of marriage is and what represents a good or a less good marriage. The explanations for marriage choices proposed by John Eekelaar and Mavis Maclean (2004) – for pragmatic, conventional and internal reasons – are highly dependent on the upbringing and experience of the partners and differ between social classes and ethnic and cultural groups. These categories can be used to explain marriage choices across borders and are useful in thinking about the marriages described in this book. In their view, 'marriage is a drama of mutual reinforcement of obligation' (Eekelaar and Maclean 2004: 534, quoting Fitzgibbon 2002) and it is hoped that this book has caught some of the drama in the stories of cross-border marriages cited as well as illuminated how the notion of obligation may be negotiated and reinforced by structures such as family, community and social and immigration policy. Just as any change in the life course is regularly assessed and re-assessed, the reasons why any-one marries are understood differently at different times and in different circumstances. The balance of Eekelaar and Maclean's three categories changes throughout a marriage and this observation applies in relation to marriages made across borders and the re-assessment of motivations for marriage may be more significant when marriages are in some way deemed to be controversial or outside the norm. In the case of cross-border marriage migrants, individual marriage choices may be very well supported inside the family and community but may be incomprehensible to the wider society, who, as we have seen, may brand them as forced, abusive or based on economic or other forms of self-interest rather than on love. When these marriages hit troubled times, they may well be reinterpreted as having been mistakes or 'forced' from the start. Add to this the power of immigration regimes which can have a marriage dissolved and an unwanted spouse removed and we can imagine how changing interpretations of how marriages came about has serious consequences (I am indebted, again, to Katharine Charsley for this insight in relation to the re-classification of marriages as 'forced'). I argue that studying marriage migration in all its guises demonstrates how the status of *migrant* affects all human relationships and puts unnecessary and unwarranted pressure on those relationships.

Is transnationalism the final destination for cross-border marriage migration?

I argue that truly transnational community links are developing in a haphazard way across the world. We see strong transnational communities in many parts of the world supported and maintained by cross-border marriage within established communities and their communities of 'home'. Transnational communities linked to South Asian countries (discussed in Chapter 6) can be found across the developed world and in many countries of the Global South. Such communities have been able to carve out economic and social niches for themselves and cross-border marriage has undoubtedly been highly significant in maintaining cultural identities and in supporting and renewing reciprocal relationships with the places they may call 'home' – as well as with transnational communities in other countries of settlement. A key question raised in the book is whether the cross-border marriages described in East Asia (in Chapter 7) will lead to the development of similar transnational structures linking, for example, Taiwan and areas in the Mekong Delta of Vietnam or Japan with parts of the Philippines.

I argue that transnational communities *will* develop in these countries and that these marriages will play a role in their development. That stated, I argue that families and communities may move towards a transnational consciousness in quite different ways to the ways we have seen in ethnically based communities. I suggest that transnational consciousnesses may, at least in the first generation, be quite one-sided and be driven by the migrant partner in the marriage more than the citizen partner.

Undoubtedly transnational links already exist between the countries of origin of migrant spouses and their countries of settlement (and these have been discussed in Chapter 7) but these are of a very different nature to the kin and community-based links explored in Chapter 6. Cross-border marriage migration in East Asia is a new phenomenon; it has not been in existence long enough for multi-generation communities to develop and importantly, the destination countries (for example, Japan, South Korea and Taiwan) have traditionally not seen themselves as countries of migration. The notion of ethnic (and racial) diversity is generally underdeveloped in the national psyche of these countries which tend to link their national ideologies to the dominant ethnic group. South Asian migrants have migrated to countries that have adopted a national ideology of multiculturalism (for example, the UK, Canada and Australia) which fostered, or at least permitted, transnational communities. In other countries where transnational South Asian communities have grown up (for example, in some African countries), migrant communities have been tolerated, but largely seen as separate from local populations. Their maintenance of close links to other countries where their families and communities were living may in itself be seen as a strategy to ensure a safe haven if 'tolerance' changes to hostility. In East Asia, the initial, pioneer migrants are female, in contrast to the male pioneer migrants of the South Asian diaspora, and while many South Asian migrants began by marrying into the local population, as the numbers of South Asian migrants grew, they sought wives from their home countries. The migration of female cross-border marriage migrants to East Asian countries has already encouraged their female family and social network members to join them and it is conceivable that continuing migration, linked to these first pioneers, could lead to the development of transnational communities such as those seen elsewhere. I am thinking here of how what are now large communities originated from just a few pioneer migrants (see Shaw 1994, for an example of how the Pakistani community in Oxford can be linked back to a few migrants) and how in parts of rural Thailand there are villages

known as 'German' and 'Swiss' villages because of the numbers of marriages between local women and men from those countries (Tosakul
Boonmathya 2006). Up until now, the migration of other women, family or friends, who migrate to marry contacts of the earlier migrants,
has led to supportive networks that have social and economic benefits.
While this may create a transnational space of sorts, it seems unlikely
that Vietnamese, Indonesian or Philippine transnational communities
will grow up in countries of East Asia. Evidence from East Asian studies indicates that the cross-border marriage migrants are not able to
pass their cultures, or even their languages, on to their children and
that, in some cases, they are not able to express their own traditions
freely. This is, of course, related to their position of relative powerlessness, as both women and migrants, but also relates to the lack of
recognition given to their cultural difference, so often stereotyped and
stigmatised but rarely valued. This experience, however, may be close
to the experience of the first South Asian migrants in Western countries and that, as we have seen, has changed. That change started for
migrants in the West when they gained formal citizenship and greater
economic, social and cultural capital. A further important change, I
argue, was the maturation of their community through their children,
who as citizens and 'natives' of their country of birth assumed and
demanded that their cultural heritage be recognised and valued. If the
children of marriage migrants in East Asia grow up demanding recognition of their dual heritage, then, I argue, transnational consciousnesses
and communities may well develop as they have in other parts of the
world.

As well as considering cross-border marriage migration in transnational, non-transnational or incipiently transnational groups, I have
also considered cross-border marriage migration in relation to forced
migration. I have included this discussion as I argue forced migration
has distinct impacts on how marriage is seen by communities and by
individuals. To date, little research has been carried out on marriage
in these communities but I argue that what there is indicates marriage
being used as both a transnational strategy and a non-transnational,
individualistic strategy to make ties and establish a family in countries
of settlement. I argue that marriage, for many refugees, represents a commitment to the country of settlement and a desire to confirm their status
in that country. For other refugees, marriage represents a reaffirmation
of loyalty and identity with the country of origin and that by marrying
in ways that reflect culture and tradition, exiles can reassert their place
within that community.

Implications for the study of gender

Any analysis of migration needs to include a gender dimension as a fundamental organising element. Spoken and unspoken attitudes to the capabilities of women and men are at the heart of how communities and societies behave, and gendered social roles are all the more powerful as they so often go unrecognised and unchallenged. Gender norms affect societies' expectations of their members as well as the aspirations and expectations of individuals. Just as in any other human activity, gendered attitudes are a powerful force, shaping migratory patterns and options, and the way women and men migrate is shaped by state policies reflecting gendered assumptions and by individuals and families acting in normative ways. It remains true that many studies of 'gender' are in fact studies of women – who, as the 'other' and the sex divergent from the male norm, become the focus of scrutiny. Truly gendered studies need to learn from the experience of both men and women as both sexes have their life choices limited by how they are perceived in relation to idealised conceptions of 'female' or 'male'. Policies promoting labour migration in much of the world are overtly gendered with male migrants being funnelled down certain routes, as construction workers, for example, and women directed in other ways, towards domestic or care work. Migration routes can, therefore, maintain the gendered status quo but yet allow migrants to enter environments where their gendered roles may not be as constrained as they were in their country of origin. Migration thus may confirm gender roles while simultaneously opening up opportunity for new gendered subjectivities. Marriage migration provides a complex field to study gender relationships as norms are challenged and reaffirmed through the experience of migration.

Marriage migration on a global scale provides an example of migration that is predominately female. Migrants who travel for marriage most often are female but it is not always clear whether women are the initiators of migration, whether they are obliged to or see little alternative to migrate, or whether they are active agents in the whole process of migration from the genesis of the idea to negotiating access to a country of settlement. Family and marriage migration provides many women with a means to travel but women may play a greater or lesser role in shaping that travel. Doreen Massey's 'power geometry' (1994) – whereby the power to decide to migrate or to stay may be externally imposed – can be seen operating in many of the examples discussed in this book and power geometries always have a gendered element. Gender is closely connected to social location and the poverty of many migrants is, in my view, closely related to the gendered restrictions they face. Rich and privileged women will always have more rights and options than poor and marginalised women even when they share similar cultural backgrounds. Migration adds a further dimension to how an individual's gender is perceived and may raise or undermine a person's social standing over and above what might be expected based on consideration of their gender alone. Gendered attributes, like cultural ones, are not immutable and women and men can break free from the limitations placed upon them by their social location. Migration may provide the stimulus to make such a break but may also just reinscribe or create new gendered norms in a different setting.

Recommendations and suggestions for further research

Chapter 4 attempted to present a summary of how cross-border marriage migration has been conceptualised in the academic literature. In my opinion, there are many gaps in the research on the subject, which is not surprising given the breadth of the field. It is only comparatively recently that nuanced and person-centred research has been carried out with cross-border marriage migrants themselves. This research, however, has yet to influence policy and practice to any great extent, and current policy, in my opinion, is still based upon stereotypical images of marriage migrants uninformed by research findings. This same observation could be levelled against migration policy and services for migrants in general. Policy and practice have developed under the assumption that public opinion is anti-migration and anti-migrant and as a result is driven by perceived political imperatives to control migration and to limit their rights. Whether public opinion is really as reactionary and as negative towards migrants is another question and I would argue that an informed public with a better understanding of the personal circumstances and experiences of migrants would be more sympathetic than politicians and policy-makers may assume. The research cited in this book brings into focus the lived realities of marriage migration and humanises a group of marginalised people, most often women, who possess agency and who are far from merely the victims of circumstance or tradition they are often assumed to be.

The issue of gender in studies of cross-border marriage migration remains under-developed and there is still a focus on heterosexual women that excludes men and gay and lesbian migrants. Research into the experience of gay and lesbian people as marriage migrants is an area to explore that at present features only in the studies of researchers within the relatively new field of sexual migration (Carrillo 2004; Cooke 2005; Manalansan IV 2006; Simmons 2008). At a global level, cross-border marriage generally results in women travelling across borders but, as we have seen, in some communities, equal numbers of men cross borders as spouses and the presumption of women as the archetypal marriage migrant may reflect cultural assumptions more than reality. If a rounded and gender-sensitive appreciation of marriage migration is to be achieved, then the experience of men as migrants and of the male and female partners of marriage migrants deserves the attention of researchers. To date, there has been little research on the outcomes of cross-border marriage on men (exceptions to this being Ballard 2004; Gallo 2006; and Charsley 2007) despite their considerable numbers. By my definition of cross-border marriage migration, significant numbers of men and women become 'transformed' or re-categorised into marriage migrants *after* they have already migrated – and men may be in the majority in this category. Through marrying a citizen partner, migrants may be able to make their migration permanent (or indeed to regularise it) and form family units in their country of migration. In this way male marriage migrants find themselves in dependent positions in relation to their citizen, female spouse necessarily upsetting the gendered power balance in many relationships.

There is also little literature describing the effect of cross-border marriage migration on the children of marriage migrants from previous relationships. There has been little research on children of mixed or dual heritage but much less on children with a 'contested' heritage by which one parent's past and origin are neither celebrated nor even acknowledged. A further potential area for research is among refugees and refugee communities, where the process and shape of migration has been imposed upon them by situations beyond their control. Marriage is a tactic and a strategy employed to escape dangerous situations and to consolidate status in a country of safety. To date, there has been little research carried out among refugee communities that explicitly focuses on the significance of marriage in flight from conflict or persecution and in subsequent attempts to rebuild communities in exile. Many studies of refugee networks and communities (for example, Farah and Mama 1999; Fuglerud 1999; Lubkeman 2000; Williams 2004) have shown that marriage may be both a means of facilitating migration as well as a means of contracting culturally, politically and socially appropriate marriages. Marriage in these studies, however, has only been described in relation to broader strategies employed by refugees, rather than as the focus of the analysis. An exception to this is the work of

Mulki Al-Sharmani who has carried out ethnographic work with Somali women in Egypt and the US and whose work studies the dynamics of transnational marriage more explicitly. I argue that studying marriage in refugee communities could have a significant role in understanding how transnational communities can develop and also how mixed relationships between refugees and members of the citizen population may fare as they negotiate ties to majority and minority communities.

The full diversity and shape of marriage migration are still not yet understood and marriage across borders no doubt takes more forms than have been discussed in this book. So-called 'temporary marriages', or *muta'a*, are common in some parts of the world and occur across borders. Such marriages are the subject of lurid press reports as they often involve vulnerable and powerless young women, in temporary relationships with older more powerful men, but these marriages have not received a great deal of attention from academic researchers. These marriages have been used by Hussein and Manthorpe as an example of how countries of the Arab world may be going through '"nuptiality transition" from one pattern of marriage to another' (2007: 469). There may be significant issues in the contracting of these marriages for the human rights of the women involved but they represent an 'exotic' form of marriage that, while important to study, should be viewed in the context of broader gender and social inequalities and not as an example of a purely cultural phenomenon. That said, Hussein and Manthorpe's notion of 'nuptiality transition' is an important one to investigate as marriage patterns change across the world.

Clearly, there is much research to be done in the field of migration for the purpose of marriage and intimate partnership but as marriage and family formation are situated close to the heart of nations and their component social groupings, research on marriage and marriage-like relationships always needs to take account of the intersectional nature of gender and power relationships. Future research needs to be sensitive to the intersection of gender, race, class, culture, and ethnicity as they are all affected by national and international policies that shape who and how individuals migrate. I argue that these complexities require researchers to study marriage migration in multiple ways that can combine to illuminate this broad field but which share a common focus on the individual situation of the migrant within the multiple structures that limit and shape opportunity. Developing intersectional approaches to the study of cross-border marriage migration must include consideration of the social positioning of marriage migrants, and it is to be hoped that future studies of women migrating for marriage will develop beyond the assumption that they are necessarily economically and socially disadvantaged and will challenge the assumption of their victimhood.

Having argued for an appreciation of the complexity and the intersectional nature of the field, I propose the following two research strategies. First, research that makes broad comparisons of marriage migration across regions focusing on understanding the human processes involved in marriage migration; and, second, further close, qualitative studies on the place of cross-border marriage migration within specific groups. I argue that both research strategies, the broad and the narrow, should include a longitudinal element. This would facilitate studies of the role of marriage in the development of transnational links, networks and communities. In this I share with Levitt and Jaworsky a concern that research 'highlights the *longue durée* and sees contemporary "globalization" as a stage in ongoing historical processes' (2007: 146). Levitt and Jaworsky are writing in reference to the study of transnationalism, arguing that communities have long been transnational in that the crossing of national, social and cultural borders has a long history. So it is with migration for marriage which, I would argue, has had an equally long history – something that has been ignored in many contemporary studies.

It has been noted several times throughout this book that migration for family formation and family reunification is one of the most significant migration streams globally, if not *the* most significant stream. This category of migration includes millions of migrants embraced within the very centre of communities where they become incorporated as members of families as well as new members of wider groups and nation-states. In these cases, the family is assumed to be capable of socialising them into the ways of their new home even while state regulation and policy may continue to classify them as contingent and dependent and as 'less' than citizens. Marriage migration, then, makes a good subject for studies of the modern family, of the institution of the family as well as of the tensions between the private space of the family and the public space of the state. Research making broad comparisons of marriage migration across regions is necessary to develop a better conceptualisation of global patterns of marriage migration – and this is something I hope to have begun in this book but which is far from complete. I have argued that there is a great deal of commonality between marriage migration in different parts of the world even though there are clear regional preferences for marriage within community or culture and between these two. I have argued that these differences are largely the product of the migration history of the countries discussed but that despite history and national ideology, the motivation for marrying across borders may be very similar. Louise Ryan's recent comparison of Irish and Polish women's use of family networks in migration (Ryan 2009) demonstrates how comparisons across ethnic groups can produce valuable insights. Research that took on the challenge of researching the broad category of marriage migration would be well placed to inform our understanding of the place of marriage and the choice of intimate partner in the strategies of migrants and other marginalised groups. It would also increase our knowledge of how the status of migrants, their gender, race, class, ethnicity and culture interact under different migration regimes and national ideologies. This book has drawn heavily on the tension between structure and agency in the lives of migrants and in particular of women migrants. The current situation across the world is that policy and other international and national structures oblige women and men, as migrants, to fit into bureaucratic categories that may or may not suit their needs and experience. These include criminalised categories – such as sex workers, the trafficked and the traffickers as well as categories of wives and/or domestic workers that may be 'chosen' for the lack of better alternatives.

The second stream of research I suggest – that closely focuses on specific groups of marriage migrants – has a solid base to build upon in the abundant studies of specific groups in different countries. I suggest that there is plenty more work to do here but that a greater emphasis on longitudinal studies would be valuable to extend knowledge of the experience of marriage migrants beyond snapshots of their lives. More long-term research would promote understandings of how individuals may or may not develop transnational identities and could investigate how they, and any children, manage their personal and social identities and relationships with both their home countries and their countries of settlement. In addition, such studies could consider the aspirations of individuals in consort with those of their families and communities as well as in opposition to them. Transnationalism, as a popular, contemporary focus of research in migration studies, remains a topic deserving further study, but I hope that in relation to cross-border marriage migration, it will be defined with more rigour than is currently the case. In my view, there are communities that have a very clear logic of transnationalism in which marriage plays a crucial part; there are other 'communities' – or perhaps that should be groups, that demonstrate *elements* of transnationalism; there are still other examples of marriage migration where transnationalism is entirely absent. Transnationalism should not be seen as the inevitable outcome of migration and, I argue, transnationalism is a process rather than a destination. Transnational communities have different shapes and features and may look very different viewed from the perspectives of individuals within communities that are notionally transnational. It is my hope that the continuing study of cross-border marriage migration can contribute to the conceptualisation of transnationalism by demonstrating its variability and subtlety.

Conclusion: towards a new conceptualisation of marriage migration

It is commonly assumed that marriage patterns across the world are changing and that lifelong monogamous partnerships are becoming less common. Western commentators may be secure in their belief that the availability of divorce, remarriage, civil partnership and co-habitation is desirable but this view is not shared by everyone. As has been argued by many of the authorities cited in this book, 'Western attitudes and laws that permit divorce and remarriage are not seen as unambiguously good and liberating' (Constable 2003: 175). Many women and men remain mistrustful of Western marriages and seek the security of more traditional forms. The research reviewed for this book has clearly shown that marriage as an institution is undergoing change and that cross-border marriages are on the fault line where new types of marriages are being negotiated. Marriages that aim for an approximation of Giddens' 'pure relationship' are challenged by both female and male partners who expect and want clear gender roles based on models of the male provider and the female producer and migrant women may look to affluent men to be the strong providers and romantic lovers that they do not find in their home countries. At the same time Western men may look for stereotypically 'amenable' foreign brides who look to them for security and domesticity. We also see women from minority groups seeking men from their community who are either 'unspoiled' by a Western upbringing or who have become freed from traditional assumptions by growing up in the West. These men may themselves prefer a wife from their country of heritage who will take on the roles they have seen their mothers play or they may be looking for a wife with a similar background to theirs. Whatever individuals are looking for in a marriage, it is certain that the drivers of these choices are not located exclusively in countries of migration. The migrant partners, who often take the risks, cross the borders and place themselves at a disadvantage to their citizen partners, are also actors playing key roles in establishing and maintaining those intimate partnerships.

Studying changing marriage patterns on a global scale encourages a more complex view of marriage migration that challenges simplistic views of marriage. Study with a global reach also places the family at the heart of studies of global migration – something that has been recognised as missing in previous studies. As Eleonore Kofman writes: 'It [the family] is not only the catalyst for a new citizenship, but also the crucible of multiple belongings, and should therefore become a priority for European research and policy' (2004: 248). I argue it is not just Europe than can benefit from such studies. A global perspective challenges the privileging of ethnicity and culture as the main markers of commonality that promotes marriage across borders and suggests that ethnicity and tradition may be just another kind of 'structure' along with others that promote or obstruct migration. It has been argued that 'marriage patterns result from both preference and opportunity' (Kalmijn 1998: 397) and as we have seen throughout this book, preference and opportunity are in part provided by circumstance but are also created by the actions of purposive agents. That said, however, I take Lois McNay's important point warning of celebrating women's achievements against oppressive structures. She writes: 'A problem with this work on the submerged practices of women and other marginal groups is that it can too easily slip into a celebration of these experiences as somehow primary or authentic' (2000: 10). A celebration of women's agency, then, needs to recognise that the lives of many women migrants, and of many men too, remain dominated by oppressive structures and global inequalities that constrain their choice and opportunity. That they are not entirely without agency is testament to their creativity and determination, but at the same time the urgent need of migrants for rights and restitution against unequal structures should be recognised. When violence and abuse occur as part of the migration experience, as is the case when migrants are trafficked, migrate through sex work or are forced into marriage, there is a tendency to cast migrants as victims. While of course recognising that they are victims of abuse and have suffered at the hands of others, I consider there is a danger in framing their experience as 'victim'. As well as downplaying their human agency, such a frame encourages the location of violence away from the global systems and inequalities that differentiate between those who can freely travel and those who cannot. Further, it is my view that the victim discourse leads to uncomfortable alliances between those who are genuinely advocating for the well-being of migrants and the victims of violence and those state agents who have 'stolen the clothes' of human rights activists to disguise other objectives such as preventing and controlling migration. While the countries of the world may adopt different policies towards family and cross-border marriage migration, a unifying characteristic is that people seeking to establish or re-establish long-term, intimate partnerships are considered as migrants first and as people second. This is not unique to streams of family migration but is no less an abuse of human rights for that.

Notes

1 Introducing Cross-Border Marriage Migration

1. It should be noted that marriage to a citizen does not automatically grant permanent residency status to a migrant – in the UK, for example, migrants on temporary visas wishing to marry a citizen must return home to apply for a marriage visa and may not switch category (Kofman *et al.* 2008).

2 Gendering Migration

1. IOM in 2005 – the more recent available figures – estimated that women accounted for 49.6 per cent of global migrants: http://www.iom.int/jahia/Jahia/about-migration/facts-and-figures/global-estimates-and-trends#4 (accessed 8 November 2009).
2. Mahler and Pessar (2006) cite examples of women's asylum claims (and other legal matters) being framed in cultural terms even when they had more general grounds for complaint. They cite Connie Oxford's work (2005) that found US immigration officials and lawyers convinced women use their experience of gendered persecution, such as female genital mutilation, as grounds for asylum even when they had sound claims based on their political activism and persecution.
3. In the UK, the most recent statements of migration policy (see http://www.ukba.homeoffice.gov.uk/) promote so-called highly skilled migration and draw heavily on policies already operating in Australia.

3 An Agency Approach to Understanding Marriage Migration

1. A similar point is made by Sallie Yea who warns against romanticised accounts of the acts of resistance made by women migrants (in her case, women from the Philippines working in the entertainment sector in South Korea) which 'overly sentimentalise migrant agency' (2004: 183).

4 An Overview of Global Cross-Border Marriage Migration

1. Hypergamy refers to marriages by which the brides move up social, economic or political scales – as opposed to isogamy, by which marriage is between equals, or hypogamy when social, economic or political status is reduced.

Constable, Nicole (2005a) uses the term 'Global hypergamy' to describe marrying 'up' on a global scale.
2. As of 2007, non-British or EU/EEA citizens wishing to marry in the UK must have residency status or a 'certificate of approval' before they can marry: http://www.ukba.homeoffice.gov.uk/visitingtheuk/gettingmarried/certificate ofapproval/ (UK Borders Agency 2007).

Bibliography

Abdi, C.M. (2007) 'Convergence of Civil War and the Religious Right: Reimagining Somali Women', *Signs: Journal in Women in Culture and Society*, vol. 33, no. 1, pp. 183–207.

Abdulrahim, D. (1993) 'Defining Gender in Second Exile: Palestinian Women in West Berlin', in G. Buijs (ed.) *Migrant Women: Crossing Boundaries and Changing Identities*, Oxford: Berg, pp. 55–82.

Abelman, N. and Kim, H. (2005) 'A Failed Attempt at Transnational Marriage: Maternal Citizenship in a Globalising South Korea', in N. Constable (ed.) *Cross-Border Marriages: Gender and Mobility in Transnational Asia*, Philadelphia, PA: University of Pennsylvania Press, pp. 101–23.

Abraham, M. (2000) 'Isolation as a Form of Marital Violence: The South Asian Immigrant Experience', *Journal of Social Distress and the Homeless*, vol. 9, no. 3, pp. 221–36.

Abraham, M. (2005) 'Domestic Violence and the Indian Diaspora in the United States', *Indian Journal of Gender Studies*, vol. 12, no. 2/3, pp. 427–52.

Ackers, L. (1998) *Shifting Spaces: Women, Citizenship and Migration within the European Union*, Bristol: Polity Press.

Ackers, L. (2004) 'Citizenship, Migration and the Valuation of Care in the European Union', *Journal of Ethnic and Migration Studies*, vol. 30, no. 2, pp. 373–96.

Agustin, L.M. (2003) 'Forget Victimisation: Granting Agency to Migrants', *Development*, vol. 46, no. 3, pp. 30–6.

Agustin, L.M. (2006) 'The Disappearing of a Migration Category: Migrants Who Sell Sex', *Journal of Ethnic and Migration Studies*, vol. 32, no. 1, pp. 29–47.

Agustin, L.M. (2007) *Sex at the Margins: Migration, Labour Markets and the Rescue Industry*, London: Zed Books.

Ahearn, L.M. (2001) 'Language and Agency', *Annual Review of Anthropology*, vol. 30, pp. 109–37.

Al-Rasheed, M. (1993) 'The Meaning of Marriage and Status in Exile: The Experience of Iraqi Women', *Journal of Refugee Studies*, vol. 6, no. 2, pp. 89–104.

Al-Sharmani, M. (2006) 'Living Transnationally: Somali Diasporic Women in Cairo', *International Migration*, vol. 44, no. 1, pp. 55–77.

Alvi, S., Clow, K.A. and DeKeseredy, W. (2008) 'Women, Abuse and Resilience in a Sample of Minority Low-Income Women', *Women's Health and Urban Life*, vol. 7, no. 2, pp. 51–67.

Anderson, B. (1991) *Imagined Communities*, London: Verso.

Anderson, B. (2000) *Doing the Dirty Work?* London: Zed Books.

Anderson, B. (2003) 'Just Another Job? The Commodification of Domestic Labour', in B. Ehrenreich and A.R. Hochschild (eds) *Global Woman: Nannies, Maids and Sex Workers in the New Economy*, London Granta, pp. 104–14.

Anderson, B. (2006) *A Very Private Business: Migration and Domestic Work*, COMPAS, University of Oxford.

Bibliography 225

Anderson, M.J. (1993) 'License to Abuse: The Impact of Conditional Status on Female Immigrants', *Yale Law Journal*, vol. 102, no. 6, pp. 1401–30.

Andrijasevic, R. (2007) 'Problematising Trafficking for the Sex Sector: A Case of Eastern European Women in the EU', in S. van Walsum and T. Spijkerboer (eds) *Women and Immigration Law: New Variations on Classical Feminist Themes*, New York: Routledge Cavendish, pp. 86–103.

Anitha, S. (2008) 'No Recourse, No Support: State Policy and Practice towards South Asian Women Facing Domestic Violence in the UK', *British Journal of Social Work*, vol. 40, no. 2, pp. 462–79.

Anitha, S., Chopra, P., Farouk, W., Haq, Q. and Khan, S. (2008) *Forgotten Women: Domestic Violence, Poverty and South Asian Women with No Recourse to Public Funds*, Manchester: Saheli.

Appadurai, A. (1996) *Modernity at Large: Cultural Dimensions of Globalization*, Minneapolis: University of Minnesota.

Archer, M. (2000) *Being Human: The Problem of Agency*, Cambridge: Cambridge University Press.

Augustine-Adams, K. (2002) ''With Notice of the Consequences': Liberal Political Theory, Marriage, and Women's Citizenship in the United States', *Citizenship Studies*, vol. 6, no. 1, pp. 5–20.

Bailey, A. and Boyle, P. (2004) 'Untying and Retying Family Migration in the New Europe', *Journal of Ethnic and Migration Studies*, vol. 30, no. 2, pp. 229–41.

Baker, P. and McEnery, T. (2005) 'A Corpus-based Approach to Discourses of Refugees and Asylum Seekers in UN and Newspaper Texts', *Journal of Language and Politics*, vol. 4, no. 2, pp. 197–226.

Ballard, R. (2004) *Riste and Ristedari: The Significance of Marriage in the Dynamics of Transnational Kinship Networks*, Manchester: The Centre for Applied South Asian Studies, University of Manchester. Available at: http://www.art.man.ac.uk/CSAS/pages/papers.

Ballard, R. (2006) 'Forced Marriages: Just Who Is Forcing Whom?', University of Roehampton, Conference Proceedings, 12 January. Available at: http://www.casas.org.uk/papers/pdfpapers/forced.pdf.

Balzani, M. (2006) 'Transnational Marriage among Ahmadi Muslims in the UK', *Global Networks*, vol. 6, no. 4, pp. 345–55.

Baumann, G. (1996) *Contesting Culture: Discourses of Identity in Multi-Ethnic London*, Cambridge: Cambridge University Press.

Beck-Gernsheim, E. (2007) 'Transnational Lives, Transnational Marriages: A Review of the Evidence from Migrant Communities in Europe', *Global Networks*, vol. 7, no. 3, pp. 271–88.

Berman, J. (2003) '(Un)Popular Strangers and Crises (Un)Bounded: Discourses of Sex-Trafficking, the European Political Community and the Panicked State of the Modern State', *European Journal of International Relations*, vol. 9, no. 1, pp. 37–86.

Bhabha, J. (1996) 'Embodied Rights: Gendered Persecution, State Sovereignty and Refugees', *Public Culture*, vol. 9, pp. 3–32.

Bhabha, J. (2007) 'Border Rights and Rites: Generalisations, Stereotypes and Gendered Migration', in S. van Walsum and T. Spijkerboer (eds) *Women and Immigration Law: New Variations on Classical Feminist Themes*, New York: Routledge Cavendish, pp. 13–34.

Bosniak, L. (1998) 'The Citizenship of Aliens', *Social Text*, vol. 16, no. 3, pp. 29–35.

Bourdieu, P. (1977) *Outline of Theory and Practice*, Cambridge: Cambridge University Press.

Bourdieu, P. (2001) *Masculine Domination*, Stanford, CA: Stanford University Press.

Bourdieu, P. (2005) 'Habitus', in J. Hillier and E. Rooksby (eds) *Habitus: A Sense of Place*, 2nd edn, Aldershot: Ashgate, pp. 43–9.

Breger, R. (1998) 'Love and the State: Mixed Marriages and the Law in Germany', in R. Breger and R. Hill (eds) *Cross-Cultural Marriage: Identity and Choice*, Oxford: Berg, pp. 129–52.

Breger, R. and Hill, R. (1998) 'Introducing Mixed Marriages', in R. Breger and R. Hill (eds) *Cross-Cultural Marriage: Identity and Choice*, Oxford: Berg, pp. 1–32.

Brennan, D. (2002) 'Selling Sex for Visas: Sex Tourism as a Stepping-stone to International Migration', in B. Ehrenreich and A. Hochschild (eds) *Global Woman: Nannies, Maids and Sex Workers in the New Economy*, London: Granta Books, pp. 154–68.

Brettell, C.B. and Hollifield, J.F. (eds) (2000) *Migration Theory*, New York: Routledge.

Buckley, S. (1997) 'The Foreign Devil Returns: Packaging Sexual Practice and Risk in Contemporary Japan', in L. Manderson and M. Jolly (eds) *Sites of Desire, Economies of Pleasure*, Chicago: University of Chicago Press, pp. 262–91.

Calavita, K. (2006) 'Gender, Migration, and Law: Crossing Borders and Bridging Disciplines', *International Migration Review*, vol. 40, no. 1, pp. 104–32.

Callamard, A. (1999) 'Refugee Women: A Gendered and Political Analysis of the Political Experience', in A. Ager (ed.) *Refugees: Perspectives on the Experience of Forced Migration*, London: Pinter, pp. 196–214.

Carrillo, H. (2004) 'Sexual Migration, Cross-Cultural Sexual Encounters and Sexual Health', *Sexuality Research and Social Policy*, vol. 1, no. 3, pp. 58–70.

Castells, M. (2000) *The Rise of the Network Society*, 2nd edn, Oxford: Blackwell.

Castles, S. (2003) 'Towards a Sociology of Forced Migration and Social Transformation', *Sociology*, vol. 37, no. 1, pp. 13–34.

Castles, S. (2007a) 'The Factors that Make and Unmake Migration Policies', in A. Portes and J. DeWind (eds) *Rethinking Migration: New Theoretical and Empirical Perspectives*, New York: Berghahn Books, pp. 29–61.

Castles, S. (2007b) 'The Migration–Asylum Nexus and Regional Approaches', in S. Kneebone and F. Rawlings-Sanaei (eds) *New Regionalism and Asylum Seekers: Challenges Ahead*, New York: Berghahn Books, pp. 25–42.

Castles, S. and Miller, M.J. (2009) *Age of Migration: International Population Movements in the Modern World*, 4th edn, London: Palgrave Macmillan.

Chant, S. and Radcliffe, S.A. (1992) 'Migration and Development: The Importance of Gender', in S. Chant (ed.) *Gender and Migration in Developing Countries*, London: Belhaven Press, pp. 1–29.

Chantler, K. (2006) 'Independence, Dependency and Interdependence: Struggles and Resistances of Minoritized Women Within and on Leaving Violent Relationships', *feminist review*, vol. 82, pp. 27–49.

Chao, E. (2005) 'Cautionary Tales: Marriage Strategies, State Discourse, and Women's Agency in a Naxi Village in South-western China', in N. Constable (ed.) *Cross-Border Marriages: Gender and Mobility in Transnational Asia*, Philadelphia, PA: University of Pennsylvania Press, pp. 34–52.

Charsley, K. (2005) 'Unhappy Husbands: Masculinity and Migration in Transnational Pakistani Marriages', *Journal of the Royal Anthropological Institute*, vol. 11, pp. 85–105.

Charsley, K. (2006) 'Risk and Ritual: The Protection of British Pakistani Women in Transnational Women', *Journal of Ethnic and Migration Studies*, vol. 32, no. 7, pp. 1169–87.

Charsley, K. (2007) 'Risk, Trust, Gender and Transnational Cousin Marriage among British Pakistanis', *Ethnic and Racial Studies*, vol. 30, no. 6, pp. 1117–31.

Charsley, K. and Shaw, A. (2006) 'South Asian Transnational Marriages in Comparative Perspective', *Global Networks*, vol. 6, no. 4, pp. 331–44.

Chen, Y. and Huang, M. (2006) 'Social Inequality and Intercultural Marriage in Taiwan', paper presented at ISA 2006 Congress: The Quality of Social Existence in a Globalising World, Durban, South Africa.

Chow, R. (1993) *Writing Diaspora: Tactics of Intervention in Contemporary Cultural Studies* Bloomington, IN: Indiana University Press.

Clegg, S. (2006) 'The Problem of Agency in Feminism: A Critical Realist Approach', *Gender and Education*, vol. 18, no. 3, pp. 309–24.

Clifford, J. (1997) *Routes: Travel and Translation in the Late Twentieth Century*, Cambridge, MA: Harvard University Press.

Cohen, E. (2003) 'Transnational Marriage in Thailand: The Dynamics of Extreme Heterogamy', in T. Bauer and B. McKercher (eds) *Sex and Tourism: Journeys of Romance, Love and Lust*, London: Haworth Hospitality Press, pp. 57–81.

Constable, N. (2003) 'A Transnational Perspective on Divorce and Marriage: Filipina Wives and Workers', *Identities: Global Studies in Culture and Power*, vol. 10, pp. 163–80.

Constable, N. (2005a) 'Introduction: Cross-border Marriages, Gendered Mobility and Global Hypergamy', in N. Constable (ed.) *Cross-Border Marriages: Gender and Mobility in Transnational Asia*, Philadelphia, PA: University of Pennsylvania Press.

Constable, N. (ed.) (2005b) *Cross-Border Marriages: Gender and Mobility in Transnational Asia*, Philadelphia, PA: University of Pennsylvania Press.

Constable, N. (2006) 'Brides, Maids and Prostitutes: Reflections on the Study of "Trafficked" Women', *PORTAL Journal of Multidisciplinary International Studies*, vol. 3, no. 2. Online.

Conway, D. (2007) 'Caribbean Transnational Migration Behaviour: Reconceptualising its "Strategic Flexibility"', *Population, Space and Place*, vol. 13, pp. 415–31.

Cooke, T.J. (2005) 'Migration of Same-Sex Couples', *Population, Space and Place*, vol. 11, pp. 401–09.

Coole, D. (2005) 'Rethinking Agency: A Phenomenological Approach to Embodiment and Agentic Capacities', *Political Studies*, vol. 53, pp. 124–42.

Crowhurst, I. (2007) 'Socio-Political and Legal Representations of Migrant Women Sex Labourers in Italy: Between Discourse and Praxis', in S. Walsum and T. Spijkerboer (eds) *Women and Immigration Law: New Variations on Classical Feminist Themes*, New York: Routledge Cavendish, pp. 241–60.

D'Cruze, S. and Rao, A. (eds) (2005) *Violence, Vulnerability and Embodiment: Gender and History*, Oxford: Blackwell.

Daniel, E.V. and Knudsen, J.C. (eds) (1995) *Mistrusting Refugees*, Berkeley, CA: University of California Press.

Dauvergne, C. (2008) *Making People Illegal*, Cambridge: Cambridge University Press.

Davin, D. (2007) 'Marriage Migration in China and East Asia', *Journal of Contemporary China*, vol. 16, no. 50, pp. 83–95.

De Certeau, M. (1984) *The Practice of Everyday Life*, Los Angeles: University of California Press.

De Hart, B. (2006a) 'Introduction: The Marriage of Convenience in European Immigration Law', *European Journal of Migration and Law*, vol. 8, no. 3–4, pp. 251–62.

De Hart, B. (2006b) 'The Morality of Maria Toet: Gender, Citizenship and the Construction of the Nation-State', *Journal of Ethnic and Migration Studies*, vol. 32, no. 1, pp. 49–68.

De Hart, B. (2007) 'The Right to Domicile of Women with a Migrant Partner in European Immigration Law', in S. van Walsum and T. Spijkerboer (eds) *Women and Immigration Law: New Variations on Classical Feminist Themes*, New York: Routledge Cavendish, pp. 142–59.

Del Rosario, T.C. (2005) 'Bridal Diaspora: Migration and Marriage among Filipino Women', *Indian Journal of Gender Studies*, vol. 12, no. 2 and 3, pp. 253–74.

Dewey, S. (2008) *Hollow Bodies: Institutional Responses to Sex Trafficking in Armenia, Bosnia, and India*, Sterling, VA: Kumarian Press.

Dona, G. and Berry, J.W. (1999) 'Refugee Acculturation and Re-Acculturation', in A. Ager (ed.) *Refugees: Perspectives on the Experience of Forced Migration*, London: Pinter, pp. 169–96.

Dutton, M.A. and Goodman, L.A. (2005) 'Coercion in Intimate Partner Violence: Toward a New Conceptualization', *Sex Roles*, vol. 52, no. 11–12, pp. 743–56.

Eastmond, M. (1993) 'Reconstructing Life: Chilean Refugee Women and the Dilemmas of Exile', in G. Buijs (ed.) *Migrant Women: Crossing Boundaries and Changing Identities*, Oxford: Berg, pp. 35–54.

Eekelaar, J. and Maclean, M. (2004) 'Marriage and the Moral Bases of Personal Relationships', *Journal of Law and Society*, vol. 31, no. 4, pp. 510–38.

Elman, R.A. (2000) 'The Limits of Citizenship: Migration, Sex Discrimination and Same-Sex Partners in EU Law', *Journal of Common Market Studies*, vol. 5, pp. 729–49.

Engebrigsten, A.I. (2007) 'Kinship, Gender and Adaptation Processes in Exile: The Case of Tamil and Somali Families in Norway', *Journal of Ethnic and Migration Studies*, vol. 33, no. 5, pp.727–46.

Faier, L. (2007) 'Filipina Migrants in Rural Japan and Their Professions of Love', *American Ethnologist*, vol. 34, no. 1, pp. 148–62.

Faier, L. (2008) 'Runaway Stories: The Underground Micromovements of Filipina Oyomesan in Rural Japan', *Cultural Anthropology*, vol. 23, no. 4, pp. 630–59.

Faist, T. (2000) 'Transnationalization in International Migration: Implications for the Study of Citizenship and Culture', *Ethnic and Racial Studies*, vol. 23, no. 2, pp. 189–222.

Fan, C.C. and Huang, Y. (1998) 'Waves of Rural Brides: Female Marriage Migration in China', *International Migration Review*, vol. 88, no. 2, pp. 227–51.

Farah, N. and Mama, M. (1999) *Yesterday, Tomorrow: Voices from the Somali Diaspora*, London: Continuum Publishing.

Farmanfarmaian, A. (1992) 'Subsystems, Subjectivity and Subversion: Iranian Refugees in Illegal Transit', *History and Anthropology*, vol. 6, no. 1, pp. 87–102.

Fernandez, S. (2009) 'The Crusade over the Bodies of Women', *Patterns of Prejudice*, vol. 43, no. 3–4, pp. 269–86.

Fischer, P.A. and Martin, R.e.a. (1997) '"Should I Stay or Should I Go?"', in T. Hammar, G. Brochmann, K. Tamas and T. Faist(eds) *International Migration, Immobility and Development*, Oxford: Berg, pp. 49–90.

Foblets, M. and Vanheule, D. (2006) 'Marriages of Convenience in Belgium: The Punitive Approach Gains Ground in Migration Law', *European Journal of Migration and Law*, vol. 8, no. 3–4, pp. 263–80.

Fortune, G. (2006) '"Mr Jones' Wives": War Brides, Marriage, Immigration and Identity Formation', *Women's History Review*, vol. 15, no. 4, pp. 587–99.

Freeman, C. (2005) 'Marrying Up and Marrying Down: The Paradoxes of Marital Mobility for Chongsonjok Brides in South Korea', in N. Constable (ed.) *Cross-Border Marriages: Gender and Mobility in Transnational Asia*, Philadelphia, PA: University of Pennsylvania Press, pp. 80–100.

Fuglerud, O. (1999) *Life on the Outside*, London: Pluto.

Fujiwara, L. (2008) *Mothers Without Citizenship: Asian Immigrant Families and the Consequences of Welfare Reform*, Minneapolis: University of Minnesota.

Gallo, E. (2005) 'Unorthodox Sisters: Gender Relations and Generational Change among Malayali Migrants in Italy', *Indian Journal of Gender Studies*, vol. 12, no. 2 and 3, pp. 217–51.

Gallo, E. (2006) 'Italy Is Not a Good Place for Men: Narratives of Place, Marriage and Masculinity among Malayali Migrants', *Global Networks*, vol. 6, no. 4, pp. 357–71.

Gardiner Barber, P. (2000) 'Agency in Philippine Women's Labour Migration and Provisional Diaspora', *Women's Studies International Forum*, vol. 23, no. 4, pp. 399–411.

Gardner, K. (2006) 'The Transnational Work of Kinship and Caring: Bengali-British Marriages in Historical Perspective', *Global Networks*, vol. 6, no. 4, pp. 373–87.

Gedalof, I. (2007) 'Unhomely Homes: Women, Family and Belonging in UK Discourses of Migration and Asylum', *Journal of Ethnic and Migration Studies*, vol. 33, no. 1, pp. 77–94.

Gennep, A. von (1960) *The Rites of Passage*, London: Routledge and Kegan Paul.

Giddens, A. (1992) *The Transformation of Intimacy*, Cambridge: Polity.

Goffman, E. (1963) *Stigma*, Englewood Cliffs, NJ: Prentice-Hall,

Gopalkrishnan, N. and Babacan, H. (2007) 'Ties That Bind: Marriage and Partner Choice in the Indian Community in Australia in a Transnational Context', *Identities: Global Studies in Culture and Power*, vol. 14, no. 4, pp. 507–26.

Gordon, M. (1964) *Assimilation in American Life: The Role of Race, Religion and National Origins*, New York: Oxford University Press.

Gorny, A. and Kepinska, E. (2004) 'Mixed Marriages in Migration from Ukraine to Poland', *Journal of Ethnic and Migration Studies*, vol. 30, no. 2, pp. 353–72.

Grabska, K. (forthcoming) 'Lost Boys, Invisible Girls: Stories of Marriage Across Borders', *Gender, Place and Culture: A Journal of Feminist Geography*.

Grewal, Z.A. (2008) 'Marriage in Colour: Race, Religion and Spouse Selection in Four American Mosques', *Ethnic and Racial Studies*, vol. 28, no. 4, pp. 1–23.

Griffiths, D.J. (2002) *Somali and Kurdish Refugees in London New Identities in the Diaspora*, Aldershot: Ashgate.

230   *Bibliography*

Grillo, R.D. (1985) *Ideologies and Institutions in Urban France: The Representation of Immigrants*, Cambridge: Cambridge University Press.

Haas, H. de (2007) 'Morocco's Migration Experience: A Transitional Perspective', *International Migration*, vol. 45, no. 4, pp. 39–70.

Hamilton, A. (1997) 'Primal Dream: Masculinism, Sin and Salvation in Thailand's Sex Trade', in L. Manderson and M. Jolly (eds) *Sites of Desire, Economies of Pleasure*, Chicago: University of Chicago Press, pp. 145–65.

Handrahan, L. (2004) 'Hunting for Women: Bride-knapping in Kyrgzstan', *International Feminist Journal of Politics*, vol. 6, no. 2, pp. 207–33.

Herman, E. (2006) 'Migration as a Family Business: The Role of Personal Networks in the Mobility Phase of Migration', *International Migration*, vol. 44, no. 4, pp. 191–229.

Hidalgo, D.A. and Bankston, C.L. (2008) 'Military Brides and Refugees: Vietnamese American Wives and Shifting Links to the Military, 1980–2000', *International Migration*, vol. 46, no. 2, pp. 167–85.

Hilsdon, A. (2007) 'Transnationalism and Agency in East Malaysia', *The Australian Journal of Anthropology*, vol. 18, no. 2, pp. 172–93.

Himelfarb Hurwitz, E.J., Gupta, J., Liu, R., Silverman, J.G. and Raj, A. (2006) 'Intimate Partner Violence Associated with Poor Health Outcomes in U.S. South Asian Women', *Journal of Immigrant and Minority Health*, vol. 8, no. 3, pp. 251–61.

Hobsbawm, E. and Ranger, T. (1983) *The Invention of Tradition*. Cambridge: Cambridge University Press.

Hoggett, P. (2001) 'Agency, Rationality and Social Policy', *Journal of Social Policy*, vol. 30, no. 1, pp. 37–56.

Holt, M. (2008) '"Marriage-like" or Married? Lesbian and Gay Marriage, Partnership and Migration', *Feminism and Psychology*, vol. 14, no. 1, pp. 30–5.

Humphrey, M. (1998) *Islam, Multiculturalism and Transnationalism: From the Lebanese Diaspora*, London: I.B. Tauris Publishers.

Hunt, L. (2008) 'Women Asylum Seekers and Refugees: Opportunities, Constraints and the Role of Agency', *Social Policy and Society*, vol. 7, no. 3, pp. 281–92.

Hussein, S. and Manthorpe, J. (2007) 'Women from the Middle East and North Africa in Europe: Understanding Their Marriage and Family Dynamics', *European Journal of Social Work*, vol. 10, no. 4, pp. 465–80.

Hwang, S., Saenz, R. and Aguirre, B.E. (1997) 'Structural and Assimilationist Explanations of Asian American Intermarriage', *Journal of Marriage and Family*, vol. 59, no. 3, pp. 758–72.

Ito, R. (2005) 'Crafting Migrant Women's Citizenship in Japan: Taking "Family" as a Vantage Point', *International Journal of Japanese Sociology*, vol. 14, pp. 52–69.

Jameson, L. (1999) 'Intimacy Transformed? A Critical Look at the "Pure Relationship"', *Sociology*, vol. 33, no. 3, pp. 477–94.

Jeffreys, S. (2009) *The Industrial Vagina: The Political Economy of the Global Sex Trade*, London: Routledge.

Johnson, E. (2007) *Dreaming of a Mail-Order Husband: Russian-American Internet Romance*, Durham, NC: Duke University Press.

Johnson-Hanks, J. (2006) *Uncertain Honor: Modern Motherhood in an African Crisis*, Chicago: University of Chicago Press.

Johnson-Hanks, J. (2007) 'On the Limits of Life Stages in Ethnography: Toward a Theory of Vital Conjunctures', *American Anthropologist*, vol. 104, no. 3, pp. 865–80.

Jones, G. (2004) 'The "Flight from Marriage" in South-East and East Asia,' in G. Jones and Ramdas, K. (eds) *(Un)Tying the Knot: Ideal and Reality in Asian Marriage*, Singapore: National University of Singapore Press.

Kalmijn, M. (1998) 'Intermarriage and Homogamy: Causes, Patterns and Trends', *Annual Review of Sociology*, vol. 24, pp. 395–421.

Kalpagam, U. (2005) '"American Varan" Marriages among Tamil Brahmans: Preferences, Strategies and Outcomes, *Indian Journal of Gender Studies*, vol. 12, no. 2 and 3, pp. 189–215.

Kaufman, J.P. and Williams, K.P. (2004) 'Who Belongs? Women, Marriage and Citizenship: Gendered Nationalism and the Balkan Wars', *International Feminist Journal of Politics*, vol. 6, no. 3, pp. 416–35.

Kempadoo, K. and Doezema, J. (eds) (1998) *Global Sex Workers: Rights, Resistance, and Redefinition*, London: Routledge.

Khoo, S. (2001) 'The Context of Spouse Migration to Australia', *International Migration*, vol. 39, no. 10, pp. 111–32.

Kivisto, P. (2001) 'Theorizing Transnational Immigration: A Critical Review of Current Efforts', *Ethnic and Racial Studies*, vol. 24, no. 4, pp. 549–77.

Kofman, E. (1999) 'Female "Birds of Passage" a Decade Later: Gender and Immigration in the European Union', *International Migration Review*, vol. 33, no. 2, pp. 269–99.

Kofman, E. (2004) 'Family-Related Migration: A Critical Review of European Studies', *Journal of Ethnic and Migration Studies*, vol. 30, no. 2, pp. 243–62.

Kofman, E. (2005) 'Citizenship, Migration and the Reassertion of National Identity Citizenship Studies', *Citizenship Studies*, vol. 9, no. 5, pp. 453–67.

Kofman, E. and Meeto, V. (2008) 'Family Migration', in *World Migration 2008: Managing Labour Mobility in the Evolving Global Economy*, Geneva: International Organization for Migration, pp. 151–72.

Kofman, E., Lukes, S., Meetoo, V. and Aaron, P. (2008) *Family Migration to United Kingdom: Trends, Statistics and Policies*, NODE Policy Report, Vienna: BMWF/ICMPD.

Kofman, E., Phizacklea, A., Raghuram, P. and Sales, R. (eds) (2000) *Gender and International Migration in Europe: Employment, Welfare and Politics*, London: Routledge.

Kojima, Y. (2001) 'In the Business of Cultural Reproduction: Theoretical Implications of the Mail-Order Bride Phenomenon', *Women's Studies International Forum*, vol. 24, no. 2, pp. 199–210.

Kunz, E.F. (1973) 'The Refugee in Flight: Kinetic Models and Forms of Displacement', *International Migration Review*, vol. VII, no. 2, pp. 125–46.

Kuper, A. (2008) 'Changing the Subject – about Cousin Marriage, Among Other Things', *Journal of the Royal Anthropological Institute*, vol. 14, pp. 717–35.

Lan, P. (2008) 'Migrant Women's Bodies as Boundary Markers: Reproductive Crisis and Sexual Control in the Ethnic Frontiers of Taiwan', *Signs: Journal in Women in Culture and Society*, vol. 33, no. 4, pp. 833–61.

Lauser, A. (2008) 'Philippine Women on the Move: Marriage across Borders', *International Migration*, vol. 46, no. 4, pp. 85–110.

Lauth Bacas, J. (2002) *Cross-border Marriages and the Formation of Transnational Families: a Case Study of Greek-German Couples in Athens*. Working Paper 02 No. 10 Transnational Communities Programme. Available at: www.transcomm.ox.ac.uk/working%20papers/.

Law, L. (1997) 'A Matter of "Choice": Discourses on Prostitution in the Philippines', in L. Manderson and M. Jolly (eds) *Sites of Desire: Economies of Pleasure*, Chicago: University of Chicago Press, pp. 233–61.

Lee, H-K. (2006) 'International Marriage and the State in South Korea', unpublished paper.

Lee, N.Y. (2006) 'Gendered Nationalism and Otherization: Transnational Prostitutes in South Korea', *Inter-Asia Cultural Studies*, vol. 7, no. 3, pp. 456–71.

Lévi-Strauss, C. (1969) *Elementary Structures of Kinship*, rev. ed, Boston: Beacon Press.

Levitt, P. and Jaworsky, B.N. (2007) 'Transnational Migration Studies: Past Developments and Future Trends', *Annual Review of Sociology*, vol. 33, no. 1, pp. 129–56.

Liao, C.M. (2007) MA dissertation, University of Kent.

Lievens, J. (1999) 'Family-Forming Migration from Turkey and Morocco to Belgium: The Demand for Marriage Partners from the Countries of Origin', *International Migration Review*, vol. 33, pp. 717–44.

Lin, G. and Ma, Z. (2008) 'Examining Cross-border Marriages in Hong Kong Since Its Return to China in 1997', *Population, Space and Place*, vol. 14, pp. 407–18.

Link, B.G. and Phelan, J.C. (2001) 'Conceptualizing Stigma', *Annual Review of Sociology*, vol. 27, pp. 363–85.

Lister, R. (1997) *Citizenship: Feminist Perspectives*, Basingstoke: Macmillan.

Liversage, A. (2009) 'Vital Conjunctures, Shifting Horizons: High-Skilled Female Immigrants Looking for Work', *Work, Employment and Society*, vol. 23, no. 1, pp. 120–41.

Lloyd, C. (2006) 'From Taboo to Transnational Political Issue: Violence Against Women in Algeria', *Women's Studies International Forum*, vol. 29, pp. 453–62.

Lu, M. (2005) 'Commercially Arranged Marriage Migration: Case Studies of Cross-border Marriages in Taiwan', *Indian Journal of Gender Studies*, vol. 12, no. 2–3, pp. 275–304.

Lubkeman, S. (2000) 'The Transformation of Transnationality among Mozambican Migrants in South Africa', *Canadian Journal of African Studies/Revue des Etudes Africaines*, vol. 34, no. 1, pp. 41–6.

Lukes, S. (2005) *Power: A Radical View*, 2nd edn, London: Palgrave Macmillan.

MacKay, D. (2003) 'Filipinas in Canada – De-Skilling as a Push Towards Marriage', in N. Piper and M. Roces (eds) *Wife or Worker: Asian Women and Migration*, New York: Rowman and Littlefield Publishers Inc, pp. 23–51.

Maclean, M. and Eekelaar, J. (2005) 'The Significance of Marriage: Contrasts between White British and Ethnic Minority Groups in England', *Law and Policy*, vol. 27, no. 3, pp. 379–98.

Mahler, S.J. and Pessar, P.R. (2006) 'Gender Matters: Ethnographers Bring Gender from the Periphery toward the Core of Migration Studies', *International Migration Review*, vol. 40, no. 1, pp. 27–63.

Maley, W. (ed.) (1998) *Fundamentalism Reborn? Afghanistan and the Taliban*, New York: New York University Press.

Malkki, L.H. (1995) *Purity and Exile: Violence, Memory and National Cosmology Among Hutu Refugees in Tanzania*, Chicago: University of Chicago Press.

Manalansan IV, M.M. (2006) 'Queer Intersections: Sexuality and Gender in Migration Studies', *International Migration Review*, vol. 40, no. 1, pp. 224–49.

Mand, K. (2005) 'Marriage and Migration through the Life Course: Experiences of Widowhood, Separation and Divorce amongst Transnational Sikh Women', *Indian Journal of Gender Studies*, vol. 12, no. 2–3, pp. 406–25.

Manderson, L. (1997) 'Parables of Imperialism and Fantasies of the Exotic: Western Representations of Thailand – Place and Sex', in L. Manderson and M. Jolly, (eds) *Sites of Desire, Economies of Pleasure*, Chicago: University of Chicago Press, pp. 123–44.

Manderson, L. and Jolly, M. (eds) (1997) *Sites of Desire, Economies of Pleasure*, Chicago: University of Chicago Press.

Marranci, G. (2006) 'Muslim Marriages in Northern Ireland', in B. Waldis and R. Byron (eds) *Migration and Marriage: Heterogamy and Homogamy in a Changing World*, Zurich: Frieburger Sozialanthropologische Studien, pp. 40–84.

Marshall, T.H. (1992) *Citizenship and Social Class*, London: Pluto Press.

Massey, D. (1994) *Space, Place and Gender*, Cambridge: Polity Press.

Matsuoka, A. and Sorenson, J. (1999) 'Eritrean Canadian Refugee Households as Sites of Gender Renegotiation', in D. Indra (ed.) *Engendering Forced Migration*, Oxford: Berghahn, pp. 218–41.

Mavroudi, E. (2007) 'Learning to Be Palestinian in Athens: Constructing National Identities in Diaspora Global Networks', *Global Networks*, vol. 7, no. 4, pp. 392–411.

McDowell, L. (ed.) (1999) *Gender, Identity and Place: Understanding Feminist Geographies*, Minneapolis: University of Minnesota.

McNay, L. (2000) *Gender and Agency: Reconfiguring the Subject in Feminist and Social Theory* Cambridge: Cambridge University Press.

Meeto, V. and Mirza, H. (2007) 'There Is Nothing "Honourable" about Honour Killings': Gender, Violence and the Limits of Multiculturalism', *Women's' Studies International Forum*, vol. 30, no. 187–200.

Menjivar, C. and Salcido, O. (2002) 'Immigrant Women and Domestic Violence: Common Experiences in Different Countries', *Gender and Society*, vol. 16, no. 6, pp. 898–920.

Menski, W. (2002) 'Comment', *Anthropology Today*, vol. 18, no. 4, pp. 20.

Min, H. and Eades, J.S. (1995) 'Brides, Bachelors and Brokers: The Marriage Market in Rural Anhui in an Era of Economic Reform', *Modern Asian Studies*, vol. 29, no. 4, pp. 841–69.

Mix, P.R. and Piper, N. (2003) 'Does Marriage "Liberate" Women from Sex Work? – Thai Women in Germany', in N. Piper and M. Roces (eds) *Wife or Worker: Asian Women and Migration*, New York: Rowman and Littlefield Publishers Inc.

Mooney, N. (2006) 'Aspiration, Reunification and Gender Transformation in Jat Sikh Marriages from India to Canada', *Global Networks*, vol. 6, no. 4, pp. 389–403.

Morokvasic, M. (1984) 'Birds of Passage Are Also Women', *International Migration Review*, vol. 18, no. 4, pp. 886–907.

Morokvasic, M. (2004) '"Settled in Mobility"': Engendering Post-Wall Migration in Europe', *Feminist Review*, vol. 77, pp. 7–25.

234 *Bibliography*

Nakamatsu, T. (2003) 'International Marriage through Introduction Agencies: Social and Legal Realities', in N. Piper and M. Roces (eds) *Wife or Worker: Asian Women and Migration*, New York: Rowman and Littlefield Publishers Inc, pp. 181–201.

Narayan, U. (1995) '"Male-Order" Brides: Immigrant Women, Domestic Violence and Immigration Law', *Hypatia*, vol. 10, no. 1, pp. 104–19.

Netting, N.S. (2006) 'Two-Lives, One Partner: Indo-Canadian Youth between Love and Arranged Marriages', *Journal of Comparative Family Studies*, vol. 37, no. 1, pp. 129–46.

Nussbaum, M.C. (2000) *Women and Human Development*, Cambridge: Cambridge University Press.

O'Connell Davidson, J. (2001) 'The Sex Tourist, His Ex-Wife and her "Other": The Politics of Loss, Difference and Desire', *Sexualities*, vol. 4, no. 5, pp. 5–24.

O'Connell Davidson, J. (2006) 'Will the Real Sex Slave Stand Up?', *Feminist Review*, vol. 83, pp. 4–22.

Ong, A. (1996) 'Cultural Citizenship as Subject-Making: Immigrants Negotiate Racial and Cultural Boundaries in the United States', *Current Anthropology*, vol. 37, no. 5, pp. 737–62.

Ong, A. (2003) *Buddha Is Hiding: Refugee, Citizenship, the New America*, Berkeley, CA: University of California Press.

Oum, Y.R. (2003) 'Beyond a Strong State and Docile Women', *International Journal of Feminist Politics*, vol. 5, no. 3, pp. 420–46.

Palriwala, R. and Uberoi, P. (2005) 'Marriage and Migration in Asia: Gender Issues', *Indian Journal of Gender Studies*, vol. 12, no. 2–3, pp. v–xxix.

Parkinson, P. (1994) 'Taking Multiculturalism Seriously: Marriage Law and the Rights of Minorities', *Sydney Law Review*, vol. 16, pp. 473–505.

Pe-Pua, R. (2003) 'Wife, Mother, and Maid: The Triple Role of the Filipino Workers in Spain and Italy', in N. Piper and M. Roces (eds) *Wife or Worker: Asian Women and Migration*, New York: Rowman and Littlefield Publishers Inc, pp. 157–80.

Pessar, P.R. and Mahler, S.J. (2001) 'Gender and Transnational Migration', paper presented at the Conference on Transnational Migration: Comparative Perspectives, Princeton University, NJ.

Phizacklea, A. (1998) 'Migration and Globalization: A Feminist Perspective', in K. Koser and H. Lutz (eds) *The New Migration in Europe: Social Constructions and Social Realities*, London: Palgrave Macmillan, pp. 22–38.

Piper, N. (1997) 'International Marriage in Japan: "Race" and "Gender" Perspectives', *Gender, Place and Culture: A Journal of Feminist Geography*, vol. 4, no. 3, pp. 321–38.

Piper, N. (2003) 'Wife or Worker? Worker or Wife: Marriage and Cross-Border Migration in Contemporary Japan', *International Journal of Population Geography*, vol. 9, pp. 457–69.

Piper, N. (2006) 'Gendering the Politics of Migration', *International Migration Review*, vol. 40, no. 1, pp. 133–64.

Piper, N. and Roces, M. (2003a) 'Introduction: Marriage and Migration in an Age of Globalisation', in N. Piper and M. Roces (eds) *Wife or Worker: Asian Women and Migration*, New York: Rowman and Littlefield Publishers Inc, pp. 1–22.

Piper, N. and Roces, M. (eds) (2003b) *Wife or Worker: Asian Women and Migration*, New York: Rowman and Littlefield Publishers Inc.

Plummer, K. (1995) *Telling Sexual Stories: Power, Change, and Social Worlds*, New York: Routledge.

Plummer, K. (2001) *Documents of Life 2: An Invitation to a Critical Humanism*, 2nd rev. edn, London: Sage.

Plummer, K. (2003) *Intimate Citizenship: Private Decision and Public Dialogues*, Seattle: University of Washington Press.

Raj, A. and Silverman, J.G. (2003) 'Immigrant South Asian Women at Greater Risk for Injury from Intimate Partner Violence', *American Journal of Public Health*, vol. 93, no. 3, pp. 435–7.

Raj, A., Silverman, J.G., McCleary-Sills, J. and Lui, R. (2004) 'Immigration Policies Increase South Asian Immigrant Women's Vulnerability to Intimate Partner Violence', *Journal of the American Medical Women's Association*, vol. 60, pp. 26–32.

Ravenstein, E.G. (1885) 'The Laws of Migration', *Journal of the Statistical Society of London*, vol. 48, no. 2, pp. 167–235.

Ravenstein, E.G. (1889) 'The Laws of Migration – Second Paper', *Journal of the Royal Statistical Society of London*, vol. 52, no. 2, pp. 242–305.

Reay, D. (2004) 'Gendering Bourdieu's Concepts of Capital? Emotional Capital, Women and Social Class', in L. Adkins and B. Skeggs (eds) *Feminism after Bourdieu*, Oxford: Blackwell, pp. 19–33.

Robinson, K. (1996) 'Of Mail-Order Brides and Boys' Own Tales: Representations of Asian-Australian Marriages', *feminist review*, vol. 52, Spring, pp. 53–68.

Roces, M. (2003) 'Sisterhood is Local: Filipino Women in Mount Isa', in N. Piper and M. Roces (eds) *Wife or Worker: Asian Women and Migration*, New York: Rowman and Littlefield Publishers Inc, pp. 73–100.

Rodriguez Garcia, D. (2006) 'Mixed Marriages and Transnational Families in the Intercultural Context: A Case Study of African-Spanish Couples in Catalonia', *Journal of Ethnic and Migration Studies*, vol. 32, no. 3, pp. 403–33.

Roer-Strier, D. and Ben Ezra, D. (2006) 'Intermarriage between Western Women and Palestinian Men: Multidirectional Adaptation Processes', *Journal of Marriage and the Family*, vol. 68, February, pp. 41–55.

Ryan, L. (2009) 'How Women Use Family Networks to Facilitate Migration: A Comparative Study of Irish and Polish Women in Britain', *The History of the Family*, vol. 14, no. 2, pp. 217–31.

Said, E.W. (1978) *Orientalism*, London: Routledge and Kegan Paul.

Sanchez Taylor, J. (2006) 'Female Sex Tourism: A Contradiction in Terms?', *feminist review*, vol. 83, pp. 42–59.

Sandy, L. (2007) 'Just Choices: Representations of Choice and Coercion in Sex Work in Cambodia', *The Australian Journal of Anthropology*, vol. 18, no. 3, pp. 194–206.

Sassen, S. (2000) 'Women's Burden: Counter-Geographies of Globalization and the Feminization of Survival', *Journal of International Affairs*, vol. 53, pp. 503–24.

Scambler, G. (2007) 'Sex Work Stigma: Opportunist Migrants in London', *Sociology*, vol. 41, no. 1079–96.

Schein, L. (1998) 'Forged Transnationality and Oppositional Cosmopolitanism', in M.P. Smith and L. Guarnizo (eds) *Transnationalism from Below*, New Brunswick, NJ: Transaction Publishers, pp. 291–313.

Schein, L. (2005) 'Marrying out of Place: Hmong/Miao Women Across and Beyond China', *Indian Journal of Gender Studies*, vol. 12, no. 2 and 3, pp. 53–79.

Schuster, L. and Solomos, J. (2002) 'Rights and Wrongs across European Borders: Migrants, Minorities and Citizenship', *Citizenship Studies*, vol. 6, no. 1, pp. 37–54.

Scott, J.C. (1985) *Weapons of the Weak*, New Haven, CT: Yale University Press.

Sharma, N. (2003) 'Travel Agency: A Critique of Anti-Trafficking Campaigns', *Refuge*, vol. 21, no. 3, pp. 53–65.

Shaw, A. (1994) 'The Pakistani Community in Oxford', in R. Ballard and M. Banks (eds) *Desh Pardesh: The South Asian Presence in Britain*, London: Hurst and Co., pp. 35–57.

Shaw, A. (2001) 'Kinship, Cultural Preference and Immigration: Consanguineous Marriage among British Pakistanis', *Journal of the Royal Anthropological Institute*, no. 7, pp. 315–34.

Shaw, A. (2006) 'The Arranged Transnational Cousin Marriages of British Pakistanis: Critique, Dissent and Cultural Continuity', *Contemporary South Asia*, vol. 15, no. 2, pp. 209–20.

Shaw, A. (2009) *Negotiating Risk: British Pakistani Experiences of Genetics*, New York: Berghahn Books.

Shaw, A. and Charsley, K. (2006) 'Rishtas: Adding Emotion to Strategy in Understanding British Pakistani Transnational Marriages', *Global Networks*, vol. 6, no. 4, pp. 405–21.

Sheel, R. (2005) 'Marriage, Money and Gender: A Case Study of the Migrant Indian Community in Canada', *Indian Journal of Gender Studies*, vol. 12, no. 2 and 3, pp. 335–56.

Shen, H. (2005) '"The First Taiwanese Wives" and "the Chinese Mistresses": The International Division of Labour in Familial and Intimate Relations across the Taiwan Strait', *Global Networks*, vol. 5, no. 4, pp. 419–37.

Sherrell, K. and Hyndman, J. (2006) 'Global Minds, Local Bodies: Kosovar Transnational Connections Beyond British Columbia', *Refuge*, vol. 23, no. 1, pp. 76–96.

Simkhada, P. (2008) 'Life Histories and Survival Strategies amongst Sexually Trafficked Girls in Nepal', *Children and Society*, vol. 22, pp. 235–48.

Simmons, T. (2008) 'Sexuality and Immigration: UK Family Reunion Policy and the Regulation of Sexual Citizens in the European Union', *Political Geography*, vol. 27, no. 2, pp. 213–30.

Skeggs, B. (2004) 'Context and Background: Pierre Bourdieu's Analysis of Class, Gender and Sexuality', in L. Adkins and B. Skeggs (eds) *Feminism after Bourdieu*, Oxford: Blackwell, pp. 19–33.

Smith, M.P. (2001) *Transnational Urbanism: Locating Globalisation*, Oxford: Blackwell Publishers Ltd.

So, C. (2006) 'Asian Mail-Order Brides, the Threat of Global Capitalism and the Rescue of the U.S. Nation-State', *Feminist Studies*, vol. 32, no. 2, pp. 395–419.

Song, M. (2009) 'Is Intermarriage a Good Indicator of Integration?', *Journal of Ethnic and Migration Studies*, vol. 35, no. 2, pp. 331–48.

Staring, R. (1998) '"Scenes from a Fake Marriage": Notes on the Flip-side of Embeddness', in K. Koser and H. Lutz (eds) *The New Migration in Europe: Social Constructions and Social Realities*, London: Palgrave Macmillan, pp. 224–41.

Bibliography 237

Summerfield, D. (2002) 'Effects of War: Moral Knowledge, Revenge, Reconciliation, and Medicalised Concepts of "Recovery"', *British Medical Journal*, vol. 325, pp. 1105–7.

Suvin, D. (2005) 'Displaced Persons', *New Left Review*, vol. 31, pp. 107–22.

Suzuki, N. (2000) 'Between Two Shores: Transnational Projects and Filipina Wives in/from Japan', *Women's Studies International Forum*, vol. 23, no. 4, pp. 431–44.

Suzuki, N. (2005) 'Tripartite Desires: Filipina-Japanese Marriages and Fantasies of Transnational Travel', in N. Constable (ed.) *Cross-Border Marriages: Gender and Mobility in Transnational Asia*, Philadelphia, PA: University of Pennsylvania Press, pp. 124–44.

Takeshita, S. (2007) *Pakistani Husbands and Japanese Wives*, IIAS Newsletter.

Taylor-Gooby, P. (2008) 'Assumptive Worlds and Images of Agency: Academic Social Policy in the Twenty-first Century?', *Social Policy and Society*, vol. 7, no. 3, pp. 269–80.

Thai, H.C. (2005) 'Clashing Dreams in the Vietnamese Diaspora: Highly Educated Overseas Brides and Low-Wage Husbands', in N. Constable (ed.) *Cross-Border Marriages: Gender and Mobility in Transnational Asia*, Philadelphia, PA: University of Pennsylvania Press, pp. 45–165.

Thai, H.C. (2008) *For Better or For Worse: Vietnamese International Marriages in the New Global Economy*, New Brunswick, NJ: Rutgers University Press.

The Times, October 2, (2004)-last update, 'Mixed Couples Cross Love Bridge to Exile', available at: http://www.timesonline.co.uk/tol/news/world/article489146.ece (accessed 29 Oct. 2009).

Timmerman, C., Lodewyckx, I. and Wets, J. (2009) 'Marriage at the Intersection Between Tradition and Globalization: Turkish Marriage Migration Between Emirdag and Belgium from 1989 to Present', *The History of the Family*, vol. 14, no. 2, pp. 232–44.

Tosakul Boonmathya, R. (2006) 'Cross-Cultural Marriages and Transnational Gender Mobility: Experiences of Village Women from North-Eastern Thailand', paper presented at international conference on Intermediated Marriages in Asia and Europe, 18–20 September.

Tsay, C. (2004) 'Marriage Migration of Women from China and Southeast Asia to Taiwan', in G. Jones and K. Ramdas (eds) *(Un)Tying the Knot: Ideal and Reality in Asian Marriage*, Singapore: National University of Singapore Press.

Turner, B.S. (2008) 'Citizenship, Reproduction and the State: International Marriage and Human Rights', *Citizenship Studies*, vol. 12, no. 1, pp. 45–54.

Turner, S. (1999) 'Angry Young Men in Camps: Gender, Age and Class Relations among Burundian Refugees in Tanzania', *UNHCR: Working Paper*, vol. 9.

Tyner, J.A. (1996) 'The Gendering of Philippine International Labor Migration', *Professional Geographer*, vol. 48, no. 4, pp. 405–17.

UK Borders Agency (2007) *What Is a Certificate of Approval?* [Homepage of UKBA], [Online]. Available at: http://www.ukba.homeoffice.gov.uk/visitingtheuk/gettingmarried/certificateofapproval/ (accessed 28 Oct. 2009).

UK Borders Agency (2008) 4 November 2008-last update, *Marriage Visa Age to Rise Later This Month* [Homepage of UKBA], [Online]. Available at: http://www.ind.homeoffice.gov.uk/sitecontent/newsarticles/marriagevisaagetorise (accessed 29 Oct. 2009).

UK Borders Agency (2009) 11 August 2009-last update, *Husbands, Wives and Civil Partners* [Homepage of UKBA], [Online]. Available at: http://www.ind.

homeoffice.gov.uk/partnersandfamilies/partners/husbandswivescivilpartners/ (accessed 28 Oct. 2009).

van Hear, N. (1998) *New Diasporas*, London: UCL Press.

van Walsum, S. and Spijkerboer, T. (2007) 'Introduction', in S. van Walsum and T. Spijkerboer (eds) *Women and Immigration Law: New Variations on Classical Feminist Themes*, New York: Routledge Cavendish, pp. 1–14.

Vertovec, S. (1999) 'Conceiving and Researching Transnationalism', *Ethnic and Racial Studies*, vol. 22, no. 2, pp. 447–62.

Voigt-Graf, C. (2005) 'The Construction of Transnational Spaces by Indian Migrants in Australia', *Journal of Ethnic and Migration Studies*, vol. 31, no. 2, pp. 365–84.

Walton-Roberts, M. (2004) 'Transnational Migration Theory in Population Geography: Gendered Practices in Networks linking Canada and India', *Population, Space and Place*, vol. 10, no. 5, pp. 361–73.

Wang, H. (2007) 'Hidden Spaces of Resistance of the Subordinated: Case Studies from Vietnamese Female Migrant Partners in Taiwan', *International Migration Review*, vol. 41, no. 3, pp. 706–27.

Wang, H-Z. and Chang, S-M. (2002) 'The Commodification Of International Marriages: Cross-Border Marriage Business in Taiwan and Vietnam', *International Migration*, vol. 40, no. 6, pp. 93–114.

Wehbi, S. (2002) "Women with Nothing to Lose': Marriageability and Women's Perceptions of Rape and Consent in Beirut', *Women's Studies International Forum*, vol. 25, no. 3, pp. 287–300.

Werbner, P. and Yuval-Davis, N. (1999) 'Introduction: Women and the New Discourse of Citizenship', in P. Werbner and N. Yuval-Davis (eds) *Women, Citizenship and Difference*, London: Zed Books, pp. 1–38.

Williams, L. (2004) 'Social Networks of Refugees: Transnationalism, Tactics and New Community Spaces', unpublished PhD in Migration Studies, Canterbury: University of Kent.

Williams, L. (2006) 'Social Networks of Refugees: Transnationalism, Tactics and New Community Spaces', *Journal of Ethnic and Migration Studies*, vol. 32, no. 5, pp. 865–79.

Williams, L. and Yu, M. (2006) 'Domestic Violence in Cross-border Marriage: A Case Study from Taiwan', *International Journal of Migration, Health and Social Care*, vol. 2, no. 3–4.

Wise, A. and Velayutham, S. (2008) 'Second-Generation Tamils and Cross-Cultural Marriage: Managing the Translocal Village in a Moment of Cultural Rupture', *Journal of Ethnic and Migration Studies*, vol. 34, no. 1, pp. 113–31.

Wray, H. (2006) 'An Ideal Husband? Marriages of Convenience, Moral Gatekeeping and Immigration to the UK', *European Journal of Migration and Law*, vol. 8, no. 3, pp. 303–20.

Wray, S. (2004) 'What Constitutes Agency and Empowerment for Women in Later Life?', *The Sociological Review*, vol. 52, no. 1, pp. 22–38.

Yang, C., Huang, I. and Tsai, H. (2009) 'Appearance and Reality of Fertility Rates for Foreign Spouses in Taiwan', paper presented at American Association for Chinese Studies 51st Annual Conference.

Yang, W. and Schoonheim, M. (2006) 'Minority Group Status and Fertility: The Case of "Foreign Brides" in Taiwan', paper presented at international conference on Intermediated Cross-border Marriages in Asia and Europe, 18–20 September.

Yang, Y. and Wang, H. (2003) 'Life and Health Concerns of Indonesian Women in Transnational Marriages in Taiwan', *Journal of Nursing Research*, vol. 11, no. 3, pp. 167–75.

Yea, S. (2004) 'Runaway Bride: Anxieties of Identity among Trafficked Filipina Entertainers in South Korea', *Singapore Journal of Tropical Geography*, vol. 25, no. 2, pp. 180–97.

Yea, S. (2008) 'Married to the Military: Filipinas Negotiating Transnational Families', *International Migration*, vol. 46, no. 4, pp. 111–44.

Yu, M. (2006) Unpublished research on transition of refuge services in Taiwan.

Yuval-Davis, N. (1997) *Gender and Nation*, London: Sage Publications.

Yuval-Davis, N. (2006) 'Intersectionality and Feminist Politics', *European Journal of Women's Studies*, vol. 13, no. 3, pp. 193–209.

Yuval-Davis, N., Anthias, F. and Kofman, E. (2002) 'Secure Borders and Safe Haven and the Gendered Politics of Belonging: Beyond Social Cohesion', *Ethnic and Racial Studies*, vol. 28, no. 3, pp. 513–35.

Zetter, R. (1991) 'Labelling Refugees: Forming and Transforming a Bureaucratic Identity', *Journal of Refugee Studies*, vol. 4, no. 1, pp. 39–62.

Zimmerman, W. and Fix, M. (2002) 'Immigration and Welfare Reforms in the United States Through the Lens of Mixed-Status Families', in S. Cohen, B. Beth Humphries and E. Mynot (eds) *From Immigration Controls to Welfare Controls*, London: Routledge, pp. 59–80.

Zolberg, A.R. (1989) 'The Next Waves: Migration Theory for a Changing World', *International Migration Review*, vol. 23, no. 3, pp. 403–30.

Index